OXFORD AND
CAMBRIDGE

THE BLUE GUIDES

BLUE GUIDE

OXFORD AND CAMBRIDGE

MERCIA MASON

*With maps, plans, and
illustrations*

ERNEST BENN LIMITED/LONDON
W.W. NORTON & COMPANY INC./NEW YORK

Wingate College Library

First Edition 1958
Second Edition 1982

Published by Ernest Benn Limited
25 New Street Square, London EC4A 3JA

© Ernest Benn Limited 1982

Printed in Great Britain

Published in the United States of America by
W.W. Norton & Company Inc.
500 Fifth Avenue, New York, N.Y. 10036

ISBN *Library* 0 510-01662-6   0 393-01547-5 (U.S.A.)
ISBN *Paperback* 0 510-01661-8   0 393-00100-8 (U.S.A.)

DEDICATION

FOR MY MOTHER
A GREAT ENCOURAGER
AND
AN INDEFATIGABLE SEEKER OF INFORMATION

PREFACE

No excuse is needed for bringing Oxford and Cambridge together between the covers of one book. They are the Heavenly Twins of university cities, and their unique status has been emphasised rather than diminished by the great increase since the 1950s in the numbers of other universities. So closely indeed are they identified in the public mind that they are often referred to simply by the composite name of 'Oxbridge'.

Ancient origins, history, organisation, migration of scholars from one to the other throughout the centuries, all these factors do give them a strong family likeness. But the traveller who is fortunate enough to have time to spend in both will before long become aware of almost as many differences as similarities. Some of these, like the 'Backs' of Cambridge, or the gardens of Oxford, are immediately obvious. Others, such as the subtle differences in the styles of the buildings, or the absolute diversity of the two university 'languages', emerge more slowly. Fully to appreciate the individuality of each place, an individuality of soul as much as of appearance, needs long familiarity with both, but even on a brief visit it is possible to catch a sense of it, in the studious hush of a secret Oxford quadrangle, or in the fresh astringent airiness of an open Cambridge court.

Not every visitor has the chance to explore both cities. The old editions of Baedeker's famous guide used to say that every tourist to England should visit Oxford 'and, if time allows, Cambridge', and—largely because of Oxford's central position, on the route to other tourist centres—this still tends to remain the pattern. But even for those who can only visit one or the other, it is still interesting to be able to make connections and comparisons, and so, with the visitor to both and the visitor to only one in mind, the introductory articles on history, organisation and architecture all treat of both places together, and in the detailed descriptions that follow frequent cross-references between the two are made.

Unlike many castles, ancient monuments, and 'stately homes', whose principal purpose nowadays is to encourage and provide for the needs of the tourist, and which are therefore organised for the tourist's convenience, the colleges of Oxford and Cambridge are essentially private places, whose raison d'être is to provide for the needs of those engaged in academic study, research, and teaching, and are therefore organised for the scholar's convenience. That visitors are allowed to wander through their quadrangles and courts—usually without even the payment of any fee—is a generous courtesy, not an obligation. It is a courtesy which should never be abused. Since the rise of mass tourism the huge numbers of visitors to both Oxford and Cambridge have caused the colleges severe problems; many have to restrict their opening hours, and the parts that visitors may see; some are finding it necessary to close entirely during the weeks of the summer examinations to ensure peace and quiet for intensive study. Sadly, too, for reasons of security and protection from damage, many halls and even chapels are open only under supervision, some not at all. So visitors may be disappointed, but they should not be surprised or resentful, if they cannot always see what they want.

The essentially private nature of the colleges, their aloofness, even, from the affairs of the citizens and visitors around them, are typified by the fact that they neither declare their identity, nor make it easy to discover their charms and treasures. It is rare to find a college with its name displayed; often the only way to discover where you are is to study the notice-board inside the gatehouse and deduce from its many flapping layers of literature which college you have reached. And once inside do not expect labels on chapel, hall, or other places of special interest. You will seldom find them. However there are always kindly people about who will direct you, or even take you there, if the directions given in the book fail.

The detailed descriptions of colleges concentrate mainly on what the ordinary unaccompanied visitor can see. Sometimes, however, places not normally open to the public, such as the Bodleian Library Arts End at Oxford, or the Thomas Gray rooms at Pembroke College, Cambridge, are also described, either because they have particular importance, or have a particular relevance to the architectural history or the personalities associated with a college. But in communities as rich in history and personalities as Oxford and Cambridge it is inevitable that almost as much has to be left out as put in. Selection has been one of the author's major problems.

At the end of the entry on each college is a list of famous people connected with it. Very stringent standards have been applied and the result is inevitably somewhat subjective and will probably satisfy no-one. Reluctantly it has been decided, to avoid any invidious choices or wounding omissions, not to include any living persons (with one—royal—exception), although often no doubt their names might be of more immediate interest than those of Elizabethan poets, or Victorian statesmen. The decision also results in women being almost totally excluded, university education for women having such a comparatively short history, and their numbers until recently having been so small. The colleges founded for women have many nationally distinguished daughters, but most of them (happily) are still alive.

Observant readers will notice that sometimes the same name occurs in more than one list. This is because the person concerned has been an undergraduate at one college, and later a fellow of another (or others).

Perhaps no book in the Blue Guide series will be subject to such informed and critical scrutiny as this one, dealing as it does with the very well-springs of scholarship and criticism. Every effort has been made to achieve absolute accuracy, but the author is only too well aware of the gap between intention and achievement. Readers will no doubt discover (perhaps with pleasure?) many mistakes. They are asked to point these out, so that future editions can be corrected. Any suggestions for improvements will be welcomed and acknowledged.

ACKNOWLEDGEMENTS

Any guide-book writer leans heavily on the work of others. The books I have chiefly consulted while working on this guide are listed in the Bibliography. I fully and gratefully acknowledge my indebtedness to their authors.

There are many other people I also wish to thank. My requests for help to University authorities or to the colleges have, almost without exception, been met with the greatest generosity and kindness. Fellows, bursars, librarians, archivists, all have taken infinite trouble to answer questions, check facts, show me round, and supply me with nuggets of fascinating information not to be found in any book. They have made what could have been an arduous task wholly delightful. To thank them all by name would almost require another book; I hope they will recognise themselves in the foregoing remarks and accept my gratitude.

My thanks also go to the staff of the Tunbridge Wells Library, who have taken a great deal of trouble to search out and obtain innumerable books, and especially to Jean Maulden in the reference department, who has piloted me through many weighty volumes.

I have had much help from the Tourist Offices in Oxford and Cambridge who have supplied me with practical information on such items as transport, recreation, visitor facilities, and opening times in their respective cities.

Finally I must thank particularly a number of friends: Christopher Gandy, who made my sojourn in Oxford so pleasant, and has patiently searched out the answers to a host of questions on both Oxford and Cambridge; Reggie and Hester Burton, my guides through the labyrinth of Oxford customs and usages; Anthony Davey and Charles Mason, my rowing coaches; the Ruggiero family who looked after me so well in Cambridge; Rosemary Paice, who has prepared the typescript with scrupulous care and skill. And lastly my husband Oliver Mason, whose knowledge and accuracy have saved me from many errors, and who has advised and encouraged me at every stage.

Any faults remaining after all this help are mine alone.

MERCIA MASON

CONTENTS

MAPS AND PLANS

GROUND PLANS

OXFORD

CAMBRIDGE

THE HISTORY OF THE UNIVERSITIES

The Middle Ages

ORIGINS

Oxford and Cambridge are two of the oldest universities in Europe, although neither is so old as they used to claim in the heady contests to establish seniority which enlivened the Middle Ages. Oxford then traced its origins to a mythical King Memphric, who founded the city in 1000 B.C., and to Brutus, an equally mythical grandson of Aeneas, who came to England after the fall of Troy, and founded the university with a group of Greek and Latin scholars who accompanied him. Less ambitiously, Oxford also claimed Alfred the Great as their founder. Cambridge countered with Prince Cantaber of Spain, in the 'year of the world' 4321, and even in the more sober assessments of 1820 a guide book to Cambridge could state that 'Its establishment as a place of instruction for youth, probably soon followed the introduction of Christianity into this island, in the fourth century, during the Saxon heptarchy'.

In fact neither university was 'founded'. Both grew up in the 12C, and began with groups of scholars congregating around famous teachers of the day. In 1167, as the result of a royal quarrel, English students were expelled from Paris, and it is probable that many migrated to Oxford, a conveniently accessible place which already had several monastic schools (St Frideswide's and Osney Abbey). Certainly by 1200 Oxford was providing a regular course of study, similar to that followed in the University of Paris.

There must also have been famous teachers at Cambridge at this time, perhaps, again, connected with monastic schools (Barnwell Priory and St Radegund's), because when in 1209 a number of students fled from Oxford after a quarrel (the first of many) with the townspeople, it was chiefly in Cambridge that they settled. Both universities grew rapidly in reputation and numbers, and received the protection and patronage of the King and, as essentially ecclesiastical establishments, of the Pope.

In the early days there were no colleges. Students lived in lodgings, or in Halls or Inns presided over by a Master. The university's affairs were regulated by the Chancellor, who also had wide authority over town matters, assisted by the Proctors, Masters, and Regent Masters (teachers in charge of a 'school'). Lectures were held in hired rooms, while the parish churches were used for ceremonial occasions and meetings. It was not until 1320, when Oxford built the Congregation House, and 1350–1400 when Cambridge built the Old Schools, that either university had any property of its own.

COLLEGES

Meanwhile, however, the first colleges had appeared: at Oxford Merton, University, and Balliol, and at Cambridge Peterhouse, were all founded by 1300; many others followed, mostly owing their establishment to rich benefactors. They provided for the communal accommodation and financial needs of teachers and masters; in effect they were 'graduate' colleges. Such undergraduates as there were continued to live mostly in hostels and Halls until the 16C. The buildings followed the monastic model, and the members were all in religious orders, and of course celibate. The academic gowns of today are the descendants of their clerical robes. Simple and austere in their inception, many of the colleges became eventually both wealthy and powerful. Indeed, their influence, as great landowners and as ecclesiastical patrons, extended far beyond the confines of their respective universities.

LEARNING

Education was directed to the needs of the Church; theological studies, however, embraced logic, philosophy, and mathematics. Students entered at about sixteen for a seven-year course in the Liberal Arts, divided into the Trivium—Grammar, Rhetoric, and Logic—and the Quadrivium—Arithmetic, Geometry, Astronomy, and Music. Their names still appear above doorways of the Old Schools in Oxford. After taking his Bachelor of Arts degree the student had to study and teach for at least a further two years to qualify for his Master's degree. To achieve a doctorate required in all about sixteen years. In days when books and writing materials were scarce and expensive both teaching and examination (of which the 'disputation' was an important part) were oral. Latin was spoken throughout. Although other subjects, notably Law and Medicine, were added to the curriculum as time went on, this pattern continued little altered until the mid 16C.

During the 14C and 15C Oxford became one of the intellectual centres of Europe and took a leading part in the development of scholastic philosophy, the revived study of Aristotle (albeit in Latin translation), and the beginnings of experimental methods of enquiry. With this period are associated the great names of Grosseteste (the first Chancellor), Roger Bacon, Duns Scotus, and William of Ockham.

In the mid 14C the university was torn by the controversies surrounding the teaching of Wyclif and his followers, known as Lollards. Regarded as heretical by conservative church authorities, they came under severe episcopal displeasure, and for a time Oxford was in considerable disfavour, and suffered some decline.

TOWN AND GOWN

The story of the universities throughout the Middle Ages is punctuated with conflicts, often bloody, between town and gown, conflicts aggravated by the growing ostentation of college wealth, and the exemption of members of the university, who came under ecclesiastical law, from lay jurisdiction. Antagonism reached its climax in Oxford in 1355 with the Massacre of St Scholastica's Day, when townsmen, summoned by the bells of St Martin's, and students, summoned by the bells of St Mary's, joined battle till the streets ran with blood. Although triumphant in the field, the townspeople later paid dearly for their victory, in fines and a yearly penance before the Vice Chancellor in St Mary's church. This ceremony was discontinued only in 1825.

At Cambridge a somewhat similar event took place in 1381 during the feast of Corpus Christi, which was an occasion for the display of much collegiate wealth. Rioters attacked colleges, seized the treasures of Great St Mary's, raided the university chest, and made a bonfire of documents outside the church. University and college authorities were forced to sign away their rights and privileges. But, as at Oxford, the university soon triumphed. The townsmen were severely punished with loss of rights, while the university's were all restored, and in addition it was given control over the town trade in food and drink, a control exercised until 1886.

The Renaissance and the Reformation

Interest in the New Learning grew throughout the 15C, stimulated by contact with the Italian universities where the Renaissance was already in full flower. At Oxford the movement towards humanistic studies and away from scholasticism was led by John Colet (who strongly influenced Erasmus during his sojourn in Oxford in 1498), by William Lily, Thomas Linacre, and William Grocyn, who first taught Greek publicly in the early 1500s, and one of whose pupils was Sir Thomas More, the 'man for all seasons'. In Cambridge the way was led by John Fisher (Vice Chancellor and later Chancellor of the university, and Bishop of Rochester, martyred in 1535). At his invitation Erasmus came to Cambridge, where he was the first to teach Greek, and in 1511 became Professor of Divinity. His presence much enhanced the university's European standing.

The religious upheavals of the 16C greatly affected Oxford and Cambridge. Many of their monastic students were dispersed and heads of colleges who would not recognise Henry VIII's supremacy (1534) were ejected. Oxford, always more religiously conservative, suffered more severely. Cambridge, under the influence of Thomas Bilney, Hugh Latimer, Nicholas Ridley, and the German protestants Martin Bucer and Paul Fagius, was in the forefront of the Reformation. After the execution of Bishop Fisher, Thomas Cromwell became Chancellor, and royal favour was shown in the establishment of five new professorships and the university's largest college—Trinity.

In 1555–56, when under Mary Tudor attempts were being made to restore the old faith, Oxford was the scene of the trial for heresy, and death at the stake, of the three bishops Cranmer, Latimer and Ridley (the 'Oxford Martyrs', though all Cambridge men). At Cambridge John Hullier endured the same terrible death on Jesus Green.

After these storms Elizabeth I's reign provided a period of tranquillity. Protestantism gradually became the established religion and from 1581 all members of the universities had to assent to the Thirty-nine Articles; Roman Catholics and Nonconformists were thus excluded for the next 300 years. The Queen took a close interest in both places, visited them several times, and provided them with new statutes, which remained in force until the 19C.

UNDERGRADUATES

During the late 16C and the 17C the number of students increased greatly, and the range of studies widened to prepare young men for the professions and public life as well as the Church. There were considerable social distinctions between the various types of students, who ranked as follows:

Gentlemen or Fellow Commoners, who paid high fees and received many of the privileges of fellows. They wore special gowns and tasselled caps.

Scholars, paid for by the foundation, but not necessarily poor.

Commoners (Oxford) and *Pensioners* (Cambridge), who paid lower fees.

Servitors (Oxford) and *Sizars* (Cambridge), who received free board and lodging and some tuition and in return acted as servants to Fellows and Fellow Commoners.

The Civil War

The Civil War of 1642–46 had disastrous effects. Oxford, always royalist and High-Church, naturally supported the King. Cambridge did likewise, though, owing to its strong Puritan elements, with less enthusiasm. Almost all the colleges surrendered their plate to provide funds for the royalist cause. Both towns became deeply embroiled in the war, Oxford as the King's headquarters, Cambridge as a Parliamentary military stronghold. At Cambridge those Masters who were suspected of High-Church or royalist leanings were expelled, and chapels were stripped of their ornaments by the notorious iconoclast William Dowsing (though some, anticipating this purge, prudently removed or concealed their treasures). During the Commonwealth similar treatment was meted out to Oxford, though it did escape the activities of Dowsing. At the Restoration in 1660 the whole process was, of course, reversed.

From the Restoration to 1800

This was initially a time of great activity, with much building and rebuilding, and some widening of the range of studies, particularly in the sciences (the Royal Society, founded in 1660, consisted largely of Oxford and Cambridge men). But during the 18C both universities sank to a low ebb; there are many contemporary comments on the idleness, heavy drinking and lack of scholarship among Fellows and undergraduates alike. Examinations deteriorated into a farcical repetition of stereotyped questions and answers; any change or reform was obstinately opposed. 'The two universities were, in the opinion of the wit and cleric, Sydney Smith, like "enormous hulks confined within mooring chains, everything flowing and progressing around them" whilst they remained immovable and decaying in mid-stream' [V.H.H. Green, 'A History of Oxford University', p 107]. They became more and more the preserve of the wealthy and privileged, as numbers dwindled and expenses increased.

Nineteenth-century Reform

At the beginning of the 19C Oxford and Cambridge were thus virtually still medieval universities. Amazing changes were to take place in the next hundred years, though reform came slowly, and often reluctantly. Some improvements were made in the examination system and some new subjects were introduced in the early 1800s, but progressive ideas were still strongly resisted, and Oxford in the 1830s and 1840s was largely absorbed in the controversies which raged round the *Tractarian* (or *'Oxford'*) *Movement*. This High-Church group, so called from the series of tracts in which its principal adherents propounded their views, was dedicated to a revitalisation of spiritual life and the refutation of the rationalist philosophies of the time. The leader of the movement, which was centred on Oriel College, was John Keble, and among its members were E.B. Pusey, Hurrell Froude, Isaac Williams, and the immensely influential John Newman. To conservative churchmen the Tractarians appeared dangerously Papistic (Newman did in fact join the Church of Rome in 1854, and eventually became a cardinal), and they rallied in opposition. In the words of the great contemporary Oxford scholar Mark Pattison, the struggle between the two factions 'entirely diverted our thoughts from the true business of the place' (Green, op. cit., p 140).

No such doctrinal battles were fought in Cambridge. There the activities of the so-called *Camden Society* (or *'Ecclesiologists'*), who like the Tractarians drew their inspiration from the pre-Reformation church, were largely confined to matters of church architecture and furnishings, though even these caused fierce controversy on occasions.

In the end reform was forced on the universities through the Parliamentary Commissions of 1850 and 1874. There were widespread changes in the fields of administration, finance, subjects of study, and examination requirements. Religious tests were abolished in 1871, and from 1874 Fellows were allowed to marry. By 1900 Oxford and Cambridge were moving into the modern world.

Women in the Universities

These liberalising measures made possible the emergence on the scene of an entirely new character—the academic woman, although it was to be a long time before her presence made much impact on these strongholds of masculinity. As late as 1938 Sir John Betjeman could write: 'I suppose it is only right to bring in undergraduettes, but in bringing them in, it would be wrong to give the impression that they play a large part in the social life of the university.' And again: 'Whether there should be women dons, or whether women should be allowed a university training at all, is a question ....'. ['An Oxford University Chest', pp 39 and 57].

The movement for the education of women had been gathering momentum since the 1840s. In their acceptance at the old universities it was for many years Cambridge which took the lead. Its Local Examinations were opened to girls in 1863 and it was a group of forward-looking Cambridge men that helped and encouraged Emily Davies to open her college for women at Hitchin in 1869. Four years later it moved to Girton, two miles from Cambridge, and its members were able (very much on sufferance and closely chaperoned) to attend university lectures, although any social mixing was strictly taboo. Newnham College (then Hall) opened in 1878, and in 1881

Wingate College Librar

women were allowed to sit the Tripos examination. And there in Cambridge the matter rested for over sixty years. Petitions for the admission of women to degrees and university membership were determinedly rebuffed, most violently in 1897 and 1920, when the controversy achieved national notoriety. Although titular degrees were granted in 1923 it was only in 1948 that women were fully admitted and in 1952 that their colleges achieved equal status with men's, and women were able to take their part in university counsels. In 1975 the first woman Vice Chancellor was elected. It seems somewhat ironical that gowns, proud symbol of the so hardly-won status of undergraduate, are now almost never worn by girls.

Oxford, always conservative, made a slower start. There the Association for the Higher Education of Women was not set up until 1878, nine years after the beginnings of Girton; the first women's colleges were established in 1879, and university examinations were not fully open to women until 1894. Thereafter, however, Oxford overtook Cambridge rapidly. Degrees for women were approved in principle in 1909, although not actually granted until 1920, when women became full members of the university. It was, however, 1959 before their colleges achieved equal status with men's. As at Cambridge this opened the doors of university office, and the first woman Proctor was elected in 1979. This had one unforeseen result. Up to then female academic dress had consisted of the appropriate gown and a soft square black cap. Such headgear cannot be raised in ceremonial greetings, so Oxford's women took to the hard 'squares' long worn by their brothers, though now seldom seen on the heads of either sex.

No Degrees for Women! The scene outside the Senate House, 1897

The women who pioneered these achievements are mentioned in the accounts of the colleges with which they are associated. Among the many men who championed their cause a few must be named: at Cambridge Henry Tompkinson, Professor Fawcett, and pre-eminently Henry Sidgwick; at Oxford Professor T.H. Green, Dr Talbot (of Keble), Dr Mark Pattison, and Professor Arthur Sidgwick (Henry's brother). In the controversies surrounding their campaign the most extraordinary arguments were brought against them, ranging from the theory that the female brain could not survive long periods of study, to objections that female hats obscured the view during scientific demonstrations. Yet within a hundred years nearly all the colleges at both universities were equally open to men and women alike.

Modern Times

Changes as far-reaching as those of the late 19C affected Oxford and Cambridge after the Second World War. State aid for higher education brought a huge increase in the number of undergraduates, and graduates reading for advanced degrees. This, and the new emphasis on scientific studies, necessitated not only much expansion and reorganisation of the university facilities and administration, but vast new building programmes as well. In all these projects the universities have had help from munificent benefactors; colleges, individual buildings, professorships, fellowships, scholarships and research programmes bear witness to their names. At Oxford Lord Nuffield, who made a fortune in motor manufacture, poured the benefits of his wealth on to the university, in spite of his well-known aversion to academics, and his low opinion of the value of academic education. On the other hand a Frenchman who had made a fortune in the Middle East, M. Antonin Besse, had such a high opinion of Oxford graduates that he gave a complete new college (St Antony's) and handsome endowments to a number of others. Yet another college, still in the embryo stage, has been given by Dr and Mrs Cecil Green of Dallas, Texas, two of many, many American benefactors, while the Nissan Motor Company of Japan has established and endowed a Centre for Japanese Studies (to be located at St Antony's College).

Prominent among Cambridge benefactors are Mr David Robinson, a Cambridgeshire businessman, who has given the college of that name, and the Cripps family, donors of new buildings at Queens', St John's, and Selwyn. Both Oxford and Cambridge have their Wolfson colleges, as well as a number of other buildings bearing this name. Both have also received much help from the Ford Foundation. These are just a few; industry has been generous to both universities, and so now, as in past generations, have countless individuals. The universities, for their part, have responded to the challenge of new needs in exciting and imaginative ways, and to changing attitudes and social 'mores' with—on the whole—sympathy and humour, so that seven hundred years of buildings, traditions, learning, and manners seem able to live together in tolerance—even in friendship.

An inter-university insult:

OXFORD

The book which is always open at the same page

CAMBRIDGE

The book which is never opened

UNIVERSITY ORGANISATION

A distinguishing feature of Oxford and Cambridge is their combination of the communal life of the colleges with the teaching and degree-conferring functions of the university. There is no university building as such, nor anything in the nature of a university campus. Both university and colleges are corporate bodies with their own quite distinct endowments, though the colleges do now contribute to the funds of the university. Each college has its own staff of tutors, enabling pupils to receive individual attention (in *tutorials* at Oxford, *supervisions* at Cambridge), but its members are entitled to attend also all university lectures. The honours lectures of the colleges are open to all members of the university.

The college community. This consists of a Head, Fellows, and Undergraduates. The Head is known as Master (the almost invariable term at Cambridge), Warden, Principal, Provost, Rector, Dean (at Christ Church), or President (at Cambridge this title occasionally denotes the Vice-Master). The Fellows are selected from distinguished graduates, not necessarily of the university or college in which they hold a fellowship. The Fellows and Tutors are popularly known as Dons. Most colleges also have a number of honorary fellows, and graduate students reading for higher degrees.

Undergraduates are either *scholars* (who form part of the foundation), or *commoners* (at Cambridge *pensioners*). They make up the great majority, and include *exhibitioners.*

Most undergraduates live in their college or one of its hostels, and are expected to dine in Hall a specified number of times during the week. The old regulations governing the time by which they had to be in their rooms in the evening, when the gates closed, have now largely vanished into history, and so, in consequence, has the ancient sport of climbing in after hours.

As it is the college rather than the university which is the focal point in Oxford and Cambridge life, it is the *Junior Common Rooms* (Oxford) and *Junior Combination Rooms* (Cambridge) and their committees which largely fulfil the functions performed at other universities by the student unions. In recent years Student Representative Councils have been established, to voice undergraduate opinion on general matters affecting daily life, and most faculties have liaison committees on which senior and junior members can meet to discuss academic affairs.

University authorities. The ultimate governing authority of the universities, consisting of all MAs who have kept their names on the books, is known as *Convocation* at Oxford, the *Senate* at Cambridge. In the past these bodies had wide voting rights, but since 1926 their function has been limited to formal matters, such as the election of the Chancellor. Legislative authority effectively rests with *Congregation* (Oxford) and the *Regent House* (Cambridge), made up of all resident doctors and MAs who hold teaching or administrative posts in the university or colleges. Measures submitted for their approval are called '*statutes*' at Oxford, '*graces*' at Cambridge. Administrative authority is exercised by the smaller elected bodies known as the *Hebdomadal* (weekly) *Council* (Oxford) and the *Council of the Senate* (Cambridge); the relationship is roughly comparable to the Government and the Cabinet.

The *Chancellor of the University*, elected (for life) by Convocation or the Senate as the case may be, is usually an eminent public figure. His rôle nowadays is purely ceremonial. In practice his executive duties are carried out by the *Vice-Chancellor*, normally (though at Oxford not necessarily) the head of one of the Colleges, who is elected by Congregation or the Council of the Senate and holds office for four years at Oxford, two at Cambridge.

University discipline is the particular responsibility of the two *Proctors* (though they have a variety of other duties), who are Fellows of colleges and hold office for a year. At Oxford they are assisted by *Pro-Proctors* and an *Assessor*.

Courses of study, appointments of teachers, and examinations are controlled by *Faculty Boards*. The range of courses open to students is extensive, and always growing; full details of everything to do with admission, courses, first and higher degrees, are given in the university handbooks, calendars and prospectuses.

The **University Year** begins in October and is divided into three terms of about eleven weeks, at Oxford *Michaelmas*, *Hilary*, and *Trinity*, at Cambridge, *Michaelmas*, *Lent*, and *Easter*. 'Full Term', during which undergraduates are required to be in residence, begins about two weeks after 'term', and ends about a week earlier. Undergraduates normally remain at the university for three or four years, depending on their course of study, and read for an honours degree (Bachelor of Arts). In contrast with the procedure at other universities, entrants to Oxford and Cambridge have to apply not to the university itself, but to the college of their choice, and normally sit a special examination set by that college (for this purpose the colleges are arranged in groups). The old examinations of 'Responsions' at Oxford and 'Little Go' at Cambridge, which qualified an applicant for admission to the university, have been superseded by exemptions granted on local examination ('A' and 'O' level) results, and at neither university is Greek or Latin any longer required. Compulsory Greek as an entry requirement was abolished in 1920 at Oxford, in 1919 at Cambridge; Latin was finally dethroned (not without a struggle) in 1960.

Examinations are held in late May and June; at Oxford Finals or '*Schools*' are taken all together, at Cambridge normally in two parts, one at the end of two years, the other at the end of the third (or fourth) year. These parts need not be in the same subject, although they are normally related; together they are known as the '*Tripos*' (perhaps from the three-legged stool on which the examiner sat in the days of oral examinations). Results are graded into classes; those passing out in mathematics at Cambridge are classed as *Wranglers* and Senior and Junior *Optimes*, though since the introduction of alphabeticallyarranged lists no longer graded as 1st, 2nd, 3rd etc within their class.

No further examination is required for a Master of Arts degree (MA) which can be obtained for a modest fee seven years after matriculation (acceptance into the university) by any BA who has kept up payment of dues.

Ceremonies and Dress. Degree-givings take place at intervals throughout the year, at Oxford in the Sheldonian Theatre, at Cambridge in the Senate House. The ceremonies, conducted in Latin, are ancient and impressive, especially when higher or honorary degrees are being conferred and the scene is enriched with the gorgeously-coloured robes and hoods of those holding or receiving doctorates. The highlight of academic ceremonial at Oxford is *Encaenia*, or *Commemoration*, held on the Wednesday following the end of Trinity term (early July). The name dates from the dedication of the Sheldonian in 1669, and the occasion is the last surviving remnant of the 'Act', the medieval ceremony of confirming degrees granted over the previous year, and of remembering founders and benefactors.

The grand summer degree-givings at Cambridge are known as *General Admissions*, those throughout the year as *Congregations*. The old name of Commencements was abandoned in 1926.

Full **academic dress** consists of the appropriate gown, for graduates a hood (slung round the neck and hanging down the back, not worn on the head) and a square hard black cap. Men wear dark suits, white shirts, white bow ties and at Cambridge 'bands' (short strips of linen at the neck); women wear dark dresses, or dark skirts with white blouses, and dark stockings. This curiously attractive costume is known as 'sub fusc'. Academic dress is worn at Oxford for ceremonial occasions: degree-giving, matriculation—when new entrants are formally presented to the Vice-Chancellor—and for examinations. At Cambridge it is worn for degree-giving only. There is no university matriculation ceremony, but some colleges conduct their own. For examinations only a gown is required. Gowns vary according to status. All undergraduate gowns are black (except at the Cambridge colleges of Caius and Trinity, where they are dark blue). At Oxford scholars wear longer ones than commoners, whose gowns are little more than loose black cotton waistcoats with long hanging bands in front. Graduates' gowns are fuller, and those of doctors of different colours, scarlet predominating. In the past undergraduates had to wear gowns for lectures, interviews, tutorials and supervisions, Chapel (surplices on Sundays, at Cambridge for all, at Oxford for Heads, Fellows and scholars), for meals in Hall, and out-of-doors in the evening. These formalities have largely disappeared, though some colleges still require gowns in Hall.

Sport and Leisure. Sport plays a large part in university life, although its position has perhaps declined as the importance of examination results has grown. All games are played, most colleges having their own sports grounds, but the athletic activity most connected in the public mind with Oxford and Cambridge is perhaps rowing. This takes place at Oxford on the Isis (Thames), mostly between Folly Bridge and Iffley, at Cambridge on the Cam between Midsummer Common and Bait's Bite Lock, beyond Fen Ditton. Rowing began in the early 19C, and the first inter-university boat race took place at Henley-on-Thames in 1829. This race (now rowed in London between Putney and Mortlake in late March or early April) gradually became a national sporting event, people who had no connection with either university being passionate supporters of one or the other boat, and flaunting dark blue favours for Oxford, light blue for Cambridge, according to a wholly arbitrary allegiance. History was made in 1981 when the Oxford crew included a woman coxwain. Inter-collegiate races, in which women now have an official part, although they do not compete against the men's crews, take place in February (known as *Torpids* at Oxford, *Lents* at Cambridge), and in early summer during *Eights Week* (Oxford, late May) and *May Week* (Cambridge, early June). The object, except in the case of the Torpids, is not to overtake but to 'bump' the boat ahead; the college crews race in several divisions on four successive days, and the top boats of the lower divisions ('sandwich boats') row also at the bottom of the divisions immediately above them. The boats start at intervals of 160 ft: if a boat succeeds in 'bumping' the one in front of it, it takes that boat's place in the next day's contest. Members of crews which move up four places or end up 'Head of the River' are awarded an oar on which is recorded the event and the names of the oarsmen and coxwain. Those who represent their university in rowing, or any other sport, are awarded a '*blue*', or for minor sports a '*half-blue*'.

During Eights Week and May Week the colleges hold sumptuous balls, usually in specially erected marquees within the grounds. Evening dress is de rigueur, and after dancing all night the tradition is to punt up or down the river in the dawn light to a bacon and egg breakfast.

Drama flourishes at both universities. Although the *Oxford University Dramatic Society* (OUDS) has a very high standard, it is Cambridge that seems to produce the actors and the shows (notably the Footlights Revue) which go on to achieve a national reputation. The *Amateur Dramatic Club* (ADC) was founded in 1855 and has its own theatre just off Jesus Lane.

In politics it is Oxford which is pre-eminent, and many famous politicians have served their apprenticeship in the Union, as the university debating societies are called. Distinguished public figures are invited as guest speakers at debates, which are sometimes regarded as being of sufficient moment to be reported in the national press.

For those who aspire to journalism there is a wide variety of publications, notably at Oxford the magazines 'Cherwell' and 'Isis', and at Cambridge 'Stop Press', 'Broadsheet', and the undergraduates' vade mecum 'Varsity Handbook' (all still in publication in 1981).

Indeed, whatever the interest, a club or society seems to exist to cater for it, and the multiplicity of meetings and entertainments offered on college notice boards is bewilderingly various. There are, too, amusements which are not announced: the thrilling hazards of night-climbing, and the associated recreation of undergraduate 'pranks'. It is perhaps less commonplace than it used to be for chamber pots, umbrellas, and gowns to appear on spires and roof-tops, but over the past years Cambridge has excelled itself with a banner slung between the pinnacles of King's College Chapel, and a car slung under St John's 'Bridge of Sighs', while Oxford successfully entrapped motorists in an inescapable circulation of the one-way road system by the judicious re-arrangement of a few traffic signs.

Among all these activities is one enjoyed and indulged in by every right-minded Oxbridgean—going on the river. Punting on the willow-lined Cherwell or Cam on sunny afternoons, or twilit evenings in early summer, must be one of the most 'unforgettable, unforgotten' memories of undergraduate days. Even here the universities must differ; Oxford punts from the sloping end, Cambridge from the flat.

Oxford punts from the sloping end, Cambridge from the flat. Above: On the Cherwell. Below: On King's Backs

THE ARCHITECTURE OF OXFORD AND CAMBRIDGE

by STEPHEN GAMES

Oxford and Cambridge offer an ideal introduction to the history of English architecture. They have both seen an almost continuous growth and development over the last 700 years, and buildings from most periods still remain. Individual buildings are among the finest anywhere in the country; together they add up to a fascinating architectural tapestry.

At heart, both Oxford and Cambridge are medieval townships and although apparently similar they have distinct identities which appeal to different people in different ways. Oxford with its noble colleges along the High Street is the more urbane of the two, Cambridge with its colleges stretching gracefully down to the river Cam the more romantic.

Cambridge lacks Oxford's busy skyline. It is flatter and smaller and has always had less colleges, though within each one there may be a wider variety in the size of courts and the styles of building. Only Christ Church, Oxford, comes near to the spaciousness of King's and Trinity, while Cambridge's smaller colleges may achieve a sense of airiness by opening up their courts on one side to give views of the outside world.

At Oxford, the colleges themselves are smaller and more tightly enclosed. There are high stone walls, including the old city wall which runs down Merton Walk and skirts the grounds of New College, and they fence the colleges off from the town, shutting out prying eyes. By contrast, Cambridge college gardens are famed for their planting and welcome the curious gaze of students and visitors as they punt past on the river or stroll along the Backs.

Oxford colleges are divided into a larger number of smaller quadrangles, making the precincts of the Bodleian Library and Oriel Lane into a dense maze of secret worlds. There is a greater similarity of buildings, partly because until the mid 19C all Oxford colleges were built in the same oolitic limestone, a good quality stone found locally.

Cambridge, whose only local stone was a poor quality clunch rubble, used red, then white, brick, or less often a stone imported from further afield. This gives it a greater variety of buildings and a less uniform, less consistent atmosphere. In this it is perhaps the more truly typical of the picturesque character of English architecture.

The location of Oxford in the area of the Cotswold Hills, and of Cambridge in the flat marshes of East Anglia, has proved a decisive factor influencing the architectural identity of each town. Cambridge colleges were built on reclaimed land outside the existing medieval town and at the convergence of two main roads, the London Road and the Colchester Road. The area between them is triangular, and triangular planning is invariably muddled and complex.

Oxford was built on slightly rising ground, well above flood level and some distance from the river Isis (Thames) and its tributary the Cherwell. In spite of its huddle of narrow streets and alleys, Oxford has a rectilinear street pattern which lends itself easily to simple, urbane planning, with ample opportunities for creating dramatic spaces.

Many Cambridge colleges are built between road and river, which gives them an ambiguity. They have to look in two directions: they have a hard face, with tough brick walls and castellated gatehouses built straight up against the street; and they have a soft face with the lawns and river gardens which give the Backs their wide open quality.

Because of their distance from the river, Oxford colleges are not distracted from their simple relationship with the street. Instead, they have a single entrance which is marked by a square stone gate tower, developed from Saxon towers. Everything else is bounded by a wall. Even at Magdalen, the only college which does front the river, there is a hard edge of buildings against the waterfront.

Oxford also has a hierarchy of streets with broad major roads intersecting at right angles and minor roads behind. The smallest are the lanes—Queen's Lane, Logic Lane, Oriel Lane—little more than alleyways dog-legging between one college and another. The grandest street, the High, is a slowly curving thoroughfare across which college buildings face each other.

Then there is St Giles, wide enough for a whole fairground in the summer, and the Broad, once the site of the town ditch but later the scene of a noble civic forum dominated by the Bodleian Library, the Sheldonian Theatre and the Old Ashmolean Museum, all university, rather than collegiate, buildings.

Cambridge has nothing like it. The college buildings face not other colleges across the narrow streets, but rambling old town buildings, which used to dominate the town far more than they do today, now that so many have been lost, and which impeded the expansion of the university. There are no major streets. The road along which most of the colleges are threaded, Trinity Street, winds about and changes its name four times within a few hundred yards. The only attempt to create a university forum—rather than the town market-place—is a small lawn in front of the Senate House.

Both universities began the same way, with teaching masters who took paying students who would later provide the trained manpower that ran the Church and the Court. An early example of their buildings can be seen in the remains of Gloucester College, founded in Oxford in 1283 and now incorporated into Worcester College. Built by Benedictines, the undressed limestone walls are typical of ordinary Cotswold housing of the day.

The Church dominated medieval society, and the earliest college buildings took the form of monastic institutions. The two largest buildings were the Hall, where everyone ate, and the Chapel. Then there would be studies and lodgings, a library, a kitchen and a lodge for the master. This order has survived to modern times at both the universities.

The first college to organise itself in this way was Merton in 1264, and Oxford continued to develop along fairly conservative lines. In a period of 200 years, from 1379 to 1566, Oxford built nine new colleges, of which eight were founded by powerful bishops and the ninth, Christ Church, by a cardinal, Thomas Wolsey. Not surprisingly, these church foundations conformed to an architectural orthodoxy, though one which was elaborated in considerable depth.

New College, built between 1379 and 1386 by William of Wykeham (Bishop of Winchester), was the first grand version of this model, with a chapel and raised hall side by side on the north of the quad, and a fortified gatehouse on the west. There are separate rooms for sleep and study, distinguishable by the alternating two- and three-light windows. Although all the rooms were part of the college community, they continued to be grouped around separate staircases each with its own front entrance, as if they were private row houses. Even grander in scale was Magdalen, built by another Bishop of Winchester nearly 100 years later, with a cloister all round the main quadrangle. Many regard it as the finest collegiate building at either university.

The Merton model, which had been so successful at Oxford and which the Bishop of Ely had recommended in the building of Cambridge's first college, Peterhouse, in 1284, had little impact on later buildings at Cambridge. Over the same 200-year period, excepting the foundation of Jesus College by a later Bishop of Ely in 1496, colleges were built by many people apart from the Church—especially clerical academics, the Crown, and women close to the Court. The result was a far greater variety of buildings, but of poorer architectural quality.

Cambridge saw six new colleges founded in the 14C but it was not until well into the 15C that planned courts came to be built—at Magdalene, King's, Christ's and Queens'. Until then, college building was crude—Old Court at Corpus Christi gives some idea still—and disorganised.

When the Crown founded colleges at Cambridge it frequently made use of existing buildings, as at Trinity, or built cheaply. Queens', founded by the Rector of St Botolph's in 1446 but taken over almost immediately by the queen of Henry VI, then by the queen of Edward IV, is a good example. Built in a reddish brick with two cloistered wings in the second court, it may look quaint to us now but it lacks any of the extravagance of Oxford. It was simply a serviceable building, based on a manor house of the period with a ceremonial gatehouse, rather than a monastery.

Cambridge continued to build sensible, generally modest, buildings on a scale that was domestic rather than grand. Henry VI's Chapel at King's College seems to be an exception—it is not. For all its soaring beauty it is a very simple building, a unique free-standing single-space structure based on a medieval hall and quite unlike the Oxford chapels, with their transepts and choir inspired by the unfinished chapel at Merton.

Other Cambridge buildings continued to break the rules to which Oxford conforms. When Dr Caius refounded Gonville College in 1557 he built the first three-sided court in the style of what were at the time the most modern French country houses. They were open on the fourth side to encourage ventilation and so prevent disease, and this was copied soon after in the new buildings of Emmanuel and Sidney Sussex.

Disease must have been combated at Cambridge fairly successfully, for Third Court at St John's, 1669, was the first college building to be built two rooms deep, meaning that they could only be ventilated on one side. According to Pevsner, the doubling-up was an afterthought after building work had begun. It is another sign of the makeshift nature of Cambridge buildings—invariably the result of lack of funds, sometimes lack of foresight, and frequently at the expense of urban cohesion.

We therefore have to take Cambridge buildings as we find them—at random: the Fellows' Building at Christ's was the first semi-Classical free-standing residential block in the 17C; Clare College, built by the Grumbold family, was a deliberately played-down reaction against Jacobean excess; Wren's chapels show the restraining influence of the Dutch; Rickman and Hutchinson's Fourth Court and Bridge of Sighs at St John's, however, show a lavish example of picturesque scene-setting though the rear is plain brick.

Perhaps because a very satisfactory architectural style was established at Oxford from early on, its development was cautious and slow. We see fan-vaulting at King's College Chapel in Cambridge in 1508, designed by John Wastell. It takes 125 years before it appears at Oxford, above the beautiful staircase to the side of Christ Church Cathedral and it was only adopted, presumably, when it was considered safely archaic. At University College, the 1716 Quad was built as an almost exact copy of Front Quad, designed in 1634 by Richard Maude with a series of little Dutch gables and Perp. hood mouldings over each window.

Gothic architecture survived far longer at Oxford than anywhere else in England, let alone Europe. Even Wren, architect of St Paul's Cathedral in London, and a man with an inquiring mind who felt more at home with Italian Baroque architecture, grudgingly returned to a kind of Gothic when asked to complete Tom Tower at Christ Church, and Hawksmoor followed his example at All Souls thirty-five years later.

Wren's earlier work, the Sheldonian Theatre, can be seen less as a contribution to mainstream Oxford architecture than as an archaeological reconstruction of an ancient Roman theatre built as an academic curiosity, just as the botanist John Tradescant brought exotic plants back from his travels abroad for the purpose of study.

Taking English architecture as a whole, there have been waves of extravagance followed by waves of simplicity. Almost without exception, Oxford benefited by the former, Cambridge by the latter. The pattern of Oxford's building activity peaked during the Middle and Late Gothic, then the Jacobean, Palladian, Baroque, and High Victorian periods, all periods of exceptional grandeur and force. The phases of Cambridge's building activity are, by contrast, Tudor, Dutch Classical, Georgian, Picturesque, and Arts & Crafts.

This does not mean, however, that there was not a certain amount of overlap and by the time we get to the 19C the divisions become less precise, especially with the Neo-Classicism of the 1820s and the Neo-Traditionalism that began in the 1890s and carried right through to as late as the 1950s.

Of those periods, the one in which Oxford is utterly unmatched is that of Jacobean Baroque in the early 17C, an architectural style which combines the heraldic devices and intricate strapwork and panelling of the Elizabethans with the Classical architecture of the Italian Renaissance. There are many small examples but the two masterpieces are Wadham College (1610–13) and the Bodleian Library (1613). The feature they share is the monumental gateway, a vast elaboration of the medieval gate towers typical of Oxford but dressed up to look Roman.

The frontispiece of the Bodleian is the grander. It is five-tiered to show each of the Classical orders (Tuscan, Doric, Ionic, Corinthian and Composite) used by the Romans. Each tier is increasingly elaborately carved, rising past a panel showing James I being attended by Fame and the University, and topped by two unequal crocketed pinnacles with a pierced strapwork crest between them.

Compare what Cambridge was doing in the same period. Cambridge had actually made its excursion into Renaissance architecture as early as 1567 with Caius's Gate of Virtue, but had no idea how to develop the idea. The Gate of Honour, 1575, is an ingenuous muddle of wrong proportions and confused motifs. And even fifty years later, in 1628, Peterhouse Chapel is still an unholy mixture of eccentric elements and fancy curves, not helped by alterations in 1709. And yet by 1631, Canterbury Quad at St John's Oxford showed a far more accurate attempt at Classical architecture, while the next year Nicholas Stone's gateway to the Botanic Garden had finally got it right.

A similar episode took place in the 18C. The growing antiquarian interest among university dons turned its attention to Andrea Palladio, the 16C Italian architect. Dean Aldrich of Christ Church and Dr Clarke of All Souls turned amateur architects and, with William Townesend, a builder, and others, provided Oxford with a wealth of Palladian buildings from 1705 until about 1770. Their purity was only matched at Cambridge with the Fellows' Building at Peterhouse, 1738.

By this time, Oxford was already creating one of the best pieces of Baroque townscaping ever seen in England, with the building by Gibbs of the Radcliffe Camera. This magnificent circular domed building sits between the semi-Gothic buildings of All Souls by Hawksmoor, for whom Gibbs had worked and who had planned a Camera of his own, and the medieval Brasenose College, now rebuilt. Though it was completely different from anything seen in Oxford before, with curved buttresses around the dome taken from Longhena's Santa Maria della Salute in Venice, it was completely at home.

It was around this time that Cambridge began to look over its shoulder at Oxford and realise that architecturally it was failing to compete. Various architects were aware of the problem and came forward with schemes of their own to transform the university.

Hawksmoor, again, suggested turning Cambridge into an Italian Baroque city with monumental vistas linked by the existing church spires. It came to nothing. Nor did a project by Capability Brown, the landscape designer, to turn all the little college gardens on the Backs into one big parkland. As with Henry VI's plans for King's College in the 16C, Cambridge's architectural history was proving to be more important for what was not built than for what was.

Another scheme which failed to materialise was Gibbs' plan for a university centre, also designed to unify the town. One part of it however was built, the Senate House 1722–30, though it looked so out of place that in 1754 the Master of Caius College next door built a pretty Palladian facade for the medieval Old Schools building by its side in an attempt to bring some Classical order to the scene.

If these ambitious schemes got nowhere, it was because Cambridge was nowhere near as rich as Oxford, where large endowments enabled college Fellows to indulge themselves in good food, good wine, good hunting and good architecture, untroubled by trifling academic concerns. The reduction in student numbers was hitting both universities severely throughout the 18C, but whereas Oxford spent its way out of the recession, Cambridge went into decline.

Some colleges at Cambridge, however, were shamed into improving the appearance of their decaying medieval buildings, and there was a strong reaction against Cambridge's traditional building material, brick, now thought second-rate. In the absence of any need for new buildings, Peterhouse refaced its old buildings in stone in 1754, followed by Christ's in 1758, Emmanuel in 1764 and several other colleges. The result was invariably an unsatisfactory combination of medieval buildings with Georgian sash windows but lacking the simple proportions which even the humblest Georgian building can boast. It was a typical case of Cambridge's make-do-and-mend attitude to building.

Colleges that did not have enough money to afford stone facings covered their brickwork or clunch in Roman cement (stucco) instead. This is what happened at Sidney Sussex College, where in the 1820s Wyatville hid the existing Elizabethan buildings behind a fake skin of gables and battlements. Had the colleges been wealthier and had to serve a larger student population, all these buildings would have been demolished and replaced.

The only way for Cambridge to stop worrying about what its existing buildings looked like was for it to turn its attention to new buildings instead. This had to wait for the climb in student numbers that affected both universities in the 19C and which in turn gave rise to calls for educational reform and a new approach to university-based, rather than collegiate, teaching.

Reform was in fact imposed on Oxford and Cambridge by Act of Parliament and it is at this point, with the universities bowing to national pressures, that their separate identities begin to blur. Yet Cambridge continued to leave its best ideas unfulfilled, especially in the neo-Greek buildings of Cockerell, Burton, and Rickman & Hutchinson, for which it was argued that Greek architecture best represented the new ideals of freedom and enlightenment being discussed in education. William Wilkins, a don at Caius, did manage to build the new college of Downing as a series of Grecian pavilions linked around three sides of a wide campus. Although it became the standard plan for American colleges, it was ignored by the rest of Cambridge.

Reform had an architectural impact in several directions: the new emphasis on science teaching at Cambridge resulted in the university laboratories on the Pembroke and Downing sites; the lifting of the restriction on marriage for dons saw the creation of a whole suburb of large brick villas in north Oxford in the 1870s and a smaller suburb of more individual houses in west Cambridge around the turn of the century; finally there was the establishment of the women's colleges.

Oxford's strong conservative church links reponded to threats of progress with an overwhelming call to revive the ecclesiastical architecture of the 14C, a movement which it pursued with its invariable vigour, insensitively destroying or improving buildings not considered sufficiently Gothic but also putting up a fantastic variety of very stylised new buildings.

For many architects working at Oxford, the Gothic revival meant the opportunity to be inventive, without the restrictions of proportions and symmetry which Classical architecture imposed on them. Among the most imaginative work was that of Butterfield, who at the new Keble College created huge expanses of flat wall in polychromatic brickwork.

Butterfield's use of brick, a material foreign to Oxford, was just one symptom of the enormous shake-up which architecture suffered under the Victorians. Even John Ruskin, the Oxford social reformer who preached about ornament, colour and texture in architecture and who commended the Gothic of Venetian palazzi and French cathedrals, found himself approving the cast-iron frame and glass roof of Woodward's University Museum.

Salvin, Waterhouse, and later Champneys and Caröe, created equally strident buildings which were frequently damaging to the character of both universities. Particularly badly hit were Balliol at Oxford, which was almost entirely rebuilt, and Caius and Pembroke at Cambridge; Waterhouse had a hand in all of them. Cambridge also had its traditions turned upside down when in 1863 Scott built a copy of Merton Chapel at St John's, Cambridge's first transeptual chapel, and one of a number of Victorian stone churches—lovely in the Midlands, wrong for East Anglia.

Victorian Gothic, however, was less well represented, and appeared later, at Cambridge although the medieval revival of the 1820s pre-dated the Oxford Tractarians. Butterfield, Burges and Street—powerful architects at Oxford—had no luck at Cambridge. Instead, Cambridge waited to develop its more domestic Arts & Crafts work, with Morris creating sumptuous medieval interiors at Jesus, Queens', Peterhouse and All Saints Church, while Blomfield's new Selwyn College was a typically sensible, modest, contrast to Keble.

There is an argument that with the abandonment of celibacy for masters of colleges in the reign of Elizabeth I, Cambridge acquired a variety of charming Master's Lodges and that the presence of women close to the university influenced its architectural decisions. True or not, it was the building of women's colleges in the 1870s and 1880s with their softer, less aggressive, designs—medieval almshouses at Girton, Queen Anne at Newnham—which contributed again to Cambridge's romantic rural atmosphere.

In the 18C and early 19C, and after the First World War, most colleges locked up their rooms and bolted the shutters for lack of students. But in the 1930s a massive expansion in student numbers began, leading to huge pressure on space. Both universities responded with a major programme, after the war, of new colleges and faculty buildings, mainly outside the historic centres, and by the conversion and enlargement of old town buildings which were adopted for modern college use.

In many cases, new buildings have proved more important in the repertoire of the architects who built them than for any contribution they might have made to the universities, though more recent buildings have captured some feeling for tradition and continuity. In general, in spite of an initial insensitivity and destructiveness in their handling of new architectural techniques, architects have quickly learnt how to slip new buildings on to difficult sites with great ingenuity, adding depth to the historic fabric of the towns.

	OXFORD	**CAMBRIDGE**

SAXON

England's earliest surviving, most basic architecture. Square towers, crude stone. Openings few and small. Plan small, square.

St Michael's Church, Cornmarket

St Bene't's, Trumpington St. Shows vestiges of Roman-style architecture, with round-headed doorway and square capitals.

Top tier of St Bene't's Church tower, Cambridge

NORMAN

Brought to England from France in 1066. Seen at best in churches and castles. Massive walls, large heavy roofs. Dressed stone provided flat surfaces for wall painting, now rare. Carved decoration, based on painting, seen in zig-zag mouldings round tops of columns, doorways, arches. All openings round-headed.

St Fridewide's Priory, now part of Christ Church Cathedral. **St Peter-in-the-East,** Queen's Lane, fantastic birds' head mouldings on south doorway. **Iffley Church,** zig-zag mouldings. **St George's Tower,** part of Oxford Castle, 1071.

Round Church (Holy Sepulchre), Bridge St. Early 12C. Rare. Only four other round churches of period in the country. Drastic rebuilding in 19C when conical roof added.

Church of the Holy Sepulchre, Cambridge

DOMESTIC NORMAN

Houses consisted of single room, or hall, often at first floor level, for all living, sleeping, eating. Stores in undercroft. Became major feature of all college buildings.

School of Pythagoras, St John's, Cambridge

School of Pythagoras, grounds of St John's College, c. 1200. May have been home of a teacher, or master, with paying resident students.

GOTHIC

Pointed arch and spire. Main structure in buttresses. Walls thinner with larger windows than before. First windows were narrow lancets, but from early 14C lancets combined and stone shafts between them thinner, ending in elaborate tracery in window heads. Planned layout of buildings. Monastic communities in first colleges, with buildings arranged round court (Cambridge) or quadrangle (Oxford).

Merton College, 1308-78. First college to lay down quadrangle plan. **Chapel,** 1290, without nave, became Oxford model. [**Exeter: Chapel,** 1854-60, brilliant copy of this period by Scott. Large rose windows, steep pitched roof, statues on buttresses, decorated trefoil parapet.]

[**St John's: Chapel,** copy of Oxford Gothic chapel by Scott, 1863-69.]

Exeter College Chapel, Oxford

EARLY PERPENDICULAR

Emerging preference for straight lines, verticality and distorted forms. Arches flatter, quatrefoils stretched, windows larger.

New College, 1379-86. Classic example of planned quadrangle. Also **Funerary Cloister,** 1400. **All Souls: Chapel,** hammerbeam roof, 1442. **Merton College,** square stone tower, 1448, developed from Saxon towers. See also numerous square gate towers at other colleges.

Merton College Chapel, Oxford

| | **OXFORD** | **CAMBRIDGE** |

PERPENDICULAR

Peculiarly English development of Gothic. Avoids curves. Emphasis on height. Complex intersecting patterns. Flat walls divided up by ribs and string courses as if windows. Intricate vaulted ceilings became fan vaults. Intricate hollow parapets. Huge glass windows, often coloured, with numerous thin shafts supported by horizontal bars. Pinnacles, square-plan spirelets, crockets.

Divinity School: lierne vault by master-mason William Orchard, c. 1483, with complicated rib and pendent bosses.

Divinity School, Oxford

King's College: Chapel, begun 1446 by Reginald Ely. Completed 1515. Unique as free-standing building. Superb fan-vaulting. Early 16C. by John Wastell.

King's College Chapel, Cambridge

DOMESTIC PERPENDICULAR

St John's College, Cambridge

Magdalen, 1474-1510, perfect example of cloistered quad, with gargoyle string course round parapet hiding gutter. Statuary and bestiary on buttresses as alternatives to spirelets. Upper storey later than lower.

Magdalen Cloister, Oxford

Queens' College, 1448, by Reginald Ely, builder of King's Chapel. Scale smaller than anything at Oxford. Cambridge's first planned college, based on manor house rather than monastery as at Oxford. Same red brick as Magdalene, and Trinity Hall. Huge turreted gatehouses —Cambridge feature. See also **St John's** (two), **Trinity** (two plus chapel), **Old Schools, Christ's** (now stone-faced), and **Jesus** (square with stepped corners).

TUDOR

After Reformation, style dictated by landed families instead of the Church. Unfortified manor houses, with castellations and other vestiges of castles used as decoration. Windows grouped into several lights. Perp. heads, but set in rectangular frame. Square hood mouldings over windows. Ornamental lanterns instead of spires.

Queens' College: President's Gallery, c. 1540. Half-timbered in original yellow and brown, not false white and black. Squarish flat-capped appearance. Tall vertical timbers, few diagonals. Leaded glass, bay windows.

President's Gallery, Queens' College, Cambridge

ELIZABETHAN

Mania for intricate flat decoration. Copious examples at both universities, mostly interiors and so difficult to find. Heraldic devices, strapwork, linen-fold, lozenges, and motifs clumsily copied from Italian Renaissance.

Jesus: First Quad, 1571, with symmetrical windows and mullions.

Main gate, Christ's College, Cambridge

Gonville and Caius, 1565-67. **Second court** (Caius), open on one side and screened by wall. Shows influence of French country houses. Became popular in later Cambridge buildings. See also **Emmanuel, Sidney Sussex, Caius: Gate of Virtue** and **Gate of Honour. Trinity Hall,** mid 16C, shows Dutch influence in stepped gable.

| | **OXFORD** | **CAMBRIDGE** |

JACOBEAN

Elements of Roman architecture employed as motifs on medieval buildings, but still essentially as decoration; columns, pediments, porticos used more sculpturally, less flat, than before. Excessively lavish at Oxford, displaying Royalist sympathies. Architectural tableaux centred round openings—fireplaces, gateways, and flat-fronted Oxford gate towers. Cambridge more eccentric, less exotic.

OXFORD

Wadham, 1610, grand four-storey frontispiece with paired columns, triumphal arch, heraldic shield. **Bodleian Library,** 1613-24, five-storey frontispiece with Tuscan, Doric, Ionic, Corinthian and Composite columns and strapwork pediment on buildings still boxy-Tudor. **St John's: Canterbury Quad,** 1631-36, shows Tudor castellated parapet and persists with hood mouldings incorporated into string course. Also elegant Renaissance cloister. **University College,** 1634-77, and **Oriel College,** 1620-42 Front Quads show Jacobean gables.

CAMBRIDGE

Peterhouse: Chapel, 1628-32, Gothic and Renaissance motifs eccentrically combined. Ogee Perp. niches, crocketed, Corinthian pilasters, rusticated facade. **Magdalene: Pepys Library,** date unknown, mock projecting gable fronts, round-arched cloister.

Detail of Bodleian Library, Oxford

EARLY RENAISSANCE

Reaction against excess, seen only at Cambridge. New mood of simple Classicism in which forms previously used with abandon now brought under control.

Fellows' Building, Christ's College, Cambridge

Trinity: Nevile's Court, 1612. Early attempt at Classical restraint. Windows regular in bays. Elegant cloister. Uninterrupted balustrade. Little decoration. **Clare College,** 1638-1700s by John Westley and the Grumbold family. Order, rhythmical facade. Tall, narrow, square bays. Regular dormer windows with hipped roofs, or pedimented gables. **Christ's: Fellows' Building,** 1640-43.

WREN

First English architect with academic knowledge of Italian Renaissance who built widely. Also influenced by Dutch, especially, and by French sources to adapt Italian and Roman models for English needs. College chapels are simple boxes, main facade on short side. Pilasters, niches, garlands, pediments, parapet urns, and lanterns used with restraint. Little other decoration.

Sheldonian Theatre, 1663-69. Faithful reconstruction of ancient Theatre of Marcellus in Rome. Ceiling painted as sky and interior meant to resemble canvas structure. **Trinity College: Chapel,** 1691-94.

Pembroke College: Chapel, 1665, Wren's first Cambridge building. **Emmanual College: Chapel,** 1666-77. **Trinity College: Library,** 1676-90, retains the cloisters and style of Nevile's Court. Excellent carving inside by Grinling Gibbons. Also fine plasterwork.

Sheldonian Theatre, Oxford

PALLADIAN

Academic interest in architecture of Andrea Palladio, 16C Italian, first published in English editions around early 18C. Palladio's country villas were rectangular boxes with main facade on long side. Proportional, symmetrical facade with central feature—portico, pediment, flight of stairs, etc. Town palazzi heavier, without central feature. Length, proportions unimportant. Windows round-headed or keystoned, large, regular, shorter at each storey.

Three amateurs led Oxford Palladianism earlier than rest of country: Dean Aldrich of Christ Church, Dr Clarke of All Souls, Wm Townesend, experienced builder. **Christ Church: Peckwater Quad,** N., E. and W. sides, 1705-14, by Aldrich. Probably also his **All Saints Church,** 1706, and (with Townesend) **Corpus Christie: Fellows' Building,** 1706. **Christ Church: Peckwater Quad** S. side (library), 1717-21, by Clarke. **Magdalen: New Building,** 1731, probably by Townesend.

East Range, Worcester College, Oxford

Senate House, 1722-30, and **King's College: Fellows' Building,** 1724, both by Gibbs. **Peterhouse: Burrough's Building,** 1738-42. **Old Schools** (E. side), 1754-58, by James Burrough, Master of Caius, and Wright. Palladian screen to mask old building and match Senate House.

	OXFORD	**CAMBRIDGE**

GEORGIAN

Simple Palladian. Terraced housing with plain rectangular fronts. Sash windows. Successful throughout Britain.

First Court and Master's Lodge, Christ's College, Cambridge

Trinity Hall, Peterhouse, Emmanuel College and others refaced their decaying medieval brick and clunch stone buildings behind new Georgian facades around 1740s.

BAROQUE

Extravagant, dramatic use of Classical elements. Expensive, and seen only at Oxford.

The **Queen's College: Front Quad**, mostly 1730s, three-sided quad completed by screen fronting the street. Possibly by Hawksmoor. Cupolas; rusticated and banded vermiculated columns on gatehouse. **Radcliffe Camera**, 1737-49, by Gibbs. Venetian in character. Curving buttresses round dome recall Longhena's church in Venice.

Radcliffe Camera, Oxford

PICTURESQUE

Growing interest in archaeology led to 200-year revival of old styles, especially Gothic. At first, used superficially as surface decoration on buildings really Georgian underneath. Created romantic settings to evoke the past.

Fourth Court, St John's College, Cambridge

All Souls: North Quad, 1715-40, by Hawksmoor in pseudo-Gothic inspired by Wren's Tom Tower at Christ Church. Also **Library**, with classical interior.

Sidney Sussex College: 16C buildings gothicised by Wyatville with stepped castellations, and stucco with raked joints to imitate stonework. **King's College: screen and hall** in flamboyant Perp. style, 1824-28, and **New Court**, 1823-27, in domestic Perp., both by Wilkins.
St John's: Bridge of Sighs and **'Wedding Cake' Cloister Court**, 1825-31, by Rickman and Hutchinson. St John's first college to require a fourth court and, for lack of space, to cross the river.

Radcliffe Observatory, Green College, Oxford

NEO-CLASSICISM

Styles from ancient Greece and Rome used by reformers to express new spirit of enlightenment in buildings that served whole university, not just colleges.

Fitzwilliam Museum, Cambridge

St Paul's Church, 1836, in Ionic style. Now converted to Arts Centre. **Ashmolean Museum**, 1841-45, by Cockerell. Imaginative handling of Greek elements.

Downing College, planned 1784, built 1800s and on, by Wilkins. Linked Grecian villas round three sides of campus. **Squire Law Library**, 1831-42, by Cockerell. **Fitzwilliam Museum**, 1837, by Basavi. Elongated portico.

GOTHIC RESTORATION

Religious movement, at first led by Cambridge Ecclesiologists, then Oxford Tractarians, aimed at rekindling medieval Christian society by recreating 14C architecture. Many buildings cruelly restored, or demolished, in misguided attempt to improve them.

Many colleges rebuilt facades, 100 years after Cambridge, in Gothic style, not Georgian. **Lincoln**, 1824, **Pembroke**, 1829-30, **All Souls**, 1826. **Balliol** almost entirely rebuilt from 1850s by Salvin, Butterfield and Waterhouse. Not a success.

Balliol College, Oxford

Round Church disfigured by Salvin.

OXFORD

CAMBRIDGE

HIGH VICTORIAN

Imaginative experimental use of Gothic in new configurations, shapes and colours. Made external appearance and planning of rooms much easier because of new freedom. Essential when designing for new needs, especially science laboratories.

University Museum, 1855, by Woodward. Influence of Ruskin in Venetian Gothic brickwork. Interior has early cast-iron Gothic nave, with glass roof. **Keble College,** 1868-82, by Butterfield. Open quads, flat expanses of polychrome brickwork. First college with corridor access. **Worcester College: Chapel and Hall,** lavish Gothic decoration by Burges, and by Kempe at **Pembroke.** North Oxford, large villas for dons, now allowed to marry and live out of college. Large estates built all at once.

Jesus: Chapel; Queen's: Hall; and **Peterhouse: Hall,** redecorated by William Morris 1864-75.
Pembroke: South Range, 1871 **Caius: Tree Court,** 1870, and **Union Society,** 1866, all by Waterhouse.

Keble College, Oxford

North Oxford villa

ARTS AND CRAFTS

Medieval revival, but more domestic flavour. Special appeal at Cambridge, where women's colleges first built.

Girton College, Cambridge

Girton College, 1873, by Waterhouse and others. Half-timbered gables, plain brickwork. More like cottage almshouses. Expansion of Cambridge later than at Oxford, dons moving west across Backs into cottagey suburb. Individual houses by Bailey Scott and others, 1900s.

JACOBEAN REVIVAL

Eclectic style, able to absorb the best features of Gothic and Classical architecture. Can be grand or domestic in flavour, highly decorative.

Town Hall, 1890s, by H. T. Hare. **Oriel,** 1908-11, by Basil Champneys.

Newnham College, Cambridge

Newnham College, 1875-1910, by Basil Champneys in mix of Jacobean and Queen Anne styles with large chimneys, dormers, small-paned windows. **Pembroke: New Building,** 1878, by G. G. Scott, and 1907 extension by Caröe with balustrading and ornamental gables. **Sidney Sussex: Garden Range,** 1891, by J. L. Pearson.

NEO-TRADITIONAL

After final Jacobean fling and shock of Great War, interwar buildings settled down to be reassuring, familiar, simple.

Campion Hall, by Lutyens, 1936. **New Bodleian Library,** 1937-40, by Scott, in square undressed limestone blocks. **Nuffield College,** designed 1939, by Harrison in Cotswolds style.

Clare: Memorial Court, 1923-24, by Scott, neo-Georgian. **Magdalene: Benson Court, Lutyens Building,** by Lutyens, 1930, in a mixture of Tudor and Jacobean styles. **Queens': Erasmus Building,** 1959, by Sir Basil Spence. Unpopular.

Nuffield College, Oxford

| | **OXFORD** | **CAMBRIDGE** |

MODERN

Vast increase in student numbers plus international trends in architecture turned Oxford and Cambridge into testing grounds for new ideas on building, planning. Late 1950s and 60s, monumental scale with new colleges and faculty buildings. Emphasis on planning. As demands met, goals grew smaller, looking at new forms of layout, organisation, then new techniques, and finally fitting in with surroundings.

St Catherine's College, 1960, by Danish architect Arne Jacobsen. Designs included furniture and cutlery.

Arts Site, 1950s, by Casson and Conder. Based on new-town shopping precincts, raised off ground on piers. **St John's: Cripps Building,** by Powell and Moya, 1963-67, superb example of same idea but more romantic. **New Hall,** founded 1954 for women, built 1962-66 by Chamberlin, Powell and Bon.

New Hall, Cambridge

ORGANISATION

English Faculty Library and Law Library, 1964, and **Zoology Laboratory,** 1970, both by Sir Leslie Martin.

Peterhouse: William Stone Building, by Sir Leslie Martin, 1963; Cambridge's only high-rise residential block. **Gonville and Caius: Harvey Court,** by Martin and St John Wilson, 1960, three-dimensional puzzle. **Christ's College: New Building,** by Denis Lasdun, 1970; multi-layered, facing one way.

New Building, Christ's College, Cambridge

MATERIALS

Thomas White Building, St John's College, Oxford

The Queen's College, Florey Building, by James Stirling, 1968-70. Red tiles, five-sided glass wall on concrete A frame. **Keble College,** 1970, and **Catholic Chaplaincy,** 1970, by Ahrends, Burton & Koralek. Curving brick. **St John's,** Arup Associates, 1974, concrete units.

History Faculty Library, Cambridge

Leckhampton, 1964, by Arup Associates. Use of prefabricated concrete. **History Faculty Library,** 1964-67, by Stirling. Red tiles, and glass.

FITTING IN

Christ Church Picture Gallery, 1964-67, by Powell & Moya. **Wadham College,** 1972, by Gillespie Kidd & Coia.

Robinson College, 1980, Gillespie Kidd and Coia. Reworking of red-brick Cambridge themes. **Trinity Hall:** new building 1976, and **Darwin College** extensions 1980, both by Roberts.

New Building, Lady Margaret Hall, Oxford

CONVERSIONS

Growing congestion led to conversion of old buildings, cottages, etc. for undergraduate accommodation, creating new trend.

Trinity College, 1967, Civic Trust Award for cottage conversions. **Blackwell's Music Shop** and **Wadham College scheme,** 1971-72, by Gillespie Kidd & Coia.

Kettle's Yard, Cambridge

Magdalene: Mallory and Benson Courts, where Redfern, then David Roberts, architecture don of college, converted old shop backs into undergraduate village. 1930s, then 50s. **Kettle's Yard,** art gallery and house, by Sir Leslie Martin. Darwin College, by Howell, Killick, Partridge and Amis, 1966.

SOVEREIGNS OF ENGLAND

Anglo-Saxons

827–836	EGBERT
837–858	ETHELWULF
866–871	ETHELRED I
871–899	ALFRED THE GREAT
899–925	EDWARD THE ELDER
925–940	ATHELSTAN
959–975	EDGAR
978–1016	ETHELRED II (THE UNREADY)
1016	EDMUND IRONSIDE
[1016–1035	CANUTE THE DANE
1035–1040	HAROLD I
1041–1042	HARDICANUTE]
1042–1066	EDWARD THE CONFESSOR
1066	HAROLD II

Normans

1066–1087	WILLIAM I (THE CONQUEROR)
1087–1100	WILLIAM II (RUFUS)
1100–1135	HENRY I
1135–1154	STEPHEN

Plantagenets

1154–1189	HENRY II
1189–1199	RICHARD I
1199–1216	JOHN
1216–1272	HENRY III
1272–1307	EDWARD I
1307–1327	EDWARD II
1327–1377	EDWARD III
1377–1399	RICHARD II

Lancastrians

1399–1413	HENRY IV
1413–1422	HENRY V
1422–1461	HENRY VI

Yorkists

1461–1483	EDWARD IV
1483	EDWARD V
1483–1485	RICHARD III

Tudors

1485–1509	HENRY VII
1509–1547	HENRY VIII
1547–1553	EDWARD VI
1553–1558	MARY I
1558–1603	ELIZABETH I

Stuarts

1603–1625	JAMES I
1625–1649	CHARLES I
[1649–1660	COMMONWEALTH]
1660–1685	CHARLES II
1685–1688	JAMES II
1688–1694	WILLIAM III AND MARY II
1694–1702	WILLIAM III
1702–1714	ANNE

Hanoverians

1714–1727	GEORGE I
1727–1760	GEORGE II
1760–1820	GEORGE III
[1810–1820	REGENCY]
1820–1830	GEORGE IV
1830–1837	WILLIAM IV
1837–1901	VICTORIA

House of Saxe-Coburg

1901–1910	EDWARD VII

House of Windsor

1910–1936	GEORGE V
1936	EDWARD VIII
1936–1952	GEORGE VI
1952–	ELIZABETH II

BIBLIOGRAPHY

The literature on Oxford and Cambridge is enormous. This bibliography touches only the fringe, and represents the books most often (though by no means exclusively) consulted during the writing of this guide. They are for the most part fairly easily available, and will probably provide for the needs of the general reader wanting further background information, or anecdotal entertainment.

Oxford

Oxfordshire	Nikolaus Pevsner and Jennifer Sherwood. Penguin Books, Buildings of England Series 1974
New British Architecture	Robert Maxwell. Thames and Hudson 1972
Clarendon Guide to Oxford	A.R. Woolley. Oxford University Press 1979
A History of Oxford University	V.H.H. Green. Batsford 1974
Oxford	Jan Morris. Faber and Faber 1965 OUP Paperback 1978
The Oxford Book of Oxford (Anthology of comments on Oxford)	Jan Morris. Oxford University Press 1978
Portrait of Oxford	Hal Cheetham. Robert Hale 1971
An Oxford University Chest (A lighthearted and idiosyncratic personal view)	John Betjeman. Reprinted by Oxford University Press 1979
The Woman at Oxford	Vera Brittain. Harrap 1960
Oxford and its Colleges	J.W. Wells. Methuen, Little Guide Series, 1897 (long out of print)

Cambridge

Cambridgeshire (2nd edn)	Nikolaus Pevsner. Penguin Books. Buildings of England Series 1970
Cambridge New Architecture A Guide to Cambridge New Architecture	N. Taylor and P. Booth. Leonard Hill Books 1970 and 1972 (out of print)
Cambridge	F.A. Reeve. Batsford 1976
Portrait of Cambridge	C.R. Benstead. Robert Hale 1968

The Colleges of Cambridge	Bryan Little. Adams and Dart 1973
Cambridge and its Colleges	Edmund Vale. Methuen, Little Guide Series 1959 (out of print)
Period Piece (Reminiscences of Cambridge and the Darwin family at the turn of the century)	Gwen Raverat. Faber and Faber 1952
That Infidel Place (History of Girton)	M.C. Bradbrooke. Chatto & Windus 1969
Women at Cambridge	Rita McWilliams Tullberg. Gollancz 1975

Much use has also been made of the University Handbooks published by OUP and CUP and the many excellent Visitors' Guides (usually anonymous) to the individual colleges and churches. These are more frequently to be found at Cambridge than at Oxford. 'Blue Guide England' by Stuart Rossiter (Ernest Benn 1980) has also been a mine of information. Two delightful books unlikely to be found, but which have given the author much pleasure, are: 'A Pictorial and Historical Gossiping Guide to Oxford' by Jas. Moore, undated but probably about 1897, and 'A Guide through the University of Cambridge', anonymous, 1820.

EXPLANATIONS

TYPE. Large type is used in describing the main outline and principal points on each route; it is also used for the introductory comments on and history of each building. Smaller type is used for diversions from the main route, places of lesser importance, and in describing architectural details where these are dealt with at length.

ASTERISKS indicate points of special interest. They are used sparingly; lack of an asterisk does not imply lack of interest or beauty. Their distribution is necessarily somewhat subjective.

PLANS (Pl. A1) after the name of a place or building refers to the grid-plan on the appropriate map. Plans of buildings, where given, are self-explanatory.

ABBREVIATIONS. In addition to those generally accepted the following also occur:

General		Architectural	
Abp	Archbishop	Norm	Norman
adm	admission	EE	Early English
Bp	Bishop	Dec.	Decorated
c.	circa (about)	Perp.	Perpendicular
C	century	Vict	Victorian
exc	except		
Pl.	plan		
pron	pronounced		

The term Gothic is applied both to medieval styles (EE, Dec., and Perp.) and also to the later reproductions of the style (eg Vict Gothic). Gothick indicates the romantic fantasy medievalism fashionable in the late 18C–early 19C.

I OXFORD

The City of Oxford

Oxford University

PRACTICAL INFORMATION

Transport

BY CAR, from London: A40/M40; about 1¼ hrs, longer at busy times.

RAILWAY STATION, Park End St. (8–10 min walk from Carfax, or 3 mins by bus). Service to and from London (Paddington) about every hour during the day (approximate time 1–1¼ hr). Tel: 722333.

BUS AND COACH STATION, Gloucester Green. *Long Distance* Service No 190 to and from London (Victoria Coach Station) half hourly during weekday daytime; variations on Sun and in evenings (approximate time 1 hr 30–40 mins depending on traffic conditions). Service Nos 390 and 790 to and from Heathrow Airport hourly (approximate time 1 hr). There are direct and frequent services between Oxford and most large or local towns, with onward connections all over the country. Detailed information from Oxford Motor Services, 395 Cowley Road, tel 774611/5; Gloucester Green Bus Station, tel 40504; Carfax Travel Bureau, tel 726172.

City Services. All parts of the city and its environs are served by bus. For Banbury Rd, Nos 580, 581, 280, 281. For Woodstock Rd, Nos 420, 421, 423. For Iffley Nos 542, 543, 440, 441. For Cowley Nos 501, 502.

A park and ride service from the outskirts to the city centre operates Mon–Sat as follows:
North side: Pear Tree, Woodstock.
West side: Seacourt, Botley Rd.
South side: Red Bridge, Abingdon Rd.

Parking. Car parks are shown on the map. The more central ones are apt to be full after about 9.30 a.m. There is a limited amount of street parking in the centre (meters; maximum stay 2 hrs) and further out free (maximum stay as indicated).

———

Main Post Office: St Aldate's St.

Information Office: St Aldate's St., tel 726871/2 (separate number for accommodation). Open all the year Mon–Sat 9–5.30; end May–late Sept Sun and Bank Holiday Mon 10.30–1, 1.30–4.

Accommodation, of which there is a great variety from large hotels to bed and breakfast, may be difficult to find in the height of the

41

season and particularly during Eights Week (late May) and Commemoration (late June/early July). Whenever possible bookings should be made well in advance. The Information Office will help (tel 726873).

Theatres: New Theatre, George St., Playhouse, Beaumont St.

Cinemas: ABC George St. and Magdalen St.

Brass Rubbing: St Mary the Virgin Church, open daily, summer 10–6, winter 11–5.

Boating is a very popular summer pastime on both rivers. On the THAMES rowing boats, punts, and canoes can be hired at Folly Bridge, Medley Boat Stn (Port Meadow) and Weirs Lane (off Abingdon Rd) and sailing dinghies at Bossoms Boatyards (Port Meadow). Salter Bros. run regular excursions from Folly Bridge (tel 43421). On the CHERWELL punts and canoes can be hired at Magdalen Bridge and the Cherwell Boat House (Bardwell Rd, off Banbury Rd). Punting is not as difficult as it looks. The first principle is to keep the pole as close as possible to the side of the boat; let it go if you are in danger of falling overboard, there is usually someone about who will retrieve it for you. A wise precaution is always to have a paddle as well. At Oxford you stand in the sloping end of the boat to punt.

Bathing: in the THAMES: at Long Bridges, reached by towpath from Folly Bridge; Tumbling Bay, reached by towpath from Botley Rd, and at Wolvercote, near Godstow. In the CHERWELL: at Parson's Pleasure, reached from South Parks Rd. Swimming pools at Hinksey Park, off Abingdon Rd, and Temple Rd, Cowley (indoor).

Sightseeing

General Advice. All the colleges display notices at their gates giving the opening times currently valid. They also indicate where the visitor may go. These directions should be strictly respected. Staircases and working libraries are **never** accessible to sightseers unless special arrangements for a particular purpose have been made in advance in writing. Visitors are particularly asked to be quiet.

Opening times. Where these are more or less permanently fixed, as with museums, galleries, old libraries round which visitors are conducted, etc, details are given in the appropriate place. The colleges themselves pose more of a problem, their opening times being liable to vary from year to year. As a rough guide, many are closed in the mornings, most are open for a few hours in the afternoon. To help in planning a tour a list (1981) is given below, but there is no guarantee that it will remain correct. The times apply only to college quadrangles and grounds; chapels, halls and other points of interest may or may not be open; where they are regularly open at fixed times this is noted in the appropriate place.

All Souls	2–5
Balliol	10–6
Brasenose	10–dusk
Christ Church	see individual entry
Corpus Christi	Term 1.30–4.30, Vacation 11.30–4.30
Exeter	9–dusk
Hertford	9.30–dusk

Jesus	2–4.30
Keble	9–dusk
Lady Margaret Hall	all day
Lincoln	2–6
Magdalen	2–6.15
Manchester	Term 9–5, Vacation 9–1
Mansfield	9–dusk
Merton	Mon–Fri 2–6, Sat and Sun 10–4
New College	Term 2–6, Vacation 11–6
Nuffield	9–dusk
Oriel	2–5
Pembroke	2–6
Queen's	Term 2–6, Vacation 9–5
St Anne's	all day
St Antony's	Mon–Sat 2–5
St Catherine's	9–dusk
St Edmund Hall	9–dusk
St Hilda's	2–5
St Hugh's	all day
St John's	Mon–Fri 2–5, Sat and Sun 10–1
St Peter's	Chapel 10–6 in term
Somerville	10–5
Trinity	2–5
University	10–6
Wadham	11–5
Wolfson	all day, grounds only, not quadrangles.
Worcester	Term 2–dusk, Vacation Mon–Sat 9–12, 2–dusk, Sun 2–dusk

Colleges may be closed during the summer examination period (mid-May–late June); many are also closed for holidays in August and at Christmas and Easter.

For visitors with very limited time there are guided walking tours lasting about 2 hrs which leave the Information Centre at 10.45 and 2.15 daily during the summer.

HISTORY

Oxford is the meeting place of two rivers. Flowing from the north-west is the Upper Thames, or Isis, and from the north the Cherwell ('Char'). Their waters join to the south of the old city centre, and together flow on south-east towards London as the Thames. These rivers still play an important part in Oxford's leisure life; in the past they were the city's raison d'être. The first settlement probably grew up at the river-crossing ('the ford for oxen') and must have been important as a meeting place of both roads and waterways, and as a defensive strongpoint in times of trouble, commanding as it did these means of communication. Even today Oxford is in some sense the crossroads of England.

Its name first appears in the Anglo-Saxon Chronicle in the year 912, when Edward the Elder 'held Lundenbyrg and Oxnaford and all the lands pertaining thereto'. By then it was one of the principal towns in the country, a busy trading centre and frequently the place where kings and their councils of state foregathered. Religious orders too had establishments here; according to legend St Frideswide had founded her priory at Oxford some time in the 8C, because it was there that a well-aimed thunderbolt rescued her from the undesired attentions of King Algar. Nothing remains of her church or convent buildings, which were burnt down by the Danes very early in the 11C.

When William of Normandy arrived in 1066 Oxford was handed over to Robert d'Oilly. He built the castle (see pp 87–8 for details) and began work on the massive walls which by the 13C enclosed the city. Churches were built, and monastic houses proliferated. St Frideswide's Priory was refounded in 1122; Osney, Godstow and Rewley abbeys followed. Various orders of friars established themselves in the area just south of the town which is now a wilderness of ring roads and car parks. Trade flourished and Oxford prospered.

But there was a cuckoo in the nest—the infant university, which soon began to dominate its adopted home. From the mid 13C the town declined as the university increased, and the history of Oxford becomes to all intents and purposes the history of Oxford University.

Town and gown were at loggerheads almost from the beginning. All through the Middle Ages the townspeople complained of the students' riotous behaviour, the university complained of the townsmen's grasping dishonesty, and the ill-feeling erupted into frequent battles. On practically every issue they supported different sides; in the Civil War the town was for Parliament, the university for the King; in the 19C the town wanted the railway, the university opposed it, and frustrated too the proposed siting of the chief GWR works near the town, which greatly needed some such source of employment. The university had a stranglehold on development and change.

Now the tables are turned, and in the 20C Oxford has become a large industrial, commercial and residential centre, where the ancient university probably impinges very little on the lives of most of its citizens apart, perhaps, from the number of visitors it attracts. This tremendous change was largely brought about in the first place by one man—William Morris (later Lord Nuffield), designer and manufacturer of the Morris car. He began, shortly before the First World War, with a small bicycle and then motor bicycle business in Longwall Street. This led in the 1920s to motor car production, first on the outskirts of Oxford itself, later in the (then) village of Cowley. Morris Motors (now part of BL) took over Oxford in the 20C as it had been taken over in the 12C by students. Indeed the old city is sometimes referred to as 'The Latin Quarter of Cowley'.

Low-lying and damp, Oxford is supposed to be an enervating place. This is not the impression it gives as traffic roars unceasingly along the streets, shopping crowds hurry along the pavements, cyclists weave their way through the narrow lanes, and tour guides whisk their charges at breathtaking speed from college to college.

OXFORD UNIVERSITY has 35 colleges, of which 7 are for graduates only: All Souls, Green, Linacre, Nuffield, St Antony's, St Cross, and Wolfson. 5 were founded for women: Lady Margaret Hall, St Anne's, St Hilda's, St Hugh's, and Somerville. All colleges are now (1981) mixed except Oriel (men only), and St Hilda's and Somerville (women only). St Hugh's admits men and women for post graduate studies, but women only as undergraduates. There are 5 Permanent Private Halls: Campion Hall, Greyfriars, and St Benet's for Jesuit, Franciscan, and Benedictine students respectively, and Mansfield College and Regent's Park College for United Reformed Church and Baptist Students respectively. The various theological colleges and 'houses' are not part of the university.

There are about 9400 undergraduate students (1979/80).

1 CARFAX, AND SOUTH AND SOUTH-EAST OF CARFAX

The centre of Oxford is CARFAX (Pl. C2, the name possibly derives from the Latin 'quadrifurcus', four forks, or the French 'quatre voies', four ways). The roads that cross here are: (N.) *Cornmarket* (buses and taxis only), which beyond Broad St. becomes Magdalen St. and then widens out into St Giles; (S.) *St Aldate's*, leading to Folly Bridge (over the Thames); (E.) *High St.* ('the High') leading to Magdalen Bridge (over the Cherwell, pron Charwell and usually referred to as 'the Cher'); (W.) *Queen St.* (pedestrians only) leading towards the modern Westgate Shopping Centre and the railway station.

It is helpful in finding the way about, and round buildings, to have this pattern and the points of the compass firmly in mind.

The majority of Oxford's most beautiful and interesting buildings, both ancient and modern, are within a $^1/_2$ m. radius of this crossroads, and of these the greater number are concentrated in the $^1/_4$ m. square immediately E. of Carfax, on each side of the High. Explorations can conveniently be divided into four groups, taking as a starting-point Carfax itself.

The 14C tower (open late Mar–end Oct, weekdays 10–6, Sun 2–6), on which is a clock with striking quarter-jacks, is all that remains of *St Martin's Church*, demolished 1896. In this church Orlando Gibbons the composer (1583–1625) was baptised, and Shakespeare is supposed to have stood sponsor to the infant William Davenant (playwright, 1606–68) whose father was landlord of the Crown Tavern opposite (now No. 3 Cornmarket), where Shakespeare almost certainly used to stay on journeys between London and Stratford. John Aubrey, the historian, records that Shakespeare 'was wont to go into Warwickshire once a yeare, and did in his journeye lye at this house in Oxon where he was exceedingly respected'.

The former inn guest room on the second floor is now known as *The Painted Room* (used as offices by the W.E.A., but open Mon–Fri 10–12, 2–4; donation appreciated). In the course of alterations in 1927, when the premises were occupied by a firm of tailors, early 17C oak panelling was discovered under the layers of wallpaper and canvas. Beneath this panelling were well-preserved wall-paintings dating from about 1550, an elegant design of trellis-work enclosing bunches of fruit and flowers. Similar paintings, dating from the 1550s and 1590s were found in 1948 in several rooms of the *Golden Cross* next door (seen on application to the Manager's office).

The Golden Cross has been an inn since the 13C, and still retains its old enclosed yard; the buildings date mostly from the 15C and 17C.

As one goes S. down ST ALDATE'S (Pl. C4) the *Information Office* is on the r. with the main Post Office and a row of telephone booths just beyond. Opposite is the Town Hall, which houses the *City Museum* (open Tues–Sat 10–5; fee). This tells the history of Oxford in a series of pictures, models, old maps, prints etc, excellently explained in English, French, German, Spanish, Japanese and Arabic. The highlight is a 'son et lumiere'-type presentation of the Massacre of St Scholastica's Day (see History, p 10).

On the corner of Pembroke St. (r.) is *St Aldate's Church*, largely rebuilt in the mid 19C, vigorously evangelical in its worship. Further on (r.) is the small *Museum of Modern Art* (open Tues–Sat 10–5, Sun 2–5). At the far end of the street is *St Ebbe's Church*, also largely rebuilt in the mid 19C, but with a massively carved Norm W. door. Beyond is the huge Westgate shopping precinct (Pl. C3/4). For more on this part of Oxford see p 88.

Behind St Aldate's Church is the entrance to **Pembroke College** (Pl. C4), founded in 1624, and named after the Earl of Pembroke, Chancellor of the University at the time; it replaced a number of medieval halls, chief of which was Broadgates Hall, whose refectory is now the Senior Common Room. Old Quad is mostly 17C but much altered about 1830, and to the W. (r.) is Chapel Quad, spacious early Vict; both are colourful with flowers. At the far end, approached up a flight of steps, is the very handsome *Hall*, with hammerbeam roof and tall Perp. windows. On the l. of the quad is the *Chapel*, a simple early 18C building elaborately decorated in 1884 by C.E. Kempe, who also designed the windows. It was colourfully restored in 1972. The altarpiece is a copy by Cranke of Ruben's 'Risen Christ'.

To the r. is the North Quad (1962); it consists of the Besse Building (named after Oxford's French benefactor M. Besse, see also pp 15–16, 94), a row of old houses originally facing Pembroke Street but now turned back to front, and a new building (1976) named after the Rt. Hon. Harold Macmillan, Chancellor of the University since 1960. The former Beef Lane is now within this quad. On the S. side are three striking bronze statues, 'Mourning Women' by J.W. Harvey (1946), a memorial to members of Pembroke's JCR who died in the Second World War.

Back in Old Quad a passage l. of the entrance leads to the Master's Lodgings, originally almshouses built by Wolsey, and to the new *Library* (1974–75) given by the McGowin family of Alabama (no adm except as stated below).

Pembroke's most famous son was Dr Johnson, who studied here for four terms in 1728–29 till poverty forced him to leave. He occupied the second-floor rooms over the gateway. Johnson retained a great affection for Oxford in spite of his brief and not always happy sojourn. His portrait by Reynolds hangs in the Senior Common Room; his teapot, cider mug, one of his 'themes' (essays), and some books are displayed in the library, and the college possesses various other Johnson memorabilia. They can only be seen however by special permission on written application.

FAMOUS MEMBERS. Broadgates Hall: Francis Beaumont, playwright, 1584–1616; John Pym, parliamentarian, 1584–1643; Sir Thomas Browne, author of 'Religio Medici', 1605–82.

Pembroke: Dr Johnson (see above), 1709–84; William Shenstone, poet, 1714–63; George Whitefield, leading Methodist, 1714–70; Sir William Blackstone, author of 'Commentaries on the Laws of England', 1723–80; John Lemprière, author of 'Bibliotheca Classica', 1765–1824; James Smithson, founder of the Smithsonian Institution in Washington, 1765–1829.

To the S. of Pembroke, in Brewer St., are the *Cathedral Choir School* and *Campion Hall*, a centre for Jesuit students, designed by Sir Edwin Lutyens in the early 1930s, and named after Edmund Campion, the Roman Catholic martyr (1581). In Rose Place is the *Old Palace* built in 16C for Robert King, last abbot of Osney and first Bishop of Oxford. With striking modern additions (1970–71, by

Ahrends, Burton and Koralek), it is now the Roman Catholic Chaplaincy to the University.

No. 83 St Aldate's is supposed to be the shop in Lewis Carroll's 'Through the Looking Glass'; its charming sign commemorates the connection. ¼ m. beyond is Folly Bridge (formerly Grand Pont, rebuilt 1825–27 by Ebenezer Perry; Pl. C6). Until the late 18C a tower and gatehouse stood on the bridge, where traditionally Roger Bacon (early scientist and astronomer, c. 1214–94) had his study (see also p 88).

Almost opposite Pembroke is the entrance to *Christ Church Meadow* (Pl. D5). Broad Walk, formerly lined by elms, runs E. to the Cherwell. A path running N. between Corpus Christi (l.) and Merton (r.) across Merton Field, where parts of the old city wall can be seen, links it with Merton St. New Walk runs to the Isis and the college boat houses (which replace the erstwhile and more picturesque college barges), where there is a pleasant riverside walk shaded with lime trees; in summer the air is heavy with their scent.

Between New Walk and St Aldate's is the *Music Faculty* building, originally St Catherine's Society and subsequently Linacre College (see p 99).

*Christ Church (Pl. C4; open Mon–Fri 9.30–4.30, Sat 9.30–12 noon, Sun all day. Entry through Meadow Gate—fee—exc Sun, when the main gate should be used), known familiarly as 'the House', from its Latin Name 'Aedes Christi', is the largest college in Oxford and has many points of comparison with Trinity College, Cambridge (see p 119). It was founded by Wolsey as Cardinal College in 1525, on the site of St Frideswide's Priory, most of which he demolished. Of the vastly ambitious buildings he planned, few were completed when he fell from favour in 1529. Henry VIII refounded it as Henry VIII College (an ecclesiastical establishment only) in 1532; this in turn was suppressed, to be refounded yet again, in 1545, as Christ Church. What Wolsey had left of the old priory church became Oxford Cathedral as well as the college chapel (a unique situation), and the Dean head of both the cathedral chapter and the college. The Dean is appointed (for life) by the Crown; the reigning sovereign is also the college Visitor. The royal connection was strengthened during the Civil War, when Charles I made the deanery his residence. Fellows of Christ Church are known, confusingly, as 'students'. The college has a long line of most distinguished members, including thirteen prime ministers, and was traditionally strongly linked with Eton and the English aristocracy.

From St Aldate's a wide pathway leads through the beautiful War Memorial Gardens (1926; wrought-iron gates by R.M.Y. Gleadowe) to *Meadow Buildings*, built in 1863 in Vict/Venetian Gothic style, and to the visitors' entrance. The buildings ahead (r.) are what remains of St Frideswide's Priory: the original 'frater' (later the Old Library, now undergraduate rooms), the cloister and the cathedral.

The small *Cloister*, whose W. side was pulled down in 1525, is in the Perp. style (1499). It was here that Cranmer was formally 'degraded' in 1556, being publicly insulted, stripped of his vestments, and having his hair shorn. A Norm

Christt Church

N

Blue Boar Street

Peckwater Quadrangle 18C

Blue Boar Quadrangle 1968

Killcanon

New Library 18C

Canterbury Quadrangle 18C

17C

Deanery Garden

Deanery

Picture Gallery 1968

17C

Oriel College

Corpus Christi College

St Aldate's Street

Great Quadrangle

16C

16C

16C-17C

16C

Cathedral 12C-16C

Tom Tower 17C

16C

16C

Hall

Tower 19C

Cloisters

Kitchen

Old Library — Former Frater of Priory

Meadow Buildings Mid 19C

Gateway to Christ Church Meadow

War Memorial Garden

Broad Walk

King Edward St.

Oriel St.

doorway leads into the EE *Chapter House*, where there is an exhibition of old plate, and a small bookstall and shop.

The **Cathedral* (open 9.30–4.30), the smallest in England, is predominantly late Norm in appearance (rebuilt 1141–80), although many additions and alterations have been made at various times, notably the 13C spire, one of the earliest in England (hence perhaps its rather squat appearance), and the 19C W. front and E. end by Sir George Gilbert Scott (1870). The visitors' doorway leads into the S. AISLE, the E. end of which is the *Lucy Chapel*. The **E. window* (c. 1330) shows, in the upper lights, the arms of England and France still separate, and in the central light the martyrdom of Becket, his head replaced, presumably in deference to Henry VIII's dislike of the saint, by a piece of plain glass. Other interesting windows are a memorial to Bp King (see Old Palace, p 51), and one by Burne-Jones portraying Faith, Hope and Charity. In this aisle are many monuments, to cavaliers killed in the Civil War and to cathedral

Oxford Cathedral: the nave arcade. From an early nineteenth century print

dignitaries, and the regimental chapel of the Oxfordshire and Buckinghamshire Light Infantry.

In the NAVE the massive piers of the arcades are alternately round and octagonal, and an illusion of height is given by the unusual placing of the triforium inside the main arches, with a secondary arch below (as at Romsey Abbey and Jedburgh). The roof is 16C timberwork, the pulpit and organ screen 17C, the stalls 19C. There are monuments to Bp Berkeley (the philosopher, 1685–1753) and Dr Pusey (high-Anglican reformer, 1800–82).

The CHOIR has a gloriously vaulted late 15C *roof (similar to the Divinity School, p 75). The E. end, by Scott, is in Norm style.

On the N. side (l.) are three parallel aisles: the North Choir aisle, the Lady Chapel, and the Latin Chapel. Between the first two are the remains of St Frideswide's shrine, and between the Lady Chapel and Latin Chapel the finely carved oak watching-chamber (15C) from which guard was kept on the treasures of the shrine. The putative saint is commemorated every 19 Oct in a special service attended by dignitaries of the cathedral, university and city, in fully-robed splendour. The Latin Chapel is so called because the daily service was said here in Latin until 1861 (except for a break during the

Commonwealth); it was also used for Divinity lectures till the late 19C. It has massive oak stalls, some probably 14C, others 16C, interesting monuments including a bust of Robert Burton (author of 'The Anatomy of Melancholy', 1577–1640), and in the N. windows some 14C stained glass. All three N. aisles have E. windows by William Morris and Burne-Jones. At the W. end of the N. aisle is a spectacular window by Abraham van Linge (c. 1630) depicting Jonah and Nineveh.

The entrance to the *Hall (open daily 9.30–12, 2–4.30 exc Sun) is in the S.E. corner of the Bell Tower (Bodley, 1879), up a stairway, built by Wyatt in 1805, beneath a beautiful fan-vaulted *roof (1640, a very late example of the style). The Hall, the largest in Oxford (115 ft by 40 ft), which was completed in Wolsey's time, has a sumptuously carved and gilded hammerbeam roof, whose central bosses bear the arms of the see of Winchester, of which, inter alia, Wolsey was bishop, encircled by the Garter. The arms of five more of Wolsey's sees, Lincoln, Bath and Wells, Durham, York, and St Alban's, and his cardinal's hat, appear in the heraldic glass (partly original) of the W. window. An impressive array of portraits includes work by Lely, Kneller, Reynolds, Gainsborough, Romney, Lawrence, Millais, Watts, Herkomer, and Graham Sutherland. Henry VIII dominates the scene, flanked by Elizabeth I and Wolsey. A bust of the reigning sovereign (college Visitor) is traditionally placed immediately below him.

Wolsey's vast kitchen, below, has been modernised and is still in use (no adm). An election slogan of 1829 reading 'No Peel' is burned into a doorway at the stair foot.

Wolsey also built the S. and two-thirds of the E. and W. sides of the GREAT QUADRANGLE (Tom Quad), including the massive gateway in whose vaulted roof are forty-eight coats of arms. The statue of Wolsey was not put up until 1791. The famous cupola-topped *Tom Tower*, designed by Wren in 1681, carries a huge bell (Great Tom, 6¼ tons, last recast 1680) taken from Osney Abbey. It rings 101 times every evening at 9.05 (9 pm by the Oxford meridian), once for each member of the original foundation, and was formerly the signal that all undergraduates should be within their colleges and the gates closed. 'It need hardly be said that the signal is not obeyed', says a guide book of 1897. The great pool, originally the college reservoir, is known as 'Mercury' from its central statue, a 1928 replacement of the 17C one by Giovanni da Bologna, toppled from its plinth by Lord Derby in 1817.

In the N.E. corner of Tom Quad is Fell's Tower (statues of John Fell, Dean 1660–86, and H.G. Liddell, Dean 1855–91). It was Dean Fell who completed the building and lay-out of Tom Quad in the late 17C. He was an energetic educational reformer and disciplinarian, hence perhaps the well-known verse beginning 'I do not like thee, Dr Fell'. Beneath it Kill Canon Passage (so called for its draughty cold) leads into PECKWATER QUAD, built on the site of Peckwater Inn, 1705–13. Here (S. side) is the *Library* (open only by special arrangement), built 1717–72 to be 'the finest library that belongs to any Society in Europe'. It has beautiful plasterwork ceilings, 18C woodwork and furnishings (including twenty-four stools by Chippendale) and some of the earliest wall bookcases to be built. It houses a priceless collection of books and MSS, and such interesting relics as Wolsey's cardinal's hat (acquired from Horace Walpole) and chair, John Evelyn's diary, Gibbon's miniature travelling library, Lewis Carroll memorabilia, and two copper braziers for charcoal. In the vestibule are busts of past royal Visitors and distinguished members of the college (one of J.L. Lowe, Dean 1939–59, by Epstein).

On the W. side is the entrance to the modern BLUE BOAR QUAD (by Powell and Moya, 1968), on the E. is CANTERBURY QUAD, built 1773–83 on the site of the old Canterbury College.

The *Picture Gallery* (open Mon–Sat 10.30–1, 2–4.30, Sun 2–4.30, entry can be made direct through Canterbury gate) contains the finest college collection in Oxford of paintings and drawings, mostly 14C–17C Italian.

FAMOUS MEMBERS are so numerous it is impossible to mention more than a random sample. Royalties: Edward VII; politicians (some Prime Ministers) Canning, Peel, Gladstone, Lord Salisbury, Lord Halifax, Lord Avon. Other notabilities: Sir Philip Sidney, poet and soldier, 1554–86; Robert Burton, writer, 1557–1640; William Penn, Quaker, founder of Pennsylvania, 'sent down' for nonconformity, 1644–1718; John Locke, philosopher, 1632–1704; John Wesley, founder of Methodism, 1703–91, and his brother Charles; John Ruskin, art pundit and social philosopher, 1819–1900; C.L. Dodgson ('Lewis Carroll'), 1832–98; W.H. Auden, poet, 1907–73.

The gate of Canterbury Quad leads out into Oriel Sq. Immediately opposite is **Oriel College** (Pl. D1) founded as 'St Mary's College' in 1324 by Adam de Brome, almoner to Edward II, and rector of St Mary the Virgin church, which was used in the Middle Ages as the college chapel, and of whose living the college is patron; de Brome is commemorated in one of its chapels. In 1326 the college was refounded by Edward II, who gave it the Hospital of St Bartholomew in Cowley as a source of income. Thereafter it was known as 'The King's College'. The name Oriel derives from a building on the site named 'La Oriole' acquired in 1329. In the 19C it was the centre of the Tractarian Movement (see History, p 13, and Famous Members, below).

The front quadrangle, built 1620–42, is in the 17C Gothic style pioneered by Merton and Wadham, with pretty Jacobean shaped gables above the windows on both outer and inner sides. A flight of steps leads up to the *Hall* (usually locked), which has a handsome hammerbeam roof. Over the hall porch are statues of Edward II and James I or Charles I, surmounted by one of the Virgin and Child, all canopied.

The *Chapel* (r.; key at porter's lodge) has its original 17C furnishings, with richly carved communion rails and a recently restored bronze lectern. All the glass, except in the ante-chapel, is late 19C.

The N. side of Back Quad (l.) is formed by the Library, a Palladian building by Wyatt (1788). Beyond is *St Mary's Quad*, formerly St Mary's Hall ('Skimmery'), absorbed into the college only in 1902. Its attractive little hall and chapel (c. 1640) are now respectively the Junior Common Room and Junior Library. Opposite is the *Rhodes building* (1901–11), which faces out on to the High. Rhodes was already diamond mining when he came up to Oriel, and owing to frequent absences in S. Africa took eight years to get his degree. He left the college £100,000 and his statue adorns the High St. front, gazing down benevolently from a lofty height on to those of Edward VII and George V.

FAMOUS MEMBERS: the great leaders of the 19C Tractarian Movement were Fellows: John Keble, Richard Whateley, Thomas Arnold (headmaster of Rugby), John Newman (afterwards cardinal), E.B. Pusey, R.H. Froude, R.W. Church. Others include: Sir Walter Raleigh, courtier, explorer, poet, 1552?–1618; Gilbert White, naturalist, and vicar of Selborne, 1720–93; Samuel Wilberforce ('Soapy Sam'), Bp of Oxford, who opposed Darwin's theories, 1805–73; Thomas Hughes, author of 'Tom Brown's Schooldays', 1822–96;

Oxford Jacobean Gothic: Oriel College, Front Quadrangle. From an early nineteenth century drawing by J.M.W. Turner

Matthew Arnold, poet, 1822–88; J.A. Froude, historian, 1818–94; Cecil Rhodes, 1853–1902.

Corpus Christi College (Pl. D3) was founded in 1517 by Richard Foxe, bishop in turn of Exeter, Bath and Wells, Durham, and Winchester, Lord Privy Seal to Henry VII and Henry VIII, and a great benefactor not only of Oxford but also Cambridge (where he was Chancellor, and Master of Pembroke College). Corpus is a small, intimate college with a strong tradition of learning established by its founder, who wished it to be 'as a hive', that 'the scholars night and day may make wax and sweet honey to the honour of God, and the advantage of themselves and all Christian men'. Provision was made for lectures in Greek, Latin, and Hebrew, whence Erasmus (a friend of Foxe) named it 'bibliotheca trilinguis'.

The gateway roof has beautiful vaulting of 1517. Above in the tower are the original rooms of the President, one with Tudor panelling and plasterwork, and an oriel window (no adm). The *FRONT QUAD is paved; in the centre is a tall sundial (1581) topped by the college emblem, a pelican (a modern replacement). The perpetual calendar round the plinth dates from 1606. On the E. side (l.) is the small *Hall* with its original hammerbeam roof, and beyond it a passage leads to the *Chapel*. Its particular features are the handsome late 17C stalls and baroque screen, the altarpiece 'after' Rubens, a striking E. window of St Christopher (1931) and a brass eagle lectern (pre-Reformation and the earliest in Oxford). The *Library*, opposite the entrance (no adm), has rich early 17C plasterwork and furnishings; the bookcases still have the rods to which books were formerly chained. Beyond, to the S.E. (l.), are a narrow quad cloistered on one side, the Fellows' or Turner buildings of 1706, and lovely gardens. Further buildings have been added at intervals, including some across Merton St. in Magpie Lane.

Unlike the other Oxford colleges Corpus did not surrender its plate to Charles I in 1642, and therefore has many priceless early pieces, including Bp Foxe's gilt and enamelled pastoral staff.

FAMOUS MEMBERS: Nicholas Udall, scholar, teacher, dramatist, 1505–56; Richard Hooker, theologian, author of 'Laws of Ecclesiastical Polity', 1554?–1600; General Oglethorpe, founder of Georgia, 1696–1785; John Keble and Thomas Arnold as undergraduates (see Oriel); Sir Henry Newbolt, poet, 1862–1938; Robert Bridges, poet, 1844–1930.

Immediately next door is ***Merton College** (Pl. D3), in all essentials the oldest in Oxford, although both University and Balliol were endowed a few years earlier. Merton was founded in 1264 by Walter de Merton, principally for the study of the 'Sciences', mathematics and natural philosophy, as opposed to theology. The original deed, complete with seals, is in the college archives. The enlarged statutes of 1274, and the whole organisation, served as a model for subsequent colleges at both Oxford and Cambridge. In 1380 a former fellow, John Wyliott, provided scholarships whose recipients were known as 'portionistae', hence their designation as 'postmasters', still used. Across the street is a house called 'Postmaster's Hall'.

The buildings are among the oldest and most interesting in Oxford, although many drastic alterations and additions were made in the 19C. The gatehouse, with carvings depicting St John the Baptist and (perhaps) Christ in the Wilderness, dates from 1418. Its statues of Walter de Merton and Henry III are reproductions.

On the S. side of FRONT QUAD (opposite the gate) is the *Hall*, originally 13C but virtually rebuilt by Wyatt in 1794 and again by Scott in 1874. The door, with elaborate ironwork, is 13C. On the W. side (r.) past the ancient Treasury or Muniment Room (1274) with high-pitched stone roof, is the entrance to the picturesque *MOB

QUAD (c. 1308). On its N. side is the *Chapel*, the oldest in Oxford, impressively lofty and large. The choir was built in 1294; the exquisite tracery of its E. window contains 13–14C glass, and the glass in the side windows is contemporary. The beautiful lectern is of spun brass of c. 1500; in the floor are memorial brasses to various Wardens, made c. 1400 and 1471. The altarpiece, a Crucifixion, is of the school of Tintoretto. Between choir and ante-chapel is a handsome Baroque screen, part of one designed by Wren, removed in the 19C and restored in 1960. The ante-chapel is formed by the transepts (14C Perp.); the intended nave, whose arch is the W. window, was never built. This window contains 15C glass, but is partly hidden by the organ and a trompe l'oeil painting (1968).

In the S. transept (r.) is a 14C piscina, curiously set high on the wall, and in the N. transept (l.) a monument to Sir Thomas Bodley (d 1613), founder of the Bodleian Library, and Anthony à Wood (d 1695), historian of Oxford and chronicler of his times.

In the S.E. corner of Mob Quad, opposite the chapel, is the *Library* (guided visits lasting $\frac{1}{2}$ hr, 2–4; apply to the Verger, in passage between Front and Mob Quads), perhaps the most interesting medieval library in England. Built 1371–78, it was the first to house the books upright in shelves, instead of lying flat in chests (one of which can be seen near the stairway). A few volumes are still chained to the shelves, which are fitted with reading boards. The furnishings, panelling, plasterwork and dormer windows are late 16C– early 17C. In the small side windows are fragments of 15C stained glass originally in the chapel. In addition to MSS, the library's historic treasures include Chaucer's astrolabe, an early Welsh Bible, and a massive chest with a complicated threefold locking mechanism in the lid. The original floor level was lower than the present one, so the traditional ghost can be seen only from his knees up.

Leading off the library are two rooms devoted to *Max Beerbohm* memorabilia.

To the W. (r.) of Mob Quad in a small garden are Grove Buildings (1864 by Butterfield, much modified in 1930). E. (l.) is FELLOWS' or GREAT QUAD, built in 1610, in the elegant late Gothic style shortly copied at Oriel, Wadham, and University Colleges, and adorned with an attractive sundial in 1974. Above Fitzjames Gateway (1497) on its N.E. side were the original Warden's lodgings, now known as the Queen's Rooms, from their occupation by Queen Henrietta Maria during the Civil War. Merton traditionally provided lodgings for royal ladies visiting Oxford. St Alban's Quad (rebuilt 1904) on the site of St Alban's Hall, incorporated into the college in 1881, gives access to the beautiful garden (adm only by special permission in writing) which has a terrace walk overlooking Merton fields and Christ Church Meadow, and a pretty early 18C stone summerhouse. Further buildings, and adaptations of old buildings, towards Rose Lane provide additional accommodation and a new Warden's Lodgings (1966).

FAMOUS MEMBERS: Thomas Bradwardine and other notable 14C philosophers and mathematicians, and possibly Wyclif, Bible translator and religious reformer, c. 1329(?)–84; Sir Thomas Bodley, 1545–1613; Lord Halsbury, Lord Chancellor, author of 'The Laws of England', 1823–1921; Max Beerbohm, writer, caricaturist, wit, 1872–1956; T.S. Eliot, poet, 1888–1965; F. Soddy, scientist, Nobel prizewinner, 1877–1956. Andrew Irvine (1902–1924) was still an undergraduate when he died climbing Mount Everest with Mallory; his last diary is in the college library.

In *Kybald St.*, a cul-de-sac off Magpie Lane (linking Merton St. with the High) are the charming old John Parsons Almshouses (1814), now part of University College. New almshouses were built in St Clement's by Helen and Frank Altschul of New York in 1959. The N. end of Merton St. emerges into the High; it is worth pausing here to look up and down this beautiful and world-famous street. To the r. past Rose Lane, which leads to Merton Field **and** Christ Church Meadow, is the **Botanic Garden** (Pl. D2, adm free; April–Sept: weekdays 8.30–5, Sun 10–12 and 2–6; Oct–Mar: weekdays 9–4.30, Sun 2–4.30; plant houses 2–4 daily). Originally the Physick Garden, linked with the Faculty of Medicine, it was founded in 1621 by Lord Danby, whose bust is over the impressive portal (by Nicholas Stone, 1630), flanked by statues of Charles I and Charles II. The common wasteland weed Oxford Ragwort was first grown here from seed brought from Mt Etna.

Across the street is **Magdalen College** (pron 'Maudlin', Pl. D2), one of the most splendid in Oxford, founded in 1458 by William Waynflete, in turn headmaster of Winchester, Provost of Eton, Bp of Winchester, and Lord Chancellor, on the site of the former Hospital of St John. The scholars are known as 'demies' (because they received only half the allowances of a Fellow); Magdalen led the way in providing places for fee-paying students. Always of aristocratic birth, they were known as 'noblemen' or 'gentleman commoners' as appropriate, and wore special silk-braided gowns. The college has always had strong links with royalty, the founder's schools, and the aristocracy. The choir school was part of the original foundation, and the chapel services are famous for their music.

Magdalen was in the forefront of the Revival of Learning and the Reformation, and strongly Puritan in the 17C. Nevertheless it loyally supported Charles I in the Civil War, giving him nearly all its silver. James II rewarded this sacrifice by forcing upon the Fellows a president unacceptable in morals, qualifications, and churchmanship. Their determined resistance led to their expulsion. Eventually, however, the King had to bow to public opinion and reinstate them. Restoration Day, 5 Oct 1688, has been celebrated ever since. In the 18C the college had a reputation for sloth and self-indulgence, for which it was severely castigated by the youthful Edward Gibbon (see below).

Being outside the city walls, Magdalen had plenty of room to expand, and both quadrangles and grounds are exceptionally spacious. James I called it 'the most absolute building in Oxford'. The chief feature of the High St. front is the graceful Perp. **TOWER, built in 1492–1505 (traditionally by Wolsey, who was then bursar), as the chapel bell tower. A hymn is sung from the top of the tower at 6 a.m. on May morning; since the late 18C this has been the college grace, though the tradition of the singing long pre-dates this.

The ornate gateway (1885) leads into ST JOHN'S QUAD; on the W. side (l.) are the Vict Gothic St Swithun's Buildings, and beyond them Longwall Quad (Giles Gilbert Scott, 1932), and the New Library built in 1851 as a hall for Magdalen College School. Immediately opposite the gateway are the President's Lodging (also Vict) and (l.) Grammar Hall, a 1614 addition to the now-vanished medieval Magdalen Hall. In the S. corner (r.) is the *outdoor pulpit*, from which a university sermon was preached on St John the Baptist's Day (24 June; now on the nearest Sunday). Originally the quadrangle was strewn with rushes (to represent the wilderness) for the occasion. Beside the pulpit is a passage to *Chaplain's Quad*, with remains of St John's Hospital and the blocked-up Pilgrim's Gate into the High.

The buildings on the E. side (r.) of St John's Quad are those planned and largely completed by Waynflete: the Chapel (entered under the Muniment Tower), and Founder's Tower, leading to the Cloisters and

Hall. The Perp. *Chapel* (1480) has suffered numerous destructions
and restorations, and is now virtually19C inside. Some of the old
stalls, with carved misericords, survive in the ante-chapel together
with other relics, including a 15C cope; also a bronze sculpture of
Christ and St Mary Magdalene by David Wynne (1964). Visitors are
welcome to choral services (evensong Sun 6 p.m., weekdays exc
Tues 6.15 p.m.: suspended in Long Vacation). The Founder's Tower
(no adm) contains state apartments, and still forms part of the
President's Lodgings. A tapestry here depicts the marriage of Henry
VIII's elder brother Arthur to Catherine of Aragon. CLOISTER QUAD

Life at Oxford in the eighteenth century. From a Rowlandson cartoon

(1490) was largely rebuilt in the 1820s; on the buttresses are grotesque figures called 'hieroglyphs'. Their symbolic significance, if any, is obscure. They were painted (officially) to honour James I's visit. Up a flight of stairs in the S.E. corner (r.) is the *Hall* (1474, much altered in 1902), which happily retains its linenfold panelling and a set of ornate early Renaissance carvings, five depicting the life of St Mary Magdalene.

Magdalen College

The Grove

New Building 18C

President's
Lodgings

Longwall
Quadrangle
20C

Grammar Hall
Early 17C

19C

Cloister
Quadrangle

St Swithun's
Buildings

Founder's Tower
Late 15C to
early 16C

New Library

19C

St John's
Quadrangle

Chapel   Hall

Chaplain's
Quadrangle

17C

High Street

Bell Tower
13C-14C

RIVER CHERWELL

The *Old Library* (no adm), on the W. side (1.) contains illuminated MSS, Wolsey's copy of the Gospels, and Waynflete's stockings, buskins, and cope. A narrow passage on the N. side leads across a wide lawn to the elegant New Building (1733); on the l. is Magdalen Grove (not open) where deer have grazed since 1700; on the r. a bridge leads to the Paddock, famous for the fritillaries which bloom there in spring, and to the *Water Walks, one of which (N.) is named after Addison, the early 18C essayist and poet.

FAMOUS MEMBERS. Richard Foxe (see Corpus Christi); John Colet, leading light in Revival of Learning, founder of St Paul's School, 1467–1519; Cardinal Wolsey 1475–1530; Cardinal Pole, controversial Abp of Canterbury, 1500–58; John Foxe (see Brasenose); Sir Thomas Bodley, founder of the Bodleian Library, 1545–1613; John Mason, a founder of New Hampshire, 1596–1635; John Hampden, parliamentarian, 1599–1643; Joseph Addison, essayist and poet, 1672–1719; William Collins, poet, 1721–59; Oscar Wilde, dramatist, 1854–1900; Compton Mackenzie, novelist, 1883–1972; C.S. Lewis (see University College); Lord Florey, scientist, Nobel prizewinner, 1898–1968. Edward Gibbon, 1737–94, author of 'Decline and Fall of the Roman Empire', left after only fourteen months (1752–53), 'the most idle and unprofitable of my whole career.'

Across Magdalen Bridge is a traffic nexus known as *The Plain* (Pl. D4). Immediately on the l. is Magdalen's Waynflete Building (1961) and Queen's Florey Building (1970), an astonishing irregular polygon of red tiles and glass on concrete stilts designed by James Stirling (cf History Faculty Building in Cambridge). Beyond, in St Clement's, is Stone's Hospital, a late 17C almshouse. On the r. are Magdalen College School and, along Iffley Road beyond the University Sports Ground, *Greyfriars*, a private Hall for Franciscan students.

In Cowley Place, on a pleasant riverside site, is **St Hilda's College** (Pl. D4), founded for women in 1893 by Miss Dorothea Beale, famous and formidable principal of Cheltenham Ladies' College:

> Miss Buss and Miss Beale
> Cupid's darts do not feel.
> How different from us,
> Miss Beale and Miss Buss.

Named after St Hilda, the 7C Abbess of Whitby who was one of

England's first women scholars, it was recognised as a Hall in 1896, and became a college in 1926. Its first home was an elegant Georgian mansion built for Dr Sibthorpe, then Professor of Botany, about 1780. Additions were made as numbers grew, in the 1880s and 1890s in Gothic style, in 1934 and after the Second World War mostly in neo-Georgian. In complete contrast is *Garden Building* (1968–70 by Alison and Peter Smithson) in markedly modern idiom.

Back across Magdalen Bridge and up the left-hand side of the High, the Vict-Gothic building on the corner of Merton St. is *The Examination Schools* (Pl. D1; no adm), extensively used for lectures as well as examinations.

A little further on is **University College** ('Univ.', Pl. D1). It was endowed by William of Durham in 1249 and was at first administered by the University (hence its name). It received its first statutes as an independent foundation in 1280. However it long held primacy among Oxford colleges on the grounds of a (purely fictitious) claim to have been founded by Alfred the Great. This claim, invented to support a lawsuit in 1381, was upheld as late as 1727, and the college celebrated its millenary in 1882. A bust of King Alfred still graces the Senior Common Room.

Nothing remains of the medieval buildings. The long curved front of the college, with its two tower gateways, is a good example of Oxford 17C Gothic. The upper (W.) gateway carries outside a statue of Queen Anne (a generous benefactor), replacing one of King Alfred, and inside a statue of James II in a Roman toga. This is a reminder of the late 17C Master, Obadiah Walker, who became a Roman Catholic, but managed to retain his post through a dispensation granted by King James. The lower gateway carries outside a statue of Queen Mary, and inside one of Dr Radcliffe, whose generous bequest financed the building in 1719 of the smaller quadrangle, named after him.

FRONT QUAD, built slowly between 1634 and 1677, is little altered, but the *Hall* was extensively remodelled inside in 1802 and enlarged in 1904. It contains some interesting modern portraits. The *Chapel* is also heavily refurbished (by Scott, 1862). The screen, stalls and reredos are late 17C, and there are dramatic windows by Abraham van Linge, 1641. In one is Jonah's ship, loyally flying the college flag. In the N.W. (r.) corner of the quadrangle a passage (doorway 3) leads to the *Shelley Memorial* (1893) where in a gloomy domed chamber a marble statue of the drowned poet rests coldly behind a grille. Shelley was 'sent down' in 1811 for producing, with his friend Hogg, a pamphlet on 'The Necessity of Atheism'.

Beyond Front Quad is a variety of further buildings: New Building, 1842, by Sir Charles Barry (architect of the Houses of Parliament), the Library, 1861, by Scott, and several modern additions tucked into any available spaces. RADCLIFFE QUAD (1716) is reached by a passage E. (l.), doorway 7, and beyond are more 19C and 20C additions, incorporating the N. end of Logic Lane.

FAMOUS MEMBERS: Lord Herbert of Cherbury, statesman and philosopher, 1583–1648; Dr John Radcliffe, popular physician and munificent benefactor of Oxford, 1650–1714; Roger Newdigate, antiquary, founder of the Newdigate Poetry Prize, 1719–1806; Shelley, Romantic poet, 1792–1822; Lord Cecil of Chelwood, international statesman, Nobel prizewinner 1864–1958; Clement Attlee, parliamentarian and Prime Minister, 1883–1967; William Beveridge, Master (see Balliol), 1879–1963; C.S. Lewis, literary critic and Christian writer, 1898–1963 (also Fellow of Magdalen).

Further up the High towards Carfax, just beyond University College, a plaque on the wall marks the site of the house where the scientist Robert Boyle (1627–91) and his assistant Robert Hook worked while in Oxford.

2 NORTH-EAST OF CARFAX

Going E. down the l. side of *THE HIGH, the first point of interest is the Covered Market, lively, colourful, odoriferous and noisy, where anything can be bought from fresh fish to old gramophone records. Beyond it on the upper corner of Turl St. ('the Turl'), is the erstwhile Mitre Hotel, a renowned coaching inn of the 17C and 18C; it is now a restaurant, with undergraduate rooms above. Opposite is *All Saints Church* (Pl. C2) with a spire by Hawksmoor which makes a significant contribution to the Oxford skyline. After the demolition of St Martin's in 1896 (see p 50) All Saints served for a time as the City Church. In the 1970s, no longer needed as a church, it was converted into the library of **Lincoln College**, whose entrance is a short distance down the Turl. Founded in 1427 by Robert Fleming, Bp of Lincoln, as a counterblast to the Wycliffite Movement, its theologians were 'to defend the mysteries of the sacred page against these ignorant laics, who profaned with swinish snouts its most holy pearls'. The religious conservatism of its foundation persisted, and during the Reformation three successive Rectors and many Fellows were expelled. Somewhat ironically Lincoln's most famous member is John Wesley, the founder of Methodism, elected to a fellowship in 1726.

The FRONT QUAD is one of the few in Oxford to retain its 15C appearance; the outer facade has battlements added in 1824, but those added inside in 1852 have happily been removed. *The Hall* (opposite the gateway) dates from 1436; in its ancient beamed roof is the original louvre through which smoke escaped. A fireplace was installed in the late 17C, but the present ornate structure is Victorian (1891). On the right is a passage over which are Wesley's rooms, restored in 1928 with gifts from the American Methodist Church, (adm on application to the Porter's Lodge).

Beyond is CHAPEL QUAD, built in 1608–31. The *Chapel* is unusually light and bright, the panelled roof decorated with shields, swags and crowns, (restored 1958), and the large windows brilliant with glass by Bernard van Linge, c. 1630. The beautifully carved woodwork is 17C, including the pulpit from which Wesley preached. In the quadrangle is an attractive modern sundial (War Memorial). The Vict-Gothic Grove Building was added, E. of the Front Quad, in 1880, and more buildings between Chapel Quad and All Saints in 1906. Finally need for additional accommodation has made the college spill over the Turl into Lincoln House (1939), and across the High into Bear Lane (1977) while All Saints Church itself (see also above) became the college *Library* (open Tues and Thur 2.30–4.30, exc when the college is closed), not inappropriately, since from its foundation Lincoln had a close connection with All Saints, whose living was in the college gift. The interior, on two levels, is remarkably beautiful, light and lofty, the ceiling decorated with elaborate plasterwork, and the giant pilasters picked out in gold. Reminders of its ecclesiastical past are the funeral hatchments, memorial tablets, and tomb of William Levins, alderman, who died in 1616 aged 100. Reminders of the college past are small exhibitions of letters, examination papers, ball programmes, and club notices.

FAMOUS MEMBERS: William Davenant, poet and playwright, Shakespeare's godson (see p 50), 1606–68; John Wesley, founder of Methodism (see above),

1703–91; Dr John Radcliffe, (see University College); Lord Morley, writer and statesman, 1838–1923.

A short way down the High from Turl St. is the church of **St Mary the Virgin** (Pl. D1), whose Dec. *tower and spire (188 ft high), one of the most splendid in England, is a conspicuous Oxford landmark. Although the parish church of Oxford, it has from earliest times been closely linked to the University. Its chapels were assigned to the different faculties for lectures, and until the 17C meetings of Congregation, examinations, learned disputations, and degree givings all took place here. Its bells summoned scholars not only to study but to battle with the townspeople (see History, p 10); they still mark such University events as the installations of the Vice-Chancellor and the Proctors (who have their own special stalls in the church), Encaenia, and meetings of Congregation and Convocation. A University sermon is delivered by a 'select preacher' on Sunday mornings in term in the presence of the Vice-Chancellor, as are the famous Bampton lectures, endowed by Dr John Bampton (d 1751). In 1555 St Mary's witnessed the trial of the Oxford Martyrs (see History, p 11), and the following year Cranmer's repudiation of his recantation. One of the grooves cut to support the platform on which he stood can be seen on a pillar l. of the Vice-Chancellor's throne, and damage to the poppyhead pew-ends may also date from this. Wesley worshipped and preached here (the last time in 1744), as in the 19C did the leaders of the controversial Oxford Movement, Keble, Pusey, and Newman, who was vicar in 1828–43 (shortly before he joined the Church of Rome).

Facing the High is the magnificent Italianate Baroque S. porch (1637) designed by Nicholas Stone and given by Dr Morgan Owen, Bp of Llandaff and chaplain to Abp Laud. That it carries a statue of the Virgin and Child formed one of the charges against Laud at his trial in 1644. The main entrance is on the N. side (in Radcliffe Sq) under the tower (which can be climbed, open all the year 10–5, in summer 10–c.7: fee). The tower and spire, Brome chapel and Congregation House, all on the N. side, date from the early 14C. (The statues on the tower replace orginals now kept in the Congregation House and the cloisters of New College.) Otherwise the church was largely rebuilt in the Perp. style, at the University's expense, in the late 15C. Part of the reredos and stalls are of this date; the rest of the woodwork is mostly 17C. The many monuments include: a slab in the floor of the choir commemorating Amy Robsart (d 1560), neglected wife of Queen Elizabeth's favourite, Leicester; tablets to Dr John Radcliffe (see University College) and the historian John Aubrey (1626–97), and the tomb of Adam de Brome (1328), vicar of the church and founder of Oriel College.

Until the building of Duke Humphrey's Library (see the Bodleian, p 75) in 1488 the upper floor of the Congregation House (N.E. side of church) was the University's only library. The room was then refurbished and used for Congregation meetings until 1637.

The church houses a *Brass Rubbing Centre* (open daily, summer 10–6, winter 11–5).

On the corner of Catte St. and the High is **All Souls College** (Pl. D1), founded in 1438 by Henry Chichele, Abp of Canterbury, with Henry VI as co-founder. It commemorated the fallen of the Hundred Years' War, and was used as a chantry for their souls (its full title is 'The College of All Souls of the Faithful Departed, of Oxford'). It has a Warden and Fellows only, and until the foundation of Nuffield College in 1937 was unique in having no undergraduates. In the 17C

More peaceful days in Oxford's 'High'. On the right are St Mary's Church, All Souls, and Queen's. From a mid-eighteenth century print

and 18C the Fellows of All Souls had a great reputation for idleness, luxury and licence, but nowadays its reputation for scholarship and distinction is unrivalled and to be elected a Fellow is a singular honour; among them are the most eminent people in many intellectual fields and from many different countries.

The entrance gateway is in the High; this and Front Quad are largely unaltered 15C work, though the statues of the founders and relief of the Resurrection on the gateway are modern replacements (1940); the originals are in the chapel undercroft and the chapel itself respectively. *The Chapel*, opposite the gateway, is reached through a beautifully fan-vaulted passage (l.). Built in the Perp. style (1442) and much restored by Scott in 1872–76, it retains its 15C hammerbeam angel roof, stalls with misericords, and the framework of a magnificent carved stone reredos. The figures in its niches are Vict and were modelled on contemporary members of the college. The originals were destroyed during the Reformation, and the ruined reredos was boarded over and decorated with a Last Judgement. This was later replaced by plasterwork; some of the painted boards hang in the ante-chapel W. of the vast black and gold Baroque screen. The ante-chapel glass is mostly 15C. GREAT (or NORTH) QUAD, reached through a passage in the N.E. (r.) corner of Front Quad, is a complete contrast, Baroque Gothic of 1715–40 by Hawksmoor. The telescope-like towers on the E. side and the ogee-capped gatehouse on the W. are unique and eye-catching. Between is a lawn of velvet perfection. The N. side is formed by the *Codrington Library* (no adm), donated together with his great collection of books by Christopher Codrington (d 1710), Governor of the Leeward Islands. It contains some 150,000 volumes, many ancient MSS, and Wren's designs for St Paul's.

Wren designed the beautiful sundial on the library S. front (previously on the chapel); its perfect accuracy is a reminder that at the time (1658) Wren was Savilian Professor of Astronomy.

FAMOUS MEMBERS: Thomas Linacre, founder of the Royal College of Physicians, c. 1460–1524; Jeremy Taylor, Anglican divine, 1613–67; Thomas Sydenham, pioneer physician, 1624–89; Christopher Wren, architect and astronomer, 1632–1723; William Blackstone, author of 'Commentaries on the Laws of England', 1723–80; T.E. Lawrence, leader of the Arab revolt against the Turks in the First World War, 1888–1935; and a host of other distinguished scholars and statesmen, too numerous to detail.

A short way down the High is the graceful classical facade of *The Queen's College* (Pl. D1), perhaps the greatest beauty of this beautiful street. It was founded in 1340 by Robert de Eglesfield of Cumberland, chaplain to Queen Philippa, wife of Edward III, under the patronage of his royal mistress; she was the first of a long line of Queens consort to take an interest in the college. His detailed provisions for its constitution were strongly religious: its theology course was to last eighteen years, its Provost and twelve Fellows were to be in Orders. Their numbers represented Our Lord and the apostles, their scarlet gowns His blood. Seventy 'poor boys' represented the disciples sent out to preach (Luke 10). These were the first undergraduates specifically provided for by an Oxford college. Strict rules of discipline were laid down: no bows and arrows, no dogs, no musical instruments except on special occasions, no playing of marbles on the steps. Although most of the founder's arrangements have long been abandoned, several old customs remain: the college is summoned to dinner by the sound of the trumpet; on feast days the founder's drinking horn—an auroch's horn mounted on eagle's feet and banded with silver—is used as a loving-cup; at Christmas a 'boar's head dinner' is celebrated (many of the original scholars were northcountrymen who could not get home for Christmas): at New Year the bursar presents to each guest at the 'Gaudy' a needle and thread ('aiguille' and 'fil', a pun on Eglesfield's name), with the words 'Take this and be thrifty'. The eight senior scholars are called 'Taberdars'.

The college was entirely rebuilt between 1671 and 1765 and is the only one in Oxford of which none of the original buildings survive. *FRONT QUAD (1710–34), 'the grandest piece of classical architecture in Oxford', is partly by Hawksmoor. Under the entrance cupola is a statue of Queen Caroline, who paid for the completion of the quadrangle. Opposite the entrance (N.) the passage leading into North Quad has on its left the *Hall* (perhaps partly by Wren), which contains a portrait of Addison by Kneller. On the right is the *Chapel*, light and spacious with a highly decorated ceiling (in the apse a painting of the Ascension by Sir James Thornhill), and magnificent Baroque screen. The side windows at the E. end are by Abraham van Linge (1635), those at the W. end come from the previous chapel (1518).

NORTH QUAD was actually built first (1671–1714), Wren being concerned with the early designs. On the left (W.) is the *Library* (no adm), a grand classical building carrying outside an array of statues and inside rich in rococo plasterwork and carved bookcases. From its S. end a narrow high-walled passage (cul-de-sac) leads past the old brewhouse into a tiny formal garden opening out on to a lawn, enclosed by cosy-looking house-backs, just behind Drawda Hall. All is peace, flowers, and pigeons. A typical Oxford anomaly, not to be missed.

Queen's Lane Quad (1790) across Queen's Lane, incorporates houses and shops already on the site. The Florey Building, for postgraduates, is described on p 64.

FAMOUS MEMBERS: Thomas Middleton, playwright, 1570–1627; William Wycherley, playwright, 1640–1716; Edmund Halley, astronomer, 1656–1742; Joseph Addison and William Collins, who both migrated to Magdalen; Jeremy Bentham, legal and social philosopher, 1748–1823; Walter Pater, critic and essayist, 1839–94 (see also Brasenose); Lord Florey (Provost), see Magdalen.

Queen's Lane (middle section closed to traffic) wanders westward into Catte St., becoming New College Lane at its W. end. On the r. is **St Edmund Hall** (Pl. D1), familiarly known as 'Teddy Hall', founded c. 1220, and the last survivor of the medieval halls. It is dedicated, probably, to St Edmund of Abingdon, Abp of Canterbury, who taught at Oxford c. 1195–1200, and it was linked to Osney Abbey until the Dissolution in 1539. It was controlled by Queen's College from 1557 to 1937, and acquired full collegiate status twenty years later.

Only a fireplace in the buttery remains of the medieval buildings; of the charming Front Quad three sides were built in the 16C and 17C, and the remaining S. side (r. of the entrance) in 1932–34. In the centre is the old well, and on the N. (l.) side a painted sundial. Opposite the entrance is the tiny panelled *Chapel*; it has 17C stalls and screen (oak on the W. side, cedar on the E.), glass by Burne-Jones, Morris, and Webb, and a striking altarpiece, 'Supper at Emmaus', by Ceri Richards (1958). E. of the chapel, ingeniously squeezed into a constricted site between the High and New College gardens, is a new quadrangle (1968–70), providing common rooms, *Hall* and sets of rooms. Its bold modern buildings (designed by Kenneth Stevens and Associates) somehow harmonise well with their ancient neighbours. The church of St Peter in the East, one of the oldest in Oxford, a little further up Queen's Lane, is now the college *Library*; only the crypt can be visited (apply at the Porter's Lodge).

The unobtrusive entrance to ***New College** (Pl. D1) belies the splendours within. This is in fact one of the grandest and most prestigious of Oxford's colleges. It was founded in 1379 by William of Wykeham, Bp of Winchester, to provide for the advanced studies of boys educated at his other great foundation, Winchester College (its original name being the St Mary College of Winchester in Oxford). His object was to repair the ravages among the ranks of the clergy of the Hundred Years' War and the Black Death (c. 1345), and produce a supply of 'men of learning, fruitful to the Church . . . the King, and the Realm'. Entry was restricted to Wykehamists until the 19C; until 1834 its members were exempt from taking University examinations, and received degrees on the Warden's word alone (a system clearly open to abuse). Although New College played a prominent part in the 16C Revival of Learning, its wealth and privilege afterwards led to a period of decline until with the University reforms of the 19C it gradually regained its pre-eminent position.

William of Wykeham laid down strict rules for its government, and his statutes set two Oxford precedents: compulsory attendance at chapel, and the college tutorial system. In the 20C it set a precedent by being the first of the men's colleges to decide to admit women (1964) although for various reasons this did not happen for another ten years.

New College is one of the few colleges where the wealth and prestige of the founder enabled his designs to be carried out in full; the principal buildings, completed about 1386, remain as a superb example of English Perp. architecture, and strikingly similar to the sister foundation. It lies just within the old city walls, which are in places incorporated into it. The turreted gate-tower carries statues of the Virgin, the angel Gabriel, and William of Wykeham; the massive oak doors are original. GREAT, or FRONT, QUAD, the first complete

quadrangle in Oxford, is impressively large; unfortunately a third storey and battlements, then sash windows, were imposed on the 14C buildings in 1674 and 1711 respectively. On the N. (l.) is the handsome *Chapel*; although the structure is of the founder's time, the interior (including the raised roof) is almost entirely Vict (by Scott, 1879). The stalls, however, retain their original arm-rests and misericords; both are richly and entertainingly carved. On the N. (l.) side of the altar are a painting of St James by El Greco, and the founder's *crozier of silver-gilt set with jewels and enamelwork. Here the stained glass is 14C, with the exception of the great W. window, depicting the Nativity and the Seven Virtues, which was painted by Thomas Jarvis to designs by Sir Joshua Reynolds (1777). It is disappointingly brown and wish-washy. The glass it displaced is in York Minster. In the floor are twenty-three 15C and 16C brasses, and high up on the S. wall two 'squints', from which the Warden could observe services and disputations (cf Christ's College, Cambridge). Below are memorials, by Eric Gill, to members of the college, both English and German, killed in the First World War. The whole is dominated by Epstein's compelling *statue of *Lazarus*. The choral services are superb (Sun 6 p.m., weekdays exc Wed 6.15; suspended in the Long Vacation).

W. (l.) of the chapel is the detached Bell Tower and the spacious Cloister, whose building necessitated the right-angled kink in New College Lane. It houses some of the statues from the tower of St Mary the Virgin church (see p 67).

The *Hall* (usually closed) adjoins the chapel. It is one of the oldest and finest in Oxford, with 16C linenfold panelling, Vict stained glass, and roof by Scott (1877). Above is the Muniment Tower (no adm) which contains the college's title deeds, admission registers, and other ancient records. The remaining 14C building is the Long Room, E. of Great Quad and backing on to Queen's Lane. Originally the latrines and cesspool, its upper floor is now a beautiful gallery and reception room.

Opposite Great Quad gateway (E.) is GARDEN QUAD, added between 1683 and 1711, and enclosed on its E. side by an elegant wrought-iron screen. The chief features of the pleasant *garden beyond are a well-preserved remnant of the old City Wall and a large artificial mound (1549), perhaps an example of the 'mounts' popular in Tudor gardens. Along the N. side of the college, facing Holywell St., are 19C additions, by Scott and Champneys, and on the E. side abutting on to Longwall St., the modern Sacher Building (by David Roberts, 1961; cf St Hugh's). The sculpture on the lawn is by Barbara Hepworth (1964).

FAMOUS MEMBERS: William Grocyn, scholar and humanist, 1446–1519; William Waynflete, founder of Magdalen College (qv), 1395–1486; Thomas Ken, one of the Seven Bishops (1688), hymn writer, 1637–1711; Sydney Smith, journalist, theologian, moral philosopher, 1771–1845; John Galsworthy, novelist and playwright, 1867–1933; A.P. Herbert, writer and politician, 1890–1971; H.A.L. Fisher, historian, 1865–1940; Maurice Bowra, classicist, Professor of Poetry, 1898–1971; numerous archbishops and bishops.

Hertford College (pron 'Harf'd', Pl. D1) lies on each side of New College Lane at its junction with Catte St., the two parts linked by the picturesque 'Bridge of Sighs' (1913). Its present foundation, made possible through the benefaction of the banker T.C. Baring, dates from 1874, and its buildings are almost entirely late Vict, in a variety of styles (by Sir T.G. Jackson). But its history goes back to 1284, when it began life as Hart Hall. It was granted collegiate status in 1740, but subsequently declined, and in 1818 was amalgamated with Magdalen Hall (see p 61), which brought to it useful endowments and distinguished scholarship.

FAMOUS MEMBERS: Of Hart Hall, John Donne, poet and divine, 1572–1631; of Hertford College first foundation, Charles James Fox, liberal statesman, 1749–1806; of Magdalen Hall, William Tyndale, translator of the Bible, pioneer of the Reformation, burned at the stake in 1536, and Thomas Hobbes, philosopher, 1588–1679; of Hertford College second foundation, Evelyn Waugh, novelist, 1903-66.

Between Hertford College and Holywell St. (N.) is the somewhat aggressive Vict-Gothic Indian Institute (Champneys 1896) now the Modern History Faculty Library. HOLYWELL itself has a number of attractive 17C and 18C houses. On the left is the *Old Music Room* (1748), the first room in England to be built solely for musical use. Its beautiful chandeliers were given by George IV, and previously hung in Westminster Hall. The Faculty of Music, formerly housed alongside, is now in St Aldate's (see p 52). In marked contrast is the modern Blackwell's Music Shop, dramatically lit inside by an inverted cone of glass.

Almost opposite is BATH PLACE, with particularly charming little houses, from which a very narrow passage threads its way past the Turf Tavern and, becoming Turf Lane, emerges into New College Lane near the house of Edmund Halley, astronomer and Savilian Professor of Geometry in 1703–42 (see also Queen's College).

On the N. side of Holywell is **Wadham College** (Pl. A8) which has its entrance in Parks Rd opposite the spacious garden of Trinity College, of which there is a good view through the 18C iron railings. Wadham, founded in 1610 by wealthy Somerset landowners Nicholas and Dorothy Wadham, is the latest of the old foundations. Its buildings, almost exactly as they were when completed in 1613, are the supreme example of the Jacobean-Gothic style, with classical touches, so popular in Oxford; their studied symmetry is particularly noticeable.

Wadham's most illustrious phase was during the Commonwealth, when many founder members of the future Royal Society, including Wren and Thomas Sydenham ('the English Hippocrates') gathered round the scientifically-minded Warden John Wilkins, Cromwell's brother-in-law (see also Trinity College, Cambridge).

The gateway to Front Quad is fan-vaulted; immediately opposite is the entrance to the chapel and the hall, a handsome portal with classical columns (cf the contemporary Bodleian Tower of the Five Orders in Schools Quadrangle), and carrying statues of the founders on each side, and James I above. The *Chapel*, actually entered from a passage in the N.E. corner (l.), is of grand and elegant proportions. The east end was considerably altered in 1832, when the reredos, stone panelling, and stalls were put in; the stucco ceiling also dates from then, replacing one of decorated wooden panels. The E. window is by Bernard van Linge (1622); the screen, pulpit, communion rail and table are all 17C, the last presented to the college in 1889 by the parish of Ilminster in Somerset, where the founders are buried. The large *Hall* has its original hammerbeam roof and louvre; the heraldic glass in the S. window commemorates benefactors of the college, that in the great bay some of its famous members.

A pleasant new copper-roofed block was added on the S.E. side (r.) in the early 1950s, and in 1971–72 old houses in Holywell were adapted and linked to new buildings to complete another quadrangle (Gillespie, Kydd and Coia). The *gardens, with sweeping lawns, stately copper beech and cedar trees, and glorious herbaceous border, are among the loveliest in Oxford. The statue of Sir Maurice Bowra (Warden, 1938–70) is by John Doubleday.

FAMOUS MEMBERS: Robert Blake, admiral, 1599–1657; Thomas Sydenham, pioneer physician, 1624–89 and Christopher Wren, architect and astronomer, 1632–1723 (both afterwards Fellows of All Souls); Arthur Onslow, Speaker of the House of Commons for 35 years, 1691–1768; T.G. Jackson, architect, 1835–1924; Thomas Beecham, conductor, 1879–1961; C. Day Lewis, poet, 1904–72.

Returning from Wadham to the Broad, you see the *New Bodleian Library* (no adm) on the right, a stolid 1930s block in Bladon stone designed by Sir Giles Gilbert Scott, and partly paid for by the Rockefeller Foundation. Of its eleven bookstacks, providing storage for some 5 million volumes, three are underground, and connected with the old library across the road by a passage and conveyor-belt. A fourth floor was added in the 1960s to house the library of the Indian Institute (see above). Across the Broad (S.) is the beautiful and impressive group of University buildings which are the very heart of Oxford.

The ***Sheldonian Theatre** (Pl. C2; open 10–12.45 and 2–4.45; 3.45 in winter) was built 1663–69, at the expense of Gilbert Sheldon, Warden of All Souls and afterwards Abp of Canterbury, to provide a venue for University occasions such as disputations and degree givings, up to that time held in St Mary's Church (see p 67). It was the first building designed by Sir Christopher Wren, then Savilian Professor of Astronomy. The annual conferment of degrees and *Commemoration* or *Encaenia* are held here at the end of the summer term (late June), the stately and complicated ceremonies made richly colourful by the full academic dress of the participants, and conducted in Latin (though nowadays translations are provided). The Theatre is also used for large public lectures, meetings and concerts.

The plan of the building, semi-circular in front, rectangular behind, was inspired by pictures of the open-air Theatre of Marcellus in Rome. It is approached up shallow steps, and partly surrounded by railings on whose stone plinths are venerable but unidentified busts, renewed in 1868 and again in 1972. Much of the outside of the Theatre is also modern restoration, the soft stone of the original having succumbed to the ravages of time and weather. The octagonal cupola replaced Wren's smaller one in 1832; it provides an excellent viewpoint (last adm 15 mins before the Theatre closes). Inside the hall is tiered seating and a gallery supported on wooden pillars painted to simulate marble. The roof is decorated with a large allegorical painting of the Triumph of Religion and Learning over Envy, Hatred and Malice (by Robert Streeter 1669).

The Theatre housed the University Press until it was moved in 1713 to the *Clarendon Building* (Pl. D1) alongside (l.). This was designed by Hawksmoor in the classical style, and largely paid for out of the profits from Lord Clarendon's 'History of the Great Rebellion' published in 1702–04. The statues on the balustrade, by Sir James Thornhill, represent the Nine Muses. Two are modern fibre-glass replacements of the original lead ones. The Press moved to Walton

St. in 1830, and after many years of use as University offices, the building is now part of the ever-extending Bodleian Library (see below).

On the right of the Sheldonian is the lovely *Old Ashmolean Museum* (Pl. C2; open Mon–Sat 10.30–1 and 2.30–4) built 1678–83 to house Elias Ashmole's collection of Natural Curiosities (moved to the Ashmolean Museum in Beaumont St. in 1840; see p 82 for details) as well as the School of Natural History and a chemical laboratory. It was the first public museum in England. Since 1937 it has been the MUSEUM OF THE HISTORY OF SCIENCE.

The nucleus of the present museum is the Lewis Evans Collection of scientific instruments (given 1925), ranging from astrolabes to photographic equipment, to which was added the Billmeir Collection in 1957. Also shown are items relating to the history of pharmacy and medicine, among them the development of penicillin.

Behind the Sheldonian lies the *Old Schools Quadrangle*, built 1613–19 in familiar Oxford Jacobean-Gothic style. Over the doorways are the names of the disciplines formerly studied here and on the E. side is the handsome gate-tower known as THE TOWER OF THE FIVE ORDERS; it is ornamented with columns of the five orders of classical architecture (Doric, Tuscan, Ionic, Corinthian, and Composite) topped by a statue of James I and above him in the parapet the Royal Stuart Arms. All the buildings are now part of the **Bodleian Library** ('Bodley'; Pl. D1). The library, one of the oldest and most important in the world, received its first collection of books and endowments from Duke Humphrey of Gloucester (1391–1447) and was housed above the Divinity School (see below), but these were dispersed during the Reformation excesses of Edward VI's reign, and in 1602 the library was refounded by, and named after, Sir Thomas Bodley, fellow of Merton College and Ambassador to the Netherlands. Beginning with 2000 books, the Bodleian now contains some 4½ million, as well as over 50,000 MSS. It is one of the six libraries which receive a copy of every book published in the UK, a right negotiated with the Stationers' Company by Sir Thomas Bodley himself. No book may be taken out, no matter how exalted the status of the would-be borrower (Charles I was refused, likewise Cromwell). Readers are admitted by ticket and must be members of the University or suitably sponsored.

The entrance is behind a bronze statue by Le Sueur of the Earl of Pembroke (one time Chancellor of the University), brought here from Wilton in 1722, and leads into the vestibule or *Proscholium* (used as a pig market under Edward VI), now the readers' and visitors' admission-hall and shop (open Mon–Fri 9–5, Sat 9–12.30). Opposite the doorway is the **Divinity School**, built mid 15C, whose exquisitely vaulted *roof, enriched with carved coats of arms, figures and natural objects, is one of Oxford's greatest glories. It was the scene in 1555 of the examination of Cranmer, Latimer, and Ridley, the 'Oxford Martyrs' (see History, p 11); later it was used as a corn-store, but was renovated by Wren, who inserted the doorway on the N. side and reinforced the walls to support the growing weight of books above. It is now used to display some of the treasures of the Bodleian.

The permanent exhibits include among manuscripts: the Chanson de Roland;

one of the original copies of the revised reissue of Magna Carta, 1217; the manuscripts of T.E. Lawrence's 'Seven Pillars of Wisdom' and Kenneth Grahame's 'Wind in the Willows'; important poetic MSS of Thomas Traherne ('Centuries of Meditations'), John Donne (his only known verse autograph), Shelley (with memorabilia) and Gerard Manley Hopkins (MS B). Printed books include the only known copies of the first work of Shakespeare's to be printed ('Venus and Adonis', 1593) and of the first edition of 'Tottel's Miscellany', 1557; and the only copy outside North America of the 'Bay Psalm Book', 1640.

Also on view is Sir Thomas Bodley's chest, with its elaborate three-fold lock mechanism (cf Merton College Old Library and St John's College Library). There are temporary exhibitions both here and in the old School of Natural Philosophy, on the S. side of Old Schools Quadrangle.

At the far end of the room a door leads into the *Convocation House* and *Apodyterium* or Vice-Chancellor's Robing Room (no adm to either); built in the mid 17C, both have fan-vaulted roofs actually inserted much later (1759). They are used for meetings of Convocation and Congregation (see University Organisation, p 17).

In 1681 Charles II summoned his third, and last, Parliament to meet him in Oxford. The Commons sat here in the Convocation House, the Lords in a room across the quadrangle approached up the stairway inscribed 'Schola Geometriae' (now the Classics Reading Room). On the King's arrival Parliament, to its intense dismay, was instantly dissolved.

The oldest part of the Bodleian library is above, in the H formed by the rooms just described, and reached up an insignificant stairway in the corner of the vestibule: 'Duke Humphrey' in the middle, over the Divinity School, the 'Arts End', added by Bodley, over the Proscholium, and the 'Selden End' added mid 17C to house books bequeathed by John Selden (d 1654). Facing the bookshelves of the **Arts End*, loaded with venerable and immensely weighty volumes, are high wooden benches and sloping reading desks calculated to keep the sleepiest student awake. The beautiful panelled ceiling is profusely decorated with the arms of the University and of Sir Thomas Bodley. Over all hangs the thrilling hush of centuries of scholarship. Unfortunately these riches can only be seen by visitors if accompanied by a senior member of the University who has arranged the visit in advance in writing.

This group of University buildings is completed by the ***Radcliffe Camera** (Pl. D1; no adm), a handsome classical rotunda rising majestically from the centre of the grass and paved square between the Old Schools and St Mary's Church, with which older neighbours it is in perfect visual harmony. It was founded as a separate library by Dr Radcliffe (see also University College) whose statue by Rysbrack stands in a niche above the entrance (inside), and was designed by James Gibbs (who also designed, inter alia, the church of St Martin-in-the-Fields in Trafalgar Sq, London, and the Senate House in Cambridge). Completed in 1749, it was originally a science library, but has long been part of the Bodleian.

On the W. side (r., facing St Mary's) of Radcliffe Sq is **Brasenose College** ('BNC'; Pl.D1) founded in 1504 by William Smythe, Bp of Lincoln, and Sir Richard Sutton (both of Lancashire). It was the direct successor to a Hall of the same name on the site, whose last Principal became the first Principal of the new college. The name probably derives from the 12C or 13C brazen knocker (possibly handle or sanctuary ring, with a lion-like mask) of the original Hall. This was carried off to Stamford in the migration of Oxford students in 1333, and only recovered in 1890. It now hangs above the high table in the Hall, and there is another small one above the main doors. The college has traditionally a great reputation for sporting prowess.

A handsome gate-tower leads into OLD QUAD. This was begun in 1509; a third storey and battlements were added 100 years later. On the N. wall (r.) is an attractive sundial (1719); instructions on how to read it correctly appear on a new aluminium panel at the entrance to the *Hall* opposite. This room was largely remodelled inside in the 18C, and has a quiet elegance. The *Chapel*, built in 1656 in an interesting mixture of Gothic and Classical styles (the only one dating from the Commonwealth years), is reached through a passage in the S.E. corner (r.) leading into small CHAPEL QUAD. It replaced the earlier chapel alongside the Hall, which then became the Senior Common Room. Its roof is spectacular: colourfully painted and apparently fan-vaulted with elaborate pendants; it is in fact plaster-work of the mid 1660s. Underneath is a 15C hammerbeam roof brought here from the old Augustinian College of St Mary in New Inn Hall St. In the ante-chapel is a memorial to Walter Pater (Fellow, 1864-94), impressively flanked by Leonardo da Vinci, Michelangelo, Plato and Dante. Beyond Chapel Quad is the Victorian NEW QUAD (Sir T.G. Jackson, 1886-1909), and the striking modern rooms skilfully inserted into the very limited space available by Powell and Moya in 1959-61, the first of their many buildings at both Oxford and Cambridge.

FAMOUS MEMBERS: John Foxe, martyrologist, 1516–87 (see also Magdalen); Robert Burton, author of 'The Anatomy of Melancholy', 1577–1640; Elias Ashmole, antiquary and founder of the Ashmolean Museum, 1617–92; William Petty, political economist, inventor and scientist, 1623–87; Thomas Traherne, mystic and poet, 1636–74; Bp Heber, hymnologist, 1783–1826; Arthur Evans, archaeologist, 1851–1941; Walter Pater, see above and Queen's College; Field-Marshal Earl Haig, (1861–1928), C-in-C of the British Expeditionary Force in the First World War; John Buchan (Lord Tweedsmuir), statesman and novelist, 1875–1940.

John Middleton, a Lancashire giant known as 'The Childe of Hale' visited the college, then full of Lancashire students, c. 1613. A life-sized portrait of him was painted, and his huge hand carved on a stone (which Pepys paid two shillings to see on his visit in 1668). The college boat is always named 'Childe of Hale' after him.

Brasenose Lane, which still has its medieval open drain (not of course in use), links Radcliffe Sq with the Turl. On the right is **Exeter College** (Pl. C2), from whose garden a huge horse-chestnut tree leans across the lane towards Brasenose. If the branches touch it, it is said, Exeter defeats BNC on the river. Exeter was founded in 1314 as Stapledon Hall by Robert de Stapledon, Bp of Exeter; it became Exeter Hall in 1404, and Exeter College in 1586 when refounded by Sir William Petrie. The democratic provisions of its first statutes perhaps reflected its first founder's allegiance to Bologna University, where he was educated, but made for a weakness and lack of continuity in its administration, which were corrected by its second founder. The strong West Country link established by Stapledon continues in the Stapledon scholarships, only open to West Country candidates.

The college has been much rebuilt and altered at various periods, and is now largely Vict in appearance. On the S. side (r.) of the quadrangle is the *Hall* (built in 1618, restored in 1818), with large, light, Perp.-style windows, fine collarbeam roof, and Jacobean screen on which is the earliest known representation of a man smoking. Opposite is the *Chapel*, built in 1854–60 by Sir George Gilbert Scott, and replacing a beautiful 17C predecessor. Scott's design was inspired by the Sainte Chapelle in Paris; its great height overwhelms the rest of the quadrangle, but the lofty multi-arched interior is undoubtedly impressive. It is richly decorated with carvings, mosaics, and a tapestry of 'The Adoration of the Magi' by Burne-Jones and William Morris, who while undergraduates here formed a life-long friendship.

Beyond the E. end of the chapel is *Palmer's Tower*, the original gatehouse of 1432, and the only old building to survive. From here passages lead r. into a 19C quadrangle and the pleasant garden; from the garden there is a good view of the Bodleian and the Divinity School, and l. into the somewhat cramped and gloomy Margary Quad, bounded on its W. side by the modern Thomas Wood building (1964). A gateway leads out into the Broad.

FAMOUS MEMBERS: Anthony Ashley-Cooper, 1st Lord Shaftesbury, politician, associated with the foundation of 'party' government and with the Habeas Corpus Act, 1621–83; Charles Lyell, geologist, 1797–1875; J.A. Froude, see Oriel; Edward Burne-Jones, Pre-Raphaelite artist, 1833–98; William Morris, artist, poet, social philosopher, 1834–96; Ray Lankester, zoologist, 1847–1929; C.H. Parry, composer, 1848–1918; J.R.R. Tolkien, philologist, author, 1892–1973.

Immediately across the Turl is **Jesus College** (Pl. C2), the first post-Reformation college in Oxford, founded in 1571, nominally by Elizabeth I, in reality by Hugh Price, treasurer of St David's, who persuaded the Queen to lend it her prestige. The college has always had a very close connection with Wales, which even as late as the early 1900s still supplied over half its members.

The Turl St. front of the college dates from the founder's time, but was refaced in the Perp. style in the 1850s; at this time there was also considerable restoration and alteration of the chapel and of the S. side (l.), which had been built early in the 17C by Sir Eubule Thelwall (Principal 1621–30) in Jacobean-Gothic. The *Chapel*, on the N. (r.) side of First Quad, was extended eastwards in 1636; it has a barrel-vaulted roof, late 17C screen, and early 17C pulpit, but is otherwise heavily Vict. On St David's Day the service is conducted in Welsh. In the ante-chapel is a bust of T.E. Lawrence (a replica of one in St Paul's Cathedral) who was an exhibitioner of the college in 1907-10. In the *Hall* (opposite the main entrance) the royal founder takes pride of place, with a carved wooden bust over the fireplace, and a portrait over the high table. (She also appears in the Senior Common Room, in a painting by Zucchero.) Other good portraits include Charles I (school of Van Dyck), Charles II (attributed to Lely), John Nash, the architect (by Lawrence), and T.E. Lawrence 'of Arabia' again. The heavily carved screen is decorated with dragons, perhaps a reminder of Welsh loyalties.

The charming INNER QUAD, built between 1646 and 1713, again in Jacobean-Gothic style, remains largely unchanged. It was mainly the work of Sir Leoline Jenkins, (Principal 1661–73), whose munificent benefactions to the college earned him the status of 'second founder'. Through a passage on its N. side (r.) are further buildings of 1905 and (unmistakably) 1971. The latter was, appropriately, opened by the Prince of Wales.

FAMOUS MEMBERS: Henry Vaughan, mystic poet, 1622–95; Richard ('Beau') Nash, social mentor of 18C Bath, 1674–1762; J.R. Green, historian, 1837–83; T.E. Lawrence, 1888–1925 (see above, also All Souls), and many Welsh prelates and statesmen.

The N. end of Turl St. (l. out of Jesus College) joins Broad St.

opposite Trinity College. *THE BROAD, as its name implies, is a wide street, gracious, treed, and unhurried. Its few shops are mostly devoted to University needs —books and academic dress. A cross in the roadway opposite Balliol marks the place where Cranmer, Latimer and Ridley were burnt at the stake in 1555–56.

Trinity College (Pl. A8), with its spacious grounds and varied yet happily harmonising buildings, is particularly attractive. It was founded in 1555 by Sir Thomas Pope, a wealthy civil servant under the regime of Mary Tudor, and was at first strongly Roman Catholic in character. But its history really begins in the late 13C, when Durham College was established to provide for students from the Benedictine priory at Durham. Parts of this first college survive in Durham Quad, which lies, unusually, some distance back from the street, and was originally approached along a narrow high-walled lane (cf Jesus College, Cambridge). Trinity traditionally drew its members from the landed gentry, and has a long list of distinguished sons. It also, in the 17C, had two remarkable and eccentric Presidents, Ralph Kettell, and Ralph Bathurst. Kettell had a particular dislike of long hair; John Aubrey (see 'Famous Members' below) records that he would come into the hall with 'a pair of scissors in his muffe, and woe to them that sate on the outside of the table.'

The beautiful iron entrance gate is a 1737 copy of the one facing on to Parks Rd (see p 73), set up at the end of the lime walk planted in 1713. To the r. are some old cottages taken over for college rooms in the 19C, and beyond them *Kettell Hall*, built for himself by the President in 1618–20. It now has the 1920s War Memorial Library (neo-classical) and modern (1964–68) buildings of CUMBERBATCH QUAD on two sides, but seems quite at ease with its 20C neighbours. The quadrangle adjoins Blackwell's bookshop, whose large underground showrooms also extend beneath it. The building along the E. side (r.) of FRONT QUAD is 19C by Sir T.G. Jackson, as is the President's Lodging just to its l. Next to this (l.) is DURHAM QUAD, the oldest part of which is the outer side of the E. range (r.). Here is the *Old Library* (no adm), whose windows contain some 15c glass. The rest is 17C and 18C. The gate-tower, with its statues of Geometry, Astronomy, Theology, and Medicine, was built by President Bathurst in the 1690s, as was the **Chapel* (r.). This has a perfect late 17C Baroque interior, almost untouched except for the insertion of Vict stained glass, and is one of the few college chapels which is 'all of a piece'. The gorgeous plasterwork ceiling has a centrepiece of the 'Ascension' by Pierre Berchet; the richly carved reredos is in the style of Grinling Gibbons, and may even be his work. It is well matched by the beautiful panelling, stalls, and screen. On the N. side (l.) of the altar is the tomb of the founder and his third wife (1567) transferred from the old chapel of 1406. The *Hall* (l.), though built in 1620, has a largely 18C interior, light, lofty, and delicately coloured. Its chief interest lies in the splendid collection of portraits, which includes a modern group representing 'Arts and Sciences at Trinity 1977'.

A passage at the N.W. corner (top l.) of the quadrangle leads into GARDEN QUAD. On the l., all among flowers, is a bust of Cardinal Newman. The buildings opposite, originally a single isolated block, are by Wren (1688) but much altered since. Open on the E. side, this quadrangle and its garden seem particularly gracious and tranquil. A gateway (Dolphin Gate, 1947) leads out into St Giles through an alleyway between the backs of Balliol and St John's. But it is hard to find.

FAMOUS MEMBERS: Lord Baltimore, one of the founders of Maryland, 1580–1632; Abp Sheldon, Warden of All Souls and builder of the Sheldonian Theatre, 1598–1677; Henry Ireton, Parliamentary leader, Cromwell's son-in-law, 1611–51; John Aubrey, antiquary and biographer, 1626–97; William Pitt, Lord Chatham, statesman, 1708–78; W.S. Landor, writer, 'sent down' for firing at the rooms of the man opposite, 1775–1864; John Newman, theologian and cardinal, 1801–90 (see also Oriel); Richard Burton, explorer, 'sent down' for trying to fight a duel, 1826–90; A. Quiller-Couch, writer, 1863–1944 (see also Jesus College, Cambridge); J. Elroy Flecker, poet, 1884–1915; Ronald Knox, Fellow (see Balliol); Terence Rattigan, playwright, 1911–79.

Immediately next door (l.) is **Balliol College** (Pl. A8). It was endowed c.1260 by John de Balliol, a powerful northern nobleman and father of the Scottish King (1292–96), as a penance imposed by the Bp of Durham for his frequent disputes with the Church. The foundation was actually established by his widow Devorguilla, at first merely as a hostel. The first statutes date from 1282. The college played an important part in the spread of the New Learning in the 15C, when a number of leading Greek scholars were among its members, notably William Gray, afterwards Bp of Ely, who bequeathed to it his superb collection of books, most of which the college still possesses. However its position of supreme academic pre-eminence, still maintained, dates from the 19C, when it was blessed with a series of outstanding Masters, the best-known of whom was Benjamin Jowett (1870–93). Through his teaching and his brilliant pupils he had a far-reaching influence on Victorian thought. His name is commemorated in Jowett Walk, between Mansfield Rd and St Cross Rd, and in the contemporary rhyme:

> Here come I, my name is Jowett;
> There's no knowledge but I know it.
> I am the Master of this college;
> What I know not isn't knowledge.

The college was almost entirely rebuilt in the 19C, the architects chiefly involved being Waterhouse (part of the front quadrangle and Hall in Garden Quad), Butterfield (chapel) and Salvin (part of the W. side (l.) of Garden Quad). The *Library* and reading-room, originally the Hall, opposite the entrance and l. in Front Quad do in fact date from the 15C, but were altered out of recognition by Wyatt in the 1790s. In Butterfield's pink and white striped *Chapel* (r. of the Library) some discarded Anglo-Flemish glass of 1528 was installed in 1912, and other windows are by Abraham van Linge (1637). Its interior is now far less colourful than Butterfield's original, much of his polychromatic alabaster-work having been plastered over, and his Gothic furnishings replaced by modern ones (1937). The spectacular silver-gilt repoussé-work *altar front is a First World War memorial. A passage in the N.W. corner (l.) leads to Garden Quad, by way of an ancient wooden door originally at the Broad St. entrance. It was to be sold for firewood in the 1860s rebuilding, but was rescued by the Revd T. Harling Newman, who 'deemed it a pity that gates which had witnessed so many deaths by burning should themselves end in flames.' Exiled for some years to Essex, the door was returned to the college in 1926.

Garden Quad presents a rather random appearance, and the Vict *Hall* looks distinctly uncomfortable, wedged between its 1960s neighbours (by Oxford Architects Partnership). It is approached by a long steep flight of steps; the organ within was given by Jowett, at whose wish the tradition of regular concerts here was established. The college has additional buildings in Manor Rd (see p 99).

FAMOUS MEMBERS: John Wyclif, Master in 1360, religious reformer and Bible translator, 1329(?)–84; Humphrey Duke of Gloucester, first founder of the

Bodleian Library, 1391–1447(?); John Evelyn, diarist, 1620–1706; Adam Smith, economist and political philosopher, 1723–90; Robert Southey, poet, 1774–1843; H.E. Manning, theologian and cardinal, 1808–92; both Abps Temple, father 1821–1902, son 1881–1944 (also Fellow of Queen's); Matthew Arnold, poet and critic, 1822–88 (also Fellow of Oriel); Algernon Swinburne, poet, 1837–1909; Arnold Toynbee, historian and expert in international affairs, 1889–1975 (also a Fellow); Lord Curzon, statesman and Viceroy of India, 1859–1925 (also Fellow of All Souls); Hilaire Belloc, writer, 1870–1953; William Beveridge, economist, creator of the Beveridge Report, 1879–1963 (also Master of University College); Julian Huxley, biologist, 1887–75; his brother Aldous Huxley, novelist ('Brave New World'), 1894–1963; Seretse Khama of Botswana, 1921–80.

The top of Broad St. just beyond Balliol joins Cornmarket St.; Carfax is to the left.

3 NORTH AND NORTH-WEST OF CARFAX

CORNMARKET ST., running northward from Carfax, consists largely of modern shops. The old Crown Tavern and Golden Cross Inn are described on p 50. In St Michael's St. (l.) is the main entrance to the *Oxford Union Society* (Pl. C2), founded as a social and debating club in 1823, a time of increasing political and social awareness and new thinking. It has long been renowned for the quality of its debates and as a training ground for future politicians; numerous distinguished MPs, ministers, and prime ministers first tried their oratorical powers in its hall. A determinedly masculine stronghold, its doors were closed to women as members until 1963. The buildings date mostly from the 1850s and 1860s; the walls and roof of the old library are decorated with scenes from the Morte d'Arthur painted by various Pre-Raphaelite artists; unfortunately owing to inadequate preparation of the plaster they have greatly deteriorated.

Debates are held on Fri at 8.15 p.m. Visitors are admitted to the gallery as spectators; application must be made to the General Office at least two days in advance.

Opposite St Michael's St. is the church of *St Michael at the North Gate* (Pl. C2), whose Saxon tower (pre-1050) once formed part of the city defences. It adjoined the Bocardo (prison), whose oaken door can be seen inside the tower on the N. side. Here Latimer and Ridley were held before their deaths at the stake in 1555, and Cranmer in 1556 (see History, p 11). The church itself, though mostly built in the 13C, has been extensively restored since a severe fire in 1953. Some of the glass is 13C, and includes (in the N. aisle) a rare lily Crucifixion. St Michael's is now the city church, and contains the city font (originally in St Martin's, then in All Saints, see p 66) which must be the one in which Shakespeare's godson was baptised.

Immediately beyond, across Broad St., in Magdalen St., is the church of *St Mary Magdalen* (Pl. A8), largely rebuilt by Scott, who added the Martyrs' aisle (N.) in 1842, when he was building the Martyrs' Memorial. In the S. chapel is a memorial to John Aubrey (d 1697) the biographer and antiquarian (see Trinity College).

The *Martyrs' Memorial*, just outside the church at the S. end of St Giles, was designed by Scott in 1841, in the style of the Waltham Eleanor Cross. It commemorates Cranmer, Latimer, and Ridley, whose statues (by H. Weeks) contemplate the swirling traffic at their feet.

On the corner of St Giles and Beaumont St. (r.) are the imposing neo-classical buildings (Pl. A8) of the *Taylor Institution* (the 'Taylorian', facing St Giles) and the ****Ashmolean Museum** (facing Beaumont St.; open 10–4, Sun 2–4) designed in 1841–45 by C.R. Cockerell, who a few years earlier had worked on the Fitzwilliam Museum at Cambridge. The Taylorian, whose facade carries statues symbolising France, Italy, Germany and Spain, was founded for the study of modern languages with a bequest from Sir Robert Taylor, an architect (d 1788). Extensions were added on the N. side in the 1930s. The Ashmolean, one of the finest museums in England outside London, houses the University's magnificent archaeological and art collections.

The history of the University museums begins in 1602, with the provision of a gallery for ancient objects within the newly built Bodleian Library. Then, in 1675, Elias Ashmole 'virtuoso and curioso', antiquarian, scientist, expert in heraldry, offered his old University the extraordinary and diverse 'closet of rarities' known as Tradescant's 'Ark', which had been left to him by John Tradescant the Younger (d 1662). These natural and historical curiosities had been collected largely by his father, John Tradescant the Elder (d 1638), naturalist, and gardener to Charles I, during his plant-hunting and other travels; the work was carried on by his son. To house the 'Ark' a new museum was built near the Bodleian and named the Ashmolean after its benefactor. It was the first public museum in Britain, and with its laboratories and library remained the centre of scientific studies in Oxford till the mid 19C. Large bequests in the 18C and 19C led to the building of the present museum in Beaumont St., to which the name 'Ashmolean' was transferred in 1899. The Old Ashmolean (see p 75) is now the Museum of the History of Science. Various extensions have been added to the Ashmolean, and the natural history and ethnographical exhibits transferred to the Science and Pitt-Rivers Museums respectively (see p 97). Reference to the floor plans will show visitors where to find the displays which particularly interest them. While it is impossible here to detail all the more important exhibits, it may be helpful, at any rate to the non-specialist visitor, to mention a few of the highlights.

Ground Floor. To the left of the entrance is the RANDOLPH GALLERY, containing classical sculptures, Greek, Hellenistic, and Roman originals, and Roman copies, mainly from the *Arundel* or *Pomfret Marbles*, including a torso of c. 480 B.C., a pedimental sculpture embodying two linear measures (Aegean of 5C B.C.) and the fragment of a frieze of an Athenian temple. In the show-cases are temporary displays of individual facets of ancient art. To the W. are the *Petrie Room* of pre-dynastic groups, mainly from Sir Flinders Petrie's Egyptian excavations; the *Chester Room*, with scarabs, beads, seals, papyri, etc; and the *Egyptian Dynastic Gallery*, which includes furnishings, bronzes, and inscriptions, mostly from excavated sites. The Egyptian Sculpture Gallery (Griffith Gallery) contains the *Shrine of Taharqa from Kawa (7C B.C.) adorned with bas-relief, and hung with wall-paintings from Tell el Amarna; finds from the Oxford excavations in Nubia; reliefs, stelae and figures (Intermediate Period and Middle Kingdom); mummy cases and

Ashmolean Museum

GROUND FLOOR

58 Japanese Art
57 Islamic Art
61 Oriental Paintings, Screens & Prints
54 Asian Ceramics
56 Later Chinese Ceramics
55 53 Sayce Room Chinese Ceramics
Access to Main Library
59 Indian Art
60 Temporary Exhibitions
5 Library Lobby Viking Antiquities
52 Ingram Gallery Chinese Ceramics
3 Sunken Court Greek Antiquities
4 Medieval Room
51 Vestibule Gandhara/Chinese Art
Randolph Lecture Room
Main Staircase
7 Chester Room
6 Petrie Room
1 Randolph Gallery Classical Sculpture
Cloakrooms
Egyptian Antiquities
8 Egyptian Dynastic Gallery
9 Griffith Gallery Egyptian Sculpture & Inscriptions
2 Ruskin Gallery
Entrance
10 Marshall Room
Worcester Porcelain

FIRST FLOOR

Near Eastern Antiquities
Cypriot Antiquities
15 Drapers Gallery
14 Myres Room
19
17 Leeds Room Roman/Anglo Saxon Antiquities
16 Beazley Room Greek Antiquities
13 Arthur Evans Room
Cretan Antiquities
Heberden Coin Room
18 Coins & Medals
12 John Evans Room
Prehistoric Europe Etruscan Antiquities
Hill Music Room Musical Instruments
24
25 Weldon Gallery European Paintings
23 Fox-Strangways Gallery Venetian Paintings
11 Tradescant Room
Pre-Raphaelite Paintings
26 Combe Room
22 Mallett Gallery Tapestry
21 Fortnum Gallery Italian Paintings
20
Main Staircase
27 Hindley Smith Gallery
32 McAlpine Gallery Temporary Exhibitions
Founders' Room Founders' Portraits
Chambers Hall Gallery English Paintings
Nineteenth Century Paintings
71
28 Eldon Gallery Prints & Drawings
30 Farrer Gallery English Silver & Italian Majolica
FIRST FLOOR
71a European Porcelain
Pissarro Room English Paintings
29
72 Madan Gallery
Dutch & Flemish Paintings, English Glass
31
Warren Room English Delftware
73 Ward Gallery Dutch Still-Life Paintings, Ceramics
SECOND FLOOR

funerary furnishings; stone fragments from Tell el Amarna; masks (New Kingdom); and painted and sculptured fragments.

From here a passage leads to the *Marshall Room* with coloured Worcester porcelain (1750–83).

North of the Randolph Gallery, the MEDIEVAL ROOM contains the
9C *'Alfred Jewel' found in 1693 near Athelney in Somerset, where
Alfred spent the winter of 878 in hiding. It bears the inscription
'Aelfred mec heht Gewyrcan' (Alfred had me made) and may be the
handle of an 'aestil' or pointer for following lines of illuminated MSS;
the similar 'Minster Lovell Jewel'; local pottery; brooches; a wooden
'Peg' tankard; medieval tiles; the ancient Odda stone, the foundation
stone of 1056 of the Saxon chapel at Deerhurst; and objects of
historical interest. In the lobby are Viking antiquities. To the right in
the Medieval Room, the SUNKEN COURT, containing large numbers
of Greek vases, is open to students on request.

Opposite the main entrance is the **Department of Eastern Art**. In the
Vestibule are examples of Gandhara sculpture and early Chinese
bronze. The *Ingram Gallery* of Chinese ceramics (400 B.C.–14C A.D.)
contains also pottery tomb figures (A.D. 618–906) and a Sung gilt
bronze Bodhisattva and 16C cast iron heads. The following rooms to
right and left show Chinese porcelains 14–20C, and Chinese
decorative arts. The end room is devoted mainly to Japanese and
Persian ceramics and other decorative arts. The *Screen Gallery* (l.)
houses Japanese fine arts, and leads into the Tibetan Room. Beyond,
the Temporary Exhibition Gallery is on the right (exhibitions here are
usually changed monthly) and on the left stone, metal and terracotta
works of India and South East Asia are displayed in two adjacent
rooms.

First Floor. The small *Founders' Room* contains portraits of the
Tradescants and of Elias Ashmole; in the corridor is a display
illustrating the early history of the Museum. A few steps down lead
to the DEPARTMENT OF ANTIQUITIES, the many superb finds arranged
for expert study rather than aesthetic appreciation. The TRADESCANT
ROOM, perhaps the most entertaining in the museum, exhibits objects
from the original collections, and historical relics such as Guy
Fawkes' lantern, Bradshaw's hat, Powhatan's mantle, etc. Displayed
in the JOHN EVANS ROOM are gold ornaments and other objects of the
European prehistoric periods with a large alcove for Italic and
Etruscan antiquities. The Cretan collection in the ARTHUR EVANS
ROOM, principally from the excavations of Sir Arthur Evans at
Knossos, is of special importance, and includes pottery, Minoan
seals, Linear B tablets, swords, jewellery, Cycladic finds from
Phylakopi in Melos and from the Diktaean Cave. Beyond is the *Myres
Room* of Cypriot antiquities, with seals, jewellery, sculpture, etc; to
the right is the *Drapers' Gallery* of finds from the Near East including
'Luristan Bronzes' and objects from Jericho. To the left the BEAZLEY
ROOM is devoted to Greek antiquities including Geometric, orientalis-
ing, black- and red-figure vases (note especially those with scenes of
men at work: a shoemaker, potters in their workshop, and a helmet
maker), bronzes, terracottas, gems and jewellery. The LEEDS ROOM
houses finds from the Roman Empire and Europe during the Dark
Ages, with particular reference to Britain. A staircase descends to the
Viking Lobby.

The Hill Music Room contains Italian and English stringed instruments
(16–18C) including 'Le Messie' by Stradivarius. The *Heberden Coin Room*
(open 10–12.30 and 2–4) contains rich collections of Greek, Roman, Oriental,

medieval European, and modern coins, and medals, a selection from all periods being on exhibition. Students may consult the main part of the collection by appointment only.

The DEPARTMENT OF WESTERN ART occupies the remainder of the upper floors. Beyond the Founder's Room (see above) is the FORTNUM GALLERY, containing the well-known Fortnum collection of Renaissance bronzes, as well as a remarkably representative collection of Italian *Paintings of the 13–17C (see also below): *Orcagna*, Birth of the Virgin; *Bronzino*, Portrait of Giov. de' Medici as a boy; *Giac. Pacchiarotti*, Virgin and Child; *Christofano Allori*, Portrait; *And. Solario*, Ecce Homo; *Davide Ghirlandaio*, Saints; *Uccello*, Hunt in a Forest; *Lor. di Credi*, Madonna and Child; *Vitt. Crivelli*, St Catherine of Alexandria; *And. Vanni*, Virgin and Child; *Fra Filippo Lippi*, Meeting of Saints; *Ghirlandaio* (attrib.), Portrait of Young Man; *Piero di Cosimo*, Forest Fire; *Pinturicchio*, Virgin and Child; cartoons by *Raphael* and *Sodoma*.

At the end is the *Mallett Gallery* with tapestries and sculpture including busts of Cromwell and Wren by *Edward Pearce* (d 1698), and of Marlborough by *Rysbrack*. The inlaid brass and tortoiseshell medailler is by *A.-C. Boulle*. Here also are a painted wooden statue of an acolyte (Netherlandish, c. 1470) and *Van Dyck*, Deposition.

The FOX-STRANGWAYS GALLERY contains small Netherlandish, German, Spanish and Italian paintings, including some lovely primitives; *Giov. Bellini*, St Jerome; *Camillo Procaccini*, Rest on Flight; *Luis de Morales*, Virgin and Child; *Simon Marmion* (?), St Francis, Virgin mourning the Body of Christ; *Veronese*, Holy Family; *Giorgione*, The Tallard Madonna; *Montagna*, Virgin and Child; *Tintoretto*, Resurrection; *Anon.*, Portrait of a Musician (? *Monteverdi*); unusual works by *Jacopo Bassano*. The WELDON GALLERY beyond is devoted to the French masters of the 16–18C, notable *Poussin* and *Claude Lorraine* and their Italian contemporaries such as *Guardi, Bernini, Barocci*, and *Canaletto*.

In the *Coombe Room* of Pre-Raphaelite paintings are works by *Rossetti* and *Millais*.

The HINDLEY-SMITH GALLERY displays English and French works of the last hundred years. *Courbet* and *Corot* are well represented, and there are works by *Toulouse-Lautrec, Matisse, Van Gogh, Pissarro, Bonnard*, and *Picasso*. The sculpture is by *Rodin, Degas* and *Daumier*. In the *Pissarro Room* are paintings from the 20C English and French Schools. Beyond this is the ELDON GALLERY with a changing selection from the rich collection of drawings, water-colours and prints.

A vestibule at the far end containing drawings by *Max Beerbohm* gives access to the *Fine Art Library* and reference collection of prints (adm to ticket-holders or on application to the attendant), and to the small *Warren Room* with English Delft ware.

In the FARRER GALLERY are the Fortnum ceramics, mainly Hispano-Moresque, Turkish and Italian, and collections of silver, including works by Huguenot craftsmen working in London (c. 1705–50; *Lamerie, Platel*, and the *Courtaulds*); also some examples of Italian sculpture, including works by the *Della Robbia*. Among the smaller works of art here are rings (Papal, 13–15C; English ecclesiastical, 13–17C); ivories and plaquettes; Limoges enamel (13–16C) including a reliquary depicting the Martyrdom and Burial of St Thomas Becket in champlevé enamel; and a fine display of timepieces (16–17C).

The Farrer Gallery leads back into the Mallett Gallery, from which a staircase showing examples of tapestry and needlework leads to the Second Floor.

The **Second Floor** contains the *Chambers Hall Gallery* devoted to the British School, including works by *Hogarth, Reynolds, Zoffany, Richard Wilson, Gainsborough, Constable, Romney, Samuel Palmer,* and *Bonington*; the *Madan Gallery* of Dutch and Flemish works of the 17C (works by *Rubens, Van Dyck, Van Goyen, Ruisdael, Paul Bril, David Teniers the Younger, Jan Van Huysum*) and the Marshall Collection of 17–18C glass; and the *Ward Gallery* of Dutch 17–18C paintings of flowers and still-life.

The *Cast Gallery* (Mon–Fri 10–11.45, 1–4) lies to the north of the Museum, approached from St John's St. It contains over 250 casts of Greek and Graeco-Roman statuary, arranged in historical sequence.

BEAUMONT STREET, laid out in 1828 and built of Bath stone, is spacious and gracious, although the Vict-Gothic Randolph Hotel (l.) is hardly in keeping with the rest. Immediately beyond it is the *Playhouse* (sympathetically designed by Sir Edward Maufe, 1938) belonging to the university and used both by the amateur Oxford University Dramatic Society (OUDS) and by professional companies. Facing the junction of Beaumont St. and Walton St. (r.) is **Worcester College** (Pl. A7), founded in 1714 on a site originally occupied by Gloucester College (1283), which provided a centre for monks of the Benedictine order studying at Oxford, each parent abbey being responsible for its own 'house' (cf Magdalene College, Cambridge, p 127). The Dissolution in 1539 brought the college to an end; it was later re-established as *Gloucester Hall*, partly dependent on St John's College, which by then owned the site. The present foundation was made possible through the benefaction of a wealthy Worcestershire landowner, Sir Thomas Cookes. The outcome of this history is visually very pleasing, medieval picturesqueness and 18C elegance sharing the front quadrangle in perfect harmony. The comparative remoteness of the college from the centre of Oxford, from which it was even more isolated before Beaumont St. was opened, earned it the soubriquet 'Botany Bay'.

The entrance front and N. (r.) side of the first quadrangle are 18C. Hawksmoor may have had a hand in their design. Building proceeded very slowly and was not completed until 1791. Both Hall and Chapel are in the entrance block; the *Hall* (l.) was decorated by Wyatt 1776–84, and although redecorated (by Burges, who did the Chapel) in 1877, has now been returned to its original style, with an entrance screen of columns, cool colours, and delicate plaster-work on the immensely high ceiling. There are few portraits; the whole effect is particularly light and airy, and is in strong contrast to the *Chapel* (r. of the entrance). This also was designed by Wyatt, and like the Hall has a screen of columns, but was completely redecorated by Burges in 1864 in the High Victorian manner, though the wealth of ornament and rich colours can hardly be seen in the gloom created by the crude heaviness of the stained-glass windows.

The N. (r.) side of the quadrangle and Provost's Lodgings are mid 18C, with a few medieval buildings wedged in between, and modern additions beyond. The S. (l.) side consists of the *medieval houses of Gloucester College; the arms of the abbeys which maintained them can be seen over some of the doors (Glastonbury, Malmesbury, St Augustine's Canterbury, Pershore), though not all are in their original positions. The W. side, opposite the entrance, is open to the beautiful *gardens, with lake and playing fields beyond, which are one of the greatest charms of this particularly attractive college. They are reached through a passage (l.). On the S. and E. sides of the garden are the Nuffield Block (1939) and New Building (1961, by Sir Hugh Casson).

FAMOUS MEMBERS: Gloucester Hall: Richard Lovelace, Cavalier poet, 1618-57; Worcester College: Thomas de Quincey, essayist and author of 'Confessions of an Opium Eater', 1785–1859.

Along Walton St., beyond Worcester (l.), is *Ruskin College* (Pl. A7), in William and Mary style, 1912, founded in 1899 by Walter Vrooman and Charles Beard, American admirers of John Ruskin, to enable working men to study history, sociology, and economics in the academic atmosphere of Oxford. It has no official connection with the University.

Further on is the famous *Oxford University Press* (Pl. A5), one of the most prestigious publishing houses in the world. It was moved from the Clarendon Building (see p 74) to this part of Oxford, known as Jericho, in the 1820s; its learned publications still bear the imprint 'Clarendon Press', and it is still controlled by the University, whose Delegates still conduct their meetings in the Clarendon Buildings.

Opposite, up Little Clarendon St., are the smart new *University Offices* (Pl. A5) built round Wellington Sq (Sir Leslie Martin, 1969–73). At the far end of Walton St., where it becomes Kingston St., a turn l. (Walton Well Rd) leads to the canal, the Thames, and *Port Meadow*, (see p 101 for details).

Worcester St., (r. as you leave Worcester College) passes the Gloucester Green Bus Station and car parks and leads to **Nuffield College** (Pl. C1), whose massive tower (housing books) and slender copper spire are a conspicuous Oxford landmark. The main entrance is in New Rd (l.). The college was endowed by Lord Nuffield in 1937 for postgraduate studies, particularly in sociology and associated subjects, and was the first to admit both men and women. Its founder was known to refer to it as 'that bloody Kremlin, where left-wingers study at my expense'. It is on the site of the old Oxford Canal basin, and although designed in 1939 was not actually built until after the war. It is in traditional Cotswold materials and style, with gabled roof-line and mullioned windows; the quadrangles, on two levels, are enlivened with ornamental pools, in the upper of which is an abstract sculpture by Hugh Dalwood (1962). The small *Chapel* is up a stairway (l.) in the lower quad; the windows, that on the N. side showing the Five Wounds of Christ, and the candlesticks were designed by John Piper, and the striking reredos (a Crucifixion) by John Hoskins. The Library (no adm) has an amusing collection of Gillray cartoons (1809) of the Life of Cobbett, with captions taken from 'The Political Register'; the reading-room walls are decorated with paintings of the Four Seasons.

The huge grassy mound on the S. side of New Rd is all there is to be seen of the *Castle*, built by Robert d'Oilly in 1071, whose site is now occupied by the County Hall and Assize Court (Vict-Norm, 1840), modern Education Offices, and Oxford prison, within whose precincts are some scant remains of the castle buildings. The castle has little history. During the struggle for the throne between Stephen and Matilda she was besieged here in 1142, eventually escaping through the snow camouflaged in white, as the romantic story goes. It may have been the birthplace of her grandson, Richard I (b 1157). It was already in ruins in the early 1300s.

Going E. up New Rd, on the l. is **St Peter's College** (Pl. C2), a pleasing if rather confusing collection of buildings reached through small flowery gardens from Bulwark Lane. Its foundation, in 1928, was inspired by F.J. Chavasse, Bp of Liverpool, to provide places for men of limited means and those wishing to be ordained in the Church of England; the project was actually carried out by his son C.M. Chavasse (later Bp of Rochester) who was the first Master. Initially it was a Private Hall, St Peter's House, and received full collegiate status in 1961. It stands on the site of Trellick's Inn (afterwards New Inn Hall), one of Oxford's oldest medieval halls, and three houses already there were incorporated into the new foundation: Hannington Hall (1832 but much altered), the old rectory (Georgian), and Canal House (1827) which was formerly the offices of the Canal Company. At the same time the church of St Peter-le-Bailey (1874, but with some materials and monuments from the former medieval church across the road) became the college *Chapel*. The themes of the glass in the E. window (John Hayward, 1964) are: the personality of St Peter; the history of the college; C.M. Chavasse. He is accompanied by his cigarette holder, his pet tortoise and squirrel, his Military Cross, his 'tin leg', and the Olympic symbol which recalls his part in the 1908 Games. His father is commemorated in a large bronze relief on the N. wall.

Opposite St Peter's, across New Inn Hall St., is the ruined gateway of St Mary's College, dissolved under Elizabeth I, an Augustinian house where Erasmus stayed in 1498-99 while preparing his Greek Testament. The site is now occupied by Frewin Hall and belongs to Brasenose College.

The area S. and W. of New Rd and the Castle was once the site of several religious houses, Osney Abbey, Rewley Abbey, and the Franciscan house of which Roger Bacon was a member (see p 52); there is a tablet to him in the wall of The Terrace at the junction of Turn Again and Old Greyfriar St (Pl. C4). All this is now recalled only in some remaining street names: Osney Lane, Paradise St., Blackfriars Rd, Friar's Wharf, Abbey Place, etc. The railway long ago cut across the old abbey sites, and between it and the city centre there has recently arisen a huge development of ring roads, houses, shops and car parks. The entrance to the multi-storey car park, seen from a raised walkway off Roger Bacon Lane, is topped by a splendid geodesic sphere looking like a vast glass football.

At Bonn Sq, New Rd becomes Queen St, which leads up to Carfax.

4 NORTH AND NORTH-EAST OF THE MARTYRS' MEMORIAL

The distances covered in this section are considerable. The earlier part of the route can easily be done on foot, but beyond about St Anne's all but the most energetic will need transport. There are frequent buses along the Woodstock and Banbury roads (for details see p 41), and it is possible to park a car in St Giles for a short period, and for longer in the more outlying areas. Much of Oxford's post-war building is included in this itinerary; for anyone at all interested in modern developments the extra effort involved in following the route is well worth while.

St Giles Fair, 1911

Unlike the three previous routes this one begins not at Carfax, but at the S. end of ST GILES, a wide thoroughfare lined with trees, many of which flower in May and June, giving a foretaste of North Oxford's riot of springtime blossom. From medieval times a great two-day fair has been held here at the feast of St Giles (Mon and Tues following the first Sun in Sept); the road is closed and all traffic diverted. On the E. (r.) side is the Martyrs' Memorial (see pp 81–82) and shortly N. of it is the entrance to St John's College.

St John's College (Pl. A8) was founded in 1555 by Sir Thomas White, a rich clothier and former Lord Mayor of London, on the site of the old Cistercian College of St Bernard founded by Abp Chichele in 1437 and closed at the Dissolution. The object was to 'strengthen the orthodox [i.e. Roman] faith' and the statutes were strongly religious in character. White was a Merchant Taylor and a number of places were, and still are, reserved for boys from the Merchant Taylors' School. The college is dedicated to St John the Baptist, patron saint of tailors. Shortly after the founder's death the Fellows acquired estates which included the Manor of Walton, now the residential area of North Oxford and thus a source of great wealth. Elizabeth I visited the college in 1567, welcomed with a Latin speech by young Edmund Campion, later executed, in 1581, for his alleged complicity in a Roman Catholic plot against the Queen. Royal visits were also paid by James I (who was entertained by a play which went on till 1 a.m.), by Charles I and by Charles II (see below). St John's was staunchly Jacobite in its loyalties, officially until George III's time, sentimentally much longer. Its most distinguished President was William Laud (1611–21), who afterwards became Abp of Canterbury and one of Charles I's chief advisers. A controversially High Churchman, he suffered execution at the hands of the Puritan faction in 1645. He was a great benefactor of the college, and is buried in the chapel between the founder and his successor as President, William Juxon (who was also later Abp of Canterbury, and as Bp of London ministered to Charles I in his last moments on the scaffold).

The oldest part of the college is FRONT QUAD, the N., S., and W. (front) sides being the remains of St Bernard's College. The third storey with dormer windows was added in the early 17C to relieve overcrowding, students at the time having to sleep two to a bed. Over the gateway is the original statue of St Bernard flanked by the two founders, Abp Chichele and Sir Thomas White; on the inner side is a statue of the patron saint by Eric Gill (1936). The old facade merges northward with the buildings, tactfully in keeping, designed by G.G. Scott the Younger in 1881.

On the N. side of Front Quad are both Chapel and Hall. The *Chapel*, though dating from 1530, has been altered many times, and is now almost wholly Vict (Blore, 1843; reredos and E. window by Kempe, 1892). Only the Baylie Chapel (N. side) built in 1662, retains its original appearance; it has a plasterwork fan-vault and contains some interesting monuments, and late 15C altar frontal and vestments. (The college has a large collection of frontals and vestments, witness to its Catholic traditions.)

The *Hall* (open 2–4), built in mid 16C, was largely remodelled inside in mid 18C. Above the plaster-panelled ceiling of 1730 the original timber roof survives; the heavy stone screen with gallery above is by James Gibbs (1742). Over the handsome marble fireplace (William Townesend 1731) hangs an 18C scagliola (imitation marble) picture of St John the Baptist, looking unusually young and cheerful, a copy after Raphael by Lamberto Gorio, brought to England in 1759. There is another picture by Gorio in the Old Library (see below), a small coloured drawing of his master F.E. Hugford (1696–1771), who perfected the technique of scagliola. The many interesting portraits include those of Henry Hudson, the navigator and explorer (Hudson's Bay), and Sir Walter Raleigh.

Opposite the main gateway a handsome portal and fan-vaulted passage lead through an even handsomer portal into *CANTERBURY QUAD, built in 1631–36 by Laud when Abp of Canterbury and Chancellor of the University. Lined by colonnades and richly decorated on the E. and W. sides in the classical Baroque manner, it presents an interesting spectrum of architectural styles, the N. and S. sides being in the more traditional and restrained Oxford Jacobean-Gothic. The bronze statues opposite and over the doorway are, respectively, of Charles I and Henrietta Maria (by Le Sueur, 1633; cf Earl of Pembroke outside the Bodleian, p 75). The King and Queen opened the new buildings, and were also entertained with a play in the Hall. The west end of the S. side was actually built as the library about 30 years before Laud extended it; the stone used came from the monastic buildings of Gloucester College (see Worcester College, p 86). The *Old Library* (adm on written application only) is a splendid room, with a ceiling of carved beams and 16C bookcases and benches. Here are displayed a number of college treasures:

Laud's crook and the staff he carried on his way to the scaffold, his skullcap and his diary; a painting on wood of Charles I and his queen, and a portrait of the King in which his features are deliniated in minutely-written psalms. When Charles II visited St John's he asked for this picture of his father, but later, on offering the hospitable Fellows whatever they wished and their choosing the picture, graciously returned it. On the staircase is the founder's chest (cf the Divinity School and Merton College Old Library) and a portrait of Dr William Paddy, physician to James I, and a great benefactor of the college.

To the S. of the Front Quad (r.) is DOLPHIN QUAD, partly late 18C, partly mid 20C by Sir Edward Maufe. This abuts on to a narrow passage and the Dolphin Gate to Trinity College (see p 80). The quad to the N. (l.) is mostly 19C and 20C work, by far the most striking building being that on the E. side, a series of interlocking polygons creating a honeycomb effect, topped by polygonal lanterns with miniature spires (Architects Copartnership, 1958–60). N. again is the Sir Thomas White Building (Arup Associates, 1974). The college also has postgraduate accommodation in Pusey Lane and Leckford Rd. The *gardens, laid out in mid 18C, are among the most beautiful in this city of beautiful gardens. The lawns rival a billiard table.

FAMOUS MEMBERS: Edmund Campion, Jesuit martyr, 1540–81; Abp Laud, 1573–1645 and Abp Juxon, 1582–1663 (see above for both); James Shirley, playwright and poet, 1596–1666; A.E. Housman, poet, 1859–1936; Gilbert Murray, classical historian and champion of international understanding, 1866–1957.

Going N. (r.) from St John's along the E. (r.) side of St Giles there are some of the handsomest Georgian houses in Oxford. Where the road forks into Woodstock Rd (l.) and Banbury Rd (r.) is *Queen Elizabeth House*, a centre for the study of Commonwealth affairs, set up in 1954 and maintained jointly by the University and the Government, and beyond, on the 'Keble Road Triangle', the towering buildings of the *Department of Engineering*, and the Nuclear Physics and other laboratories. In the fork itself is St Giles Church, mostly 12C and 13C, a still point between rivers of traffic.

On the W. (l.) side of St Giles, almost opposite St John's, is the Taylor Institution (see p 82). Beyond it is *Blackfriars*, established in the 1920s for Dominican monks studying in Oxford; the spacious chapel, in Perp.-Gothic style, is welcoming and serene. Next door is *Pusey House*, also in Gothic style, a High Anglican theological centre founded in 1884; its name commemorates Edward Pusey, one of the leaders of the Tractarian Movement (see History, p 13). In Pusey St. is *Regents Park College*, a training centre for the Baptist ministry, established in London in the 19C and moved to Oxford in 1938. It is not a college proper, but a Permanent Private Hall of the University, as is *St Benet's*, further up St Giles, set up in 1847 as an Oxford centre for Benedictines from Ampleforth. In Pusey Lane (l. off Pusey St.) is the Oriental Institute (1958–60).

Continuing l. up Woodstock Rd there is first the vast pile of St Aloysius Roman Catholic Church (1873–75), then the entrance to **Somerville College** (Pl. A5; grounds open daily 10–5, chapel and hall by arrangement at the Porter's Lodge), founded in 1879 for women students, who for long had to brave the opposition of the more conservative elements in the university (for details of the women's education movement see History, p 13). It still admits only women. Unlike Lady Margaret Hall, founded a year earlier for Church of England girls, Somerville was deliberately undenominational (the chapel was not built till 1935; see below). Beginning as Somerville

Hall and named after Mary Somerville, a distinguished mathematician (d 1872), its title was changed to 'College' in 1894. It became a fully independent self-governing body in 1926, soon after women were admitted as members of the university. It has always had a formidable reputation for academic excellence, and the roll of its past members now outstanding in academic and public life is impressive indeed. It seems a far cry from Ruskin's patronising comment in a birthday book of 1881: 'So glad to be old enough to be let come and have tea at Somerville, and to watch the girlies play at ball'.

The buildings are somewhat confusing. The first quadrangle (*Darbishire*) is one of the newest, built in 1933 by Morley Horder. Of Bladon stone and of two storeys only and to a comfortably domestic uniform design, it is in marked contrast to the second (*Middle*) quad, which is dominated on the l. by the sheer yellow brick cliff of St Aloysius Church, and on the r. by rather aggressively Vict-Gothic ranges designed by Sir T.G. Jackson (1881) and Walter Cave (1895) as extensions to Walton House, the college's first residence. Through the arch (S.) is the third (*Garden*) quad, again with buildings of various dates and styles, mostly red brick neo-Queen Anne, set pleasantly round spacious treed lawns. Immediately E. (l.) through the arch on the first floor is the *Hall*, beautifully panelled and hung with portraits.

On the W. side is the library (Basil Champneys, 1903), on the S. the startling Wolfson Block (Arup Associates, 1959), and Vaughan, Margery Fry-Elizabeth Nuffield houses providing both graduate and undergraduate accommodation. Standing alone and lonely is the undenominational *Chapel* (1935), as austere within as without. The sculptures in the grounds are by Wendy Taylor, Sam Werthmann, and Polly Ionides.

FAMOUS MEMBERS: Rose Macaulay, novelist, 1889–1958; Dorothy Sayers, novelist and religious writer, 1893–1957; Barbara Ward (Lady Jackson) DBE, author and economist, 1914–81; and many distinguished scholars and political figures still living.

Immediately N. of Somerville is the Radcliffe Infirmary, built in the late 18C with funds bequeathed by Dr Radcliffe (see University College, p 65 and Radcliffe Camera, p 76), a dignified stone edifice in classical style, round which has grown up a collection of heterogeneous 19C and 20C accretions. It is a great teaching hospital, and fittingly the *Radcliffe Observatory* (Pl. A3) immediately adjacent has become the centre-piece of a new college devoted entirely to advanced medical studies. Originally to be called Radcliffe College, this embryonic foundation was renamed **Green College** after Dr and Mrs Cecil Green of Dallas, Texas, who largely financed the project. The beautiful Observatory was built in the 1770s (again with funds from Dr Radcliffe) and mostly designed by James Wyatt. It has long single-storey wings with alternating windows and arched niches, and at the centre a second storey topped by a polygonal tower, inspired by the Temple of the Winds in Athens, and decorated with reliefs of the winds and their Greek names. Above is a copper-covered globe supported by lead figures of Atlas and Hercules.

Opposite is **St Anne's College** (Pl. A3; grounds open daily). It was founded in 1879 as the Society of Oxford Home Students, for women studying in Oxford but not living in college; it gradually acquired a number of hostels, and eventually few students actually lived at home, but there were no college buildings until the 1930s. It became St Anne's Society in 1942 and received full collegiate status in 1952. Men are now admitted. Perhaps because of its rather informal

Wolfson Building, St Anne's College

background, its reputation was one of sociability and versatility, which its present appearance somehow seems to reflect. It is one of the very few colleges to announce its name at the main gate.

The buildings are of considerable variety, yet together make up a very harmonious group and provide accommodation to suit differing tastes. Until the 1930s the site, between the Woodstock and Banbury roads, was occupied by Vict houses with large gardens, used as hostels. These have been left in situ, and their modern neighbours have grown around them; the gardens likewise have been allowed to preserve their domestic intimacy; there are no quadrangles as such.

The *Founder's Gatehouse* (1966 by Howell, Killick, Partridge and Amis, who also designed Wolfson and Rayne buildings) is an evocation in modern terms of the traditional towered college gateway. To the S. (r.) is the *Dining Hall* (Gerald Banks, 1959), whose N. and E. sides are almost entirely of glass, which allows a good view of the interior, lined with wood slats and decorated with a vast abstract mural (Stefan Knapp). The glass cupola above makes a pleasing contribution to the skyline.

N. (l.) are the older college buildings, Hartland House (by Giles Gilbert Scott, 1938, extended in 1951 and 1972), housing library, common rooms and study-rooms. Ahead are the new residential blocks, Wolfson, 1964, and Rayne, 1968.

N. across Bevington Rd is **St Antony's College** (Pl. A3; open Mon–Sat 2–5; visitors should call at the Porter's Lodge), a graduate college specialising in modern history, economics and politics, and accommodating a centre for Japanese studies (see History, p 16). It was founded in 1948 by Monsieur Antonin Besse, a French shipping magnate, who also gave generous benefactions shared by various of the less well-off colleges. It first occupied the buildings of a former Anglican convent, the chapel of which is now the Library (J.L. Pearson, 1891). The New Building (1968–70) is by Howell, Killick, Partridge and Amis. In the entrance hall are bronzes of the founder and his wife by Oscar Nemon.

On the E. side of Banbury Rd is *Wycliffe Hall*, an evangelical Church of England theological college. About 5 mins walk N. is **St Hugh's College** (Pl. A1), founded for women as St Hugh's Hall in 1886 by Elizabeth Wordsworth, Principal of Lady Margaret Hall, and daughter of the Bp of Lincoln, after whose predecessor, St Hugh of Lincoln, the Hall was named. It became a college in 1911 and was incorporated by Royal Charter in 1926. Originally occupying various houses in Norham Rd and Gardens it moved to its present site in 1916. During the Second World War it was requisitioned as a military hospital. Men are now admitted as postgraduates.

The buildings (seen by arrangement with the Domestic Bursar), face S. with their backs to St Margaret's Rd. They are neo-Georgian, red brick and bow-windowed. The Library (W.), built in 1936, is named after the first Principal, Miss C.A.E. Moberley; the *Hall* (E.) was extended in 1958; it contains some interesting portraits. Above the entrance gate is the small *Chapel* where Miss B.E. Gwyer, a former Principal, is commemorated outside by a bust (by *Miriam Coatman*) and inside by an engraved glass panel (1976, by *Laurence Whistler*). The bold new Wolfson Building (1964) in very red red brick is by David Roberts (cf Magdalen, Sacher Building, and much work at Cambridge). The Kenyon New Building (1966), also by David Roberts, won an architectural award.

The colourful terraced gardens (open during daylight hours exc Aug, Christmas and Easter) were partly the creation of Miss Annie M.A.H. Rogers (d 1937) a pioneer of women's education in Oxford, and a famous Oxford 'character'.

Just S. of St Hugh's, across Banbury Rd, Bardwell Rd leads past the famous Dragon School (for boys aged 8–13) to ***Wolfson College** (see plan of Environs; about $^1/_2$ m., grounds open daily, quadrangles and buildings by prior arrangement only). Beginning life in 1965 as Iffley College, a society for graduates reading for advanced degrees, it became Wolfson College in 1966, when benefactions from the Wolfson and Ford Foundations made large-scale development possible. The majority of members are scientists or mathematicians, and the first President was the philosopher Sir Isaiah Berlin.

The college occupies a spacious well-treed site beside the Cherwell; it has its own small marina, and a footbridge over the river leads to open water-meadows and a pleasant riverside path. The low white concrete buildings banded with grey panels, by Powell and Moya (cf Brasenose and Christ Church, and the Cripps Building of St John's College, Cambridge) have won a number of architectural awards. They provide accommodation ranging from small family houses to bed-sitting room units, large common and study rooms, library, and a wood-panelled dining-hall with pyramid-shaped roof.

Turning S. (l.) from Wolfson, back towards the centre, Lady Margaret Hall can be reached either by cutting through Dragon School Lane (about ¹/₂ m.) or by returning to Banbury Rd and turning l. down Norham Gardens opposite St Anne's (about 10 mins walk from this point), passing en route the Department of Education and *St Stephen's House*, a High Anglican theological college.

Lady Margaret Hall ('L.M.H.'; Pl. B1; open daily exc Aug, Christmas and Easter; visitors to the Hall and Chapel should call at the Porter's Lodge) was founded for Church of England girls in 1878, amid the controversy surrounding women's education (see History, p 13) and owed much to the championship of Dr E.S. Talbot, Warden of Keble College, after whom one of the buildings is named, and who at a great age dedicated the chapel in 1933. The college itself is named after Lady Margaret Beaufort (d 1509) 'a scholar, a gentlewoman, and a saint', founder of St John's and Christ's Colleges, Cambridge, and of professorships in Divinity at both universities. It grew rapidly both in numbers and reputation, and was incorporated by Royal Charter in 1926. Men are now admitted.

The first students were accommodated in the brick villa which still stands l. of the entrance gate. In 1881 this was extended by Basil Champneys (cf Newnham College, Cambridge) in the Georgian style which set the pattern for most of the college's future development, so that although the buildings are of many different dates they form together a mellow and integrated whole. The only exceptions are the painfully out-of-keeping residential blocks of 1972, five-storey towers of bright red brick and glass.

The handsome entrance leads into Wolfson Quad; to E. (r.) are the residential blocks of Wordsworth (1886), Talbot (1910), and Toynbee (1915); to S. (l.) is Lodge (1926); all are by Sir Reginald Blomfield. Opposite (N.) is the Library (by Raymond Erith) built only in 1957, but in perfect agreement with its older neighbours. It is named after Lynda Grier, a former Principal. A passage opposite the entrance leads to a second quadrangle with the Deneke Building E. (r.), housing the large dining-hall, and the Chapel, both by Sir Giles Gilbert Scott, 1931–33. The *Chapel* (access through the Deneke Building) is in the Byzantine style, and contains a painting of the Flagellation of Christ attributed to *Taddeo Gaddi* (14C, Florentine), a beautiful triptych by *Burne-Jones* (1863) and handsome carved stalls. The gardens are exceptionally spacious and peaceful; to E. a long path near the river leads to the college landing stage and punts.

On the N. side of L.M.H. a gateway leads out into Benson Pl and Norham Rd, a short way up which (r.) is *Maison Française*. Founded in 1946 as a centre of Anglo-French cultural studies and friendship, it moved from Woodstock Rd to its present elegant home in 1963. In front is a sculpture, 'Flore', by *Maillol*.

The *University Park* (the Parks), with numerous playing-fields including the University Cricket Ground, tennis courts and croquet lawns, lies immediately S. During the Civil War Charles I's artillery was encamped here; during the Second World War parts were used for vegetable-growing in the voluntary 'Dig for Victory' campaign. The Parks are criss-crossed by footpaths and bounded on the E. side by the Cherwell, which can be crossed either by Rainbow Bridge, beyond which the path leads to Marston, or in the S.E. corner near the men's bathing place *Parson's Pleasure*. Here the river divides, and paths lead either along the near bank (Cherwell Water Walks) or between the two streams (Mesopotamia) to emerge (about 1 m.) into Marston Rd.

On the W. side of the Parks, in Parks Rd about 3 mins walk from the end of Norham Gardens, is **Keble College** (Pl. A6) founded in 1870 as a memorial to the Revd John Keble (1792–1866), one of the leaders of the Oxford Tractarian Movement (see History, p 13), to provide 'persons desirous of academical education and willing to live economically, with a college wherein sober living and high culture of the mind may be combined with Christian training based upon the principles of the Church of England.' Denominational restrictions were not, however, imposed. Money for the foundation was raised by public subscription, the Chapel, Hall and Library being given entirely by the Gibbs family of Tyntesfield, Somerset, enthusiastic Tractarians. Initially it was governed by a council and Warden who appointed tutors; Fellows were elected in 1930, and it became fully independent and of equal status with the older colleges in 1952. Its past members include many famous church leaders, bishops and archbishops.

The original buildings (1868–82) are all by William Butterfield, himself a High Churchman and much associated with the Camden Society (Cambridge equivalent of the Tractarians). They are in his characteristic style, asymmetrical Gothic, red brick diversified with polychrome patterns and stone dressings (it has been described as 'The Fair Isle Jersey'). The rooms open off corridors instead of staircases as is traditional in the older colleges. *Liddon Quad* (r. of the entrance) is dominated by the vast *Chapel, whose soaring interior is a riot of colour and decoration, with more polychrome brickwork, carved stonework, a floor of encaustic tiles laid in patterns of increasing elaboration as they approach the altar, and above the blind arcading mosaic panels of biblical scenes, inspired by Giotto's frescoes of the life of St Francis at Assisi. These and the stained glass are by A. Gibbs. The nave seats face E., a departure

High Victorian Gothic at Keble College

from the usual college chapel arrangement of stalls. In 1892 a small side chapel was added to house Holman Hunt's famous picture 'The Light of the World', presented by Mrs Combe, widow of the Superintendent of the Oxford University Press; Butterfield would not allow it to be hung in the chapel 'a place of Worship, not a gallery'. Also in this chapel is Keble's sick communion set (seen by prior arrangement only).

On the S. (l.) side of Liddon Quad is the *Library* (no adm, but glass doors afford a glimpse inside). The furnishings are by Butterfield, and it possesses a valuable collection of illuminated MSS and early printed books bequeathed by Sir Charles Brooke. Beyond it is the *Hall*, containing portraits of Keble and many other saintly-faced men associated with the college, and a huge painting 'A Tale from Boccaccio' by *G.F. Watts* (1817–1904), on indefinite loan from the Tate Gallery. S. (l.) again is *Pusey Quad* and the Warden's Lodging, and W. (on to Blackhall and Museum Rds) are award-winning buildings (1970) by Ahrends, Burton and Koralek; they face inwards, yellow brick with slit windows to the outer side, glass to the inner (cf Queen's College, Florey Building, p 64).

Almost opposite Keble is the **University Museum** (Pl. A6; open Mon–Sat 10–4), built in 1855 to meet the growing need for scientific facilities. The object was to assemble 'all the materials explanatory of the organic beings placed upon the globe'; lecture rooms and laboratories were also provided. It is perhaps more interesting to the general visitor for its architecture than its exhibits, spectacular and curious as some of these, especially the skeletons, are. The moving spirit in its inception was Dr Henry Acland (later Regius Professor of Medicine). John Ruskin, his close friend and Slade Professor of Fine Art, had a strong influence on the choice of Italian Gothic for the design (by Benjamin Woodward, of the Dublin firm of Sir Thomas Deane, Son and Woodward), and took a great interest in every stage of the building.

It is of red and brown stone, with steeply pitched roof and central tower; the window arches carry tracery and are richly decorated with carved natural objects. The cathedral-like *interior is constructed of cast-iron and glass, with a lofty central 'nave' and side 'aisles' which carry, above, an arcaded gallery whose pillars are each of different stone, a practical geology lesson. The ubiquitous decoration also serves an instructional purpose, all the flowers, fruit, foliage and animals, whether in iron or stone, being faithful copies of nature. The stone-carvers were the Irish O'Shea brothers, whose fiery tempers were legendary; on the mouldings of the outer portal can still be seen the mutilated remains of their caricatures of Oxford worthies, alternating with the heads of parrots and owls, which they were subsequently made to obliterate.

The small octagonal building (r.) is a copy of the Abbot's Kitchen at Glastonbury; it was the original Chemistry Laboratory. Next to it is the Radcliffe Science Library (Sir Thomas Jackson 1901 and Sir Hubert Worthington 1934), whose underground extension is beneath the Museum forecourt. Behind is the *Pitt-Rivers Museum of Ethnology and Pre-History* (open Mon–Sat 2–4) built in 1885 to house the collection of General A.H. Lane-Fox Pitt-Rivers (new accommodation is being built in Bradmore Rd).

Round this nucleus has grown up the great complex of the Science Area, extending to the bottom of South Parks Rd. Although some buildings date from the late 19C and early 20C, the great majority belong to the post-Second World War years, the architectural partnerships mainly responsible being *Lanchester*

A Cathedral of Science: the iron and glass 'nave' of the University Museum

and Lodge, and *Ramsey, Murray, White and Ward*. Characteristically of Oxford, flowering trees are planted along all the fronts and road-ways.

On the S. side of South Parks Rd is *Rhodes House* (Pl. A6) built in 1929 (Sir Herbert Baker) as the HQ of the Rhodes Trust and centre for Rhodes Scholars and Commonwealth, American and African studies. It houses the appropriate department of the Bodleian Library. It is a Cotswold-style building, entered through a massive pillared portico and copper-domed rotunda topped by a bronze bird copied from the carved stone birds found at Zimbabwe. In the circular vestibule are memorials to Rhodes Scholars of all nationalities who fell in the First and Second World Wars.

Beyond Rhodes House, in Mansfield Rd (r.; closed to through traffic) is **Mansfield College** (Pl. B5/7). Founded in Birmingham in 1838 as a theological college for the Congregational (now United Reformed) Church, it moved to Oxford in 1886; since 1955 it has been a Permanent Private Hall of the University, and its members now read a variety of subjects. The buildings, set round very spacious lawns, are in the Gothic style (Basil Champneys, 1887–89). In the chapel (r.) is a series of stained-glass windows and statues representing figures from church history. The Library (opposite the entrance; no adm) has interesting timberwork and a ceiling of painted panels.

Next door is **Manchester College** (Pl. B7) also founded as a Nonconformist (Unitarian) training college. Beginning in Manchester in 1786, it moved several times before settling in Oxford in 1888. The Vict-Gothic buildings are by Thomas Worthington, and his son Percy designed the Arlosh Hall (1915). In the Chapel are windows by *Burne-Jones* and *Morris*.

At the bottom of South Parks Rd a path straight ahead leads to the Cherwell and Parson's Pleasure bathing pool (see above). To the r. is the impressive white concrete building, partly mounted on stilts, of the *Departments of Zoology and Psychology* (1965–70 by Sir Leslie Martin, who also designed the new pathology block in the Science Area). Opposite this is **Linacre College** (Pl. B5), modestly housed in early 19C buildings formerly Cherwell Edge, a Roman Catholic convent. Founded in 1926 as a society for graduates, mostly of other universities, wishing to study at Oxford, and named after Thomas Linacre (Renaissance scholar and physician, d 1524; see also All Souls College, p 68) it became a college in 1965.

St Cross Rd runs S. between college playing fields to the junction with Manor Rd (l., about ¼ m.). Here is the Martin Building of Balliol, named after its designer Sir Leslie Martin, and across the road Holywell Manor (early 15C but radically altered in 1926). On the l. of Manor Rd are the striking new *English Faculty* and *Law Libraries* and *Institute of Statistics* (also by Sir Leslie Martin, 1964). At the end of the road is **St Catherine's College** (Pl. B8). Beginning in 1868 as a society for non-collegiate students (cf St Anne's), both undergraduate and graduate, it became a college in 1963. The emphasis is on the sciences, although a proportion of the entrants have to read arts subjects. The buildings, furniture, and gardens were all designed by the Danish architect Arne Jacobsen (1960–64); it is the only Oxford college to have this complete unity of conception.

The plan is strictly geometrical throughout. Built of specially-made small yellow bricks, it is a long rectangle running N. and S., with residential accommodation along each side, common rooms and huge *Hall* (tapestries behind the high table designed by Tom Phillips) across the N. end, and beyond the central circular lawn separate blocks for lecture rooms and the library, named respectively after the Bernard Sunley Trust and the Wolfson Foundation, two of the college's principle benefactors. Between them rises a tall thin campanile; near by is *Epstein*'s bronze bust of Einstein. Both library and rooms have windows to floor level. The total lack of privacy thus achieved is overcome by the occupants with a variety of ingenious devices. The gardens between the buildings are set with rows of parallel walls imprisoning small trees and shrubs. Outside the rectangle, on the E. side, are water gardens, with a sculpture by *Barbara Hepworth*, and the Music Room, an interesting double hexagon design. Beyond, across a meadow, flows the Cherwell.

As its chapel the college uses St Cross Church (12–13C) in St Cross Rd. On its S. side, housed at present in a former schoolroom, is the nucleus of **St Cross College** (Pl. B8), founded for graduates in 1965. Most of its members hold university appointments. About 5 mins walk further on are Holywell St., leading to the Broad, and Longwall St., leading to the High.

ENVIRONS OF OXFORD

For those who have time and want a change from intensive sightseeing, there are a number of places, many within walking distance of the centre, which are pleasant to visit.

South Side

A path beside the Thames, accessible near Folly Bridge, leads downstream to Abingdon, passing a number of locks and weirs, and beyond Sandford winding through quiet watermeadows, with Radley College (boys' public school) away to the W. and the beautiful park and woods of Nuneham Courtenay across the river (E.). At *Iffley* (about 1½ m.) is one of three locks built on the Thames in 1632 (rebuilt in 1923). The others are at Sandford and the Swift Ditch. Over the river, which can be crossed here, is the village, an oasis of peace in spite of urban development and heavy traffic all round. In the main street, opposite the stone-built, thatched old school, is the former Dame School, inscribed 'Mrs Sarah Nowells School 1822'. The Norm *Parish Church is one of the finest in England. All the doorways are richly carved, as are some of the windows and the tower arches inside. The top stage of the tower, with its vigorous carvings, is a 1975 restoration. In the churchyard is a font-bowl of unknown date, and an extremely ancient yew tree.

Immediately E. of Iffley is *Cowley* (about 1m.), with the vast British Leyland works developed from the Morris Motors started so modestly just before the First World War by Lord Nuffield.

S.W. of Oxford is *Boar's Hill*, a semi-rural residential area at the top of which (Old Boar's Hill) is *Jarn's Mound*, a wild garden and wood made by the archaeologist Sir Arthur Evans (d 1941). The mound itself, approached up very steep steps, provides a splendid view of the city.

West Side

Immediately W. of the town the Thames flows through *Port Meadow*. This rather desolate expanse, frequently flooded, belongs to the Freemen of Oxford, who from the time of Edward the Confessor (d 1066) have enjoyed the right of free pasture here; once a year grazing animals are rounded up by a posse of Freemen led by the Sheriff, who is also Curator of the Meadow, and a nominal fine imposed on the owners. It can be reached from Walton Well Rd (Pl. A5) by a bridge over the canal, from which paths lead to *Wolvercote* (about 1½ m.) or, more pleasantly, straight ahead and then across and beside the river.

A path l. (about ½ m. from the bridge) leads to *Binsey*, a tiny village set round a wide green. The small 12–13C church is ½ m. beyond; in the churchyard is a holy well associated with the legend of St Frideswide. The path beside the river continues to *Godstow Lock* (about 2½ m.) with the remains of a Benedictine nunnery, where Fair Rosamund, mistress of Henry II, was educated, and where she was

buried after her death at Woodstock (possibly at the hands of the jealous Queen).

Opposite is the famous *Trout Inn*, with a riverside terrace. The towpath continues to Eynsham and beyond.

From here a narrow road leads (about 1m.) to *Wytham* (pron Wit'm) a completely unspoilt village of stone and thatch cottages; in the inn car park is a circular dovecot. Village and beautiful woods belong to the University (access to the woods only by permit from the secretary to the University Chest). To the S.W. is the country described in Matthew Arnold's 'Scholar Gipsy': *Bablock Hythe*, *Fyfield*, and *Cumnor Hill* (now a residential suburb). In Cumnor church is a contemporary statue of Elizabeth I and a memorial to Amy Robsart (see also the church of St Mary the Virgin, p 67).

Stanton Harcourt (W.) is the original seat of the Harcourt family, who moved to Nuneham Courtenay in 1750. The church has a very rare mid 13C chancel screen, and in the Harcourt Chapel magnificent family monuments, that of Margaret Harcourt (1471) being one of the three known effigies of ladies wearing the Order of the Garter. Alongside the church the remains of the medieval manor gatehouse, Pope's Tower (so called because Alexander Pope lodged there in 1717–18), and kitchen make a picturesque group.

East Side

S. of Headington is *Shotover Country Park* (about 4m.), a large area of open common and woodland good for picnics and walks, with views of Oxford from the very steep approach road.

North Side

Elsfield village (about 4m.) was the home from 1920 until his death in 1940 of Lord Tweedsmuir, distinguished as a scholar, statesman, and Governor General of Canada, but best known as John Buchan, author of 'The Thirty-Nine Steps' and numerous other exciting books. *Water Eaton* (little more than a manor-house and chapel) and *Islip* are attractive places on the Cherwell, and can be reached by boat.

II CAMBRIDGE

The City of Cambridge   Cambridge University

PRACTICAL INFORMATION

Transport

BY CAR, from London: A1, A1(M), A505, A10; or M11. About 1¼ hrs, longer at busy times.

RAILWAY STATION, Station Rd, off Hills Rd (1¼ m. from the city centre, 8 mins by frequent bus service). Service to and from London (Liverpool St.) about every hour during the day (about 65 mins), or London (King's Cross), about 80 mins. Tel. 311999.

BUS AND COACH STATION, Drummer St. *Long Distance* Express Services Nos 098, 095, 097 to and from London (Victoria Coach Station), approximate journey time 2–2½ hrs. Express Service 079 to and from Heathrow Airport, approximate journey time 2¼ hrs. There are direct services between Cambridge and most large or local towns, with onward connections in all directions. Detailed information from Eastern Counties Bus Co Ltd., Drummer St., tel 353418.

City Service: All parts of the city and its environs are served by bus.

For Newnham and Grange Rd areas Nos 118, 119, 120, 196.
For Castle St. and Huntingdon Rd (Girton) Nos 189, 190, 191.
For Madingley Rd No 196.
A park and ride service operates on Sat from the southern side of the city (Cattle Market, Cherry Hinton Rd).

Parking: Car parks are shown on the map. The more central ones are often full after about 9.30 a.m. There is some limited street parking in the centre (meters).

Main Post Office: St Andrew's St.

Information Office: Wheeler St., tel 358997; after 3 and weekends 353363 (separate number for accommodation). Open Mar–Oct Mon–Fri 9–6, Sat 9–3, Nov–Feb Mon–Fri 9–3.30, Sat 9–3. May–Sept also on Sun 10.30–3.30.

Accommodation of all kinds is plentiful but should always be booked in advance if at all possible, especially in the peak summer period, during May Week (June/early July), and during the July festivals, when rooms can be very hard to find. The Information Office runs an accommodation service (tel 67800).

Theatres: Arts Theatre, Peas Hill; ADC Theatre, Park St. (University Amateur Dramatic Club, and other amateur groups).

A music and drama festival and a folk festival are held in July. There are numerous concerts and recitals all the year round.

Cinemas: Arts, Market Passage; Victoria, Market Square; ABC, St Andrew's St.

Brass Rubbing: The Wesley Church Library, King St. Open Tues–Sat 10–5, also Mon in July and Aug.

Boating is a popular recreation in summer and a good way of seeing the 'Backs' or getting to Grantchester. Rowing boats, punts, and canoes can be hired at Quayside (off Bridge St.) and Mill Lane for the Backs, and at Mill Lane, upper river, for Grantchester (about 2 hrs there and back). Motor boats can be hired below Jesus Lock, and in summer there are regular motor-launch excursions. For advice to novices in the art of punting see p 42. At Cambridge you stand on the flat end of the boat to punt.

Bathing: In the *river* at Sheep's Green, *Swimming-pools*: Jesus Green, open air; Parkside Pool, off Gonville Place, indoor and heated (open all the year round).

Sightseeing

Most of the colleges are normally open all day; their chapels also are usually open. Halls are often closed unless the staff are about (mid morning and early afternoon). Staircases and working libraries are **never** accessible to sightseers unless special arrangements for a particular purpose are made in advance in writing. Visitors are courteously asked to be quiet, and not to walk on the grass. Cambridge lawns are sacred to the feet of resident Fellows.

Where opening times are restricted or permanently fixed details are given under the appropriate entry. An increasing number of colleges close during the summer examination period (mid May–late June); some also close for holidays in August and at Christmas and Easter.

From Easter to October there are guided tours of the colleges, starting from the Information Centre in Wheeler St.

HISTORY

Cambridge, on the southern edge of the Fens, has a definitely East Anglian character, compounded of wide skies, flat expanses—it is nowhere more than 50 ft above sea level—and light reflected by the waters of river, brooks, channels, and winter-flooded fields. And often an icy east wind blows 'straight from the steppes of Russia'.

Excavations on the higher ground north of the river (Castle Hill area) have revealed evidence of Belgic settlements pre-dating the arrival of the Romans in c. A.D. 43. The Romans established a camp here, and round it and on the south side of the river (Market Hill area) there gradually grew up a prosperous town, for the Cam was navigable from this point northward to the sea, while to the south and west Roman roads linked it with the rest of the country.

Early names for the river were Rhee and, more frequently, Granta (now usually applied to the two branches above Cambridge), whence derived the town's Saxon name of Grantabrycge (Granta-bridge). Through a number of variations this eventually developed into Cambridge, from which (and not the other way round) the river took its present name.

Soon after the Conquest the Normans built the castle (1068) of which now only the mound remains, and made Cambridge their base of operations against Saxons holding out, under Hereward the Wake's leadership, in the fastnesses of the fens. It became the chief centre of their authority in the area. Churches were built, religious houses established (Barnwell Priory, St Radegund's, and various friaries), and some time in the 12C the defences were strengthened by the construction of the King's Ditch. This artificial 'moat' enclosed the south and east sides of the town, and followed roughly the line of Mill Lane, Pembroke St., Lion Yard, Hobson St. and Park Parade, where it rejoined the river.

Cambridge flourished as a commercial centre, and the great annual fair held on Stourbridge Common, east of the town, attracted traders not only from all over England, but from the Continent as well. The dues from this fair were, in 1211, granted by King John to the leper hospital maintained by the monks of Barnwell Priory. After the Dissolution Henry VIII granted them to the town; from then on the conduct and revenues of the fair became one of the many points of dispute between the town and university authorities. It was the great event of the Cambridge year, formally visited by both Mayor and Vice-Chancellor with their several entourages, and it flourished until well into the 19C.

Scholars began to arrive in Cambridge very early in the 13C, and as at Oxford the university soon acquired a position of pre-eminence and authority over the town which was to be for centuries the source of endless conflict. The university's encroachments caused much damage to the town's prosperity; land alongside the river, where there had previously been busy wharves and warehouses, was acquired for college buildings, and areas of pasture taken over as recreation grounds for the students.

A matter of common concern was the frequent outbreaks of plague, which attacked citizens and scholars alike. Miasma from the fens was regarded as the cause, but the true source of infection was the water supply from the polluted river, and the filthy King's Ditch, used as an open sewer and as a repository for the town's rubbish. Dr Perne of Peterhouse realised this truth when he wrote, in 1574, 'Our synnes is the principall cause [of sickness]. The other cause I conjecture is the corruption of the King's Ditch'. He suggested a scheme (in fact mooted by Matthew Parker of Corpus Christi some years earlier) for a fresh water supply which would also flush out the ditch, and this was eventually carried out in 1610, in a rare instance of co-operation between town and university (see p 150 for details).

Little changed in Cambridge until the 19C, when enclosure of open fields made expansion possible beyond the former town boundaries. The railway arrived in 1845, and thereafter river trade declined. But

with the development of scientific studies in the university and the building of research laboratories new science-based industries grew up to supply their needs, and such industries, later widely diversified, became an important source of employment and prosperity in Cambridge. In the 20C the town grew to envelop many surrounding villages, and has now a population of some 99,000. In 1951 it was granted the status of city.

Happily the expansion has taken place round the perimeter, so that the many open spaces in the centre, which are such a distinctive and attractive part of the Cambridge scene, remain as from time immemorial common pasture land. Horses graze on Coe Fen and Lammas Land, and cattle browse on Midsummer Common. 'Rus in urbe' indeed.

CAMBRIDGE UNIVERSITY has 26 colleges, of which 2 are for graduates: Darwin, and Wolfson (which admits a few mature students as undergraduates). Three were founded for women: Girton, New Hall, and Newnham. Girton now admits men also. All but 4 of the former men's colleges now admit women; the exceptions are: Magdalene, Pembroke, Peterhouse, and St John's. There are 5 Approved Societies or Foundations, primarily for graduades: Clare Hall, Homerton College, Hughes Hall, Lucy Cavendish College (women only) and St Edmund's House. The last 2 accept a few mature undergraduate students.

There are about 9400 undergraduates in the university.

Historic Cambridge is an easy place to explore; about a mile long, and half a mile wide, all within walking distance. It is bounded to the west by the river; the colleges and university buildings lie mostly beside and between two roughly parallel roads running south to north—*Regent St.*, which becomes first *St Andrew's St.* then *Sidney St.*, and *Trumpington St.*, which continues as *King's Parade, Trinity St.* and *St John's St.* These long roads converge at *Bridge St.* and cross the river at Magdalene Bridge. Here the river takes a sweeping eastward bend, so forming, with the big expanses of open common-land on its righthand bank, the northern boundary of the old city. In finding the way about both the city and individual colleges it is useful to keep this north–south pattern of river and roads firmly in mind.

Most of the modern university and college developments are immediately across the river to the west, along *Queen's Rd* and *Grange Rd*. Even here the distances are not very great. It is only to visit the few colleges which lie to the north-west beyond Magdalene Bridge that transport is really needed.

Market Hill is a convenient point from which to start explorations.

1 NORTH OF MARKET HILL

MARKET HILL (Pl. B7) and its immediate environs are the civic and shopping centre of Cambridge. Though it does in fact slope slightly down from W. to E., the word 'hill' is used here, as elsewhere in Cambridge, to denote an open space. It is the scene of a colourful market. On the S. side (l. going up the hill) is the Guildhall, below which (l.) Guildhall St., with a sculpture, 'Talos', by Michael Ayrton, leads to the multi-storey car park, and to Wheeler St., in which is the *Tourist Information Office.*

Past the turn to Guildhall St. is the curiously named *Petty Cury* (pedestrians only) and *Lion Yard*, formerly the 'yard' of the Red Lion Inn, now a covered shopping precinct, in whose central square a large red lion mounted on a white pole looks down benignly on shoppers and on visitors to the public library.

On the N. side (r.), on the corner of St Mary's St. and Rose Crescent, is *Bacon's tobacco shop*, celebrated by the scholar and parodist Charles Calverley (d 1884); his bust and the appropriate verses appear on a wall plaque. Above the Guildhall (l.) in Peas Hill, is *St Edward's Church* (Pl.B7; entrance in St Edward's Passage, where there are some picturesque old houses and a large fig tree).

Only the base of the tower remains of the original church, built in 1175. The rest was rebuilt in the Dec. style, c. 1400. The pale, slender piers of the nave, and lofty pointed arches, make the interior particularly attractive and spacious. The chancel aisles were added in 1446 to serve as chapels for Trinity Hall (N. side) and Clare College (S. side), whose members had previously worshipped in St John Zachary, demolished when King's College was built. The living is in the gift of Trinity Hall, and carries the designation of 'chaplaincy'. Many alterations were made in the mid 19C (E. window by Sir George Gilbert Scott) and the font was given by the Cambridge Camden Society (the 'Ecclesiologists', see History, p 13). In the late 1940s new windows were installed in the nave aisles (designed by Sir Albert Richardson), those on the S. side commemorating Hugh Latimer and Thomas Bilney, leading figures in the early Reformation; the original pulpit, from which they preached, was also reinstated. At the W. end of the S. aisle is a tablet to F.D. Maurice (1802–72) theologian and social reformer, who founded the Working Men's College, and the first college for women (Queen's College, London). He was chaplain in the last year of his life.

Just beyond St Edward's is the *Arts Theatre*, built and presented to Cambridge by the famous economist John Maynard Keynes (d 1946). It has special links with the church.

On the upper (W.) side of Market Hill is **St Mary the Great** ('Great St Mary's'), the university church and principal parish church of Cambridge. In the past it was used, as was normal, for many secular purposes for which a large meeting place was needed. The university held disputations here, and it was used for degree-giving ceremonies until the Senate House was built in 1730.

Although there has been a church on the site at least since the 12C, the present building dates from the late 15C–early 16C; two kings, Richard III and Henry VII, and many eminent statesmen and ecclesiastics, contributed to its cost. Henry VII also gave the timber for the roof, which, skilfully preserved in the 18C by James Essex, can still be seen in its Tudor magnificence. St Mary's has the lofty simplicity of the late Perp. style; the characteristic adornments of the period—wall-paintings, carvings, and stained-glass windows—were mostly removed, as being idolatrous, during the Reformation. Many leading reformers preached here, some of whom later died at the stake during Mary Tudor's efforts to restore the old faith. The bodies of the German theologians Bucer and Fagius, buried here and in St Michael's respectively, were exhumed and burned on Market Hill, and both churches were cleansed of their presence in an elaborate ceremony. When Elizabeth I came to the throne their ashes were given reverent reburial. (Brass floor plate in the chancel, S. side.)

In the 17C galleries were built to accommodate the large congregations which gathered on special occasions or to hear the university sermon (attendance at which was compulsory for undergraduates), and an enormous three-decker pulpit, designed by James Essex, and nicknamed 'Golgotha', was installed at the W. end. Its woodwork was used to make vestry and side chapel screens when both it and some of the galleries were removed during the vigorous alterations carried out in the 19C, largely influenced by the tenets of the Camden Society (see History, p 13).

The entrance is through the S. porch; ahead l. is the font (1632), Gothic in design, Renaissance in decoration. Near it hangs the vicar's mace, which with the carved Madonna and Child, and the processional cross and candle-holders (in the N. aisle), are the work of a local craftsman, Loughnan Pendred. Behind is the *tower*, which can be climbed for a splendid view (usually open; small fee). The great organ at the W. end was built for the church of St James's Piccadilly, London, by Bernard Schmidt ('Father Smith') and bought by the university in 1692. In the floor near the W. end of the N. aisle (l.) is a slab commemorating the death of Andrew Skinner in '1710–11', the double date caused by the discrepancy between the legal and the historical year at that time. At the E. end of the aisle is the hearse cloth of Henry VII, used when his requiems were sung. The *pulpit*, on the N. side of the chancel steps, can be pulled out on rails into the middle of the nave; it is one of the few movable pulpits in England. Behind the *high altar* is a spectacular gilded wood-sculpture of Christ in Majesty (Alan Durst, 1960). Most of the *windows* date from the 19C restoration. Those in the aisle carry the arms of the original benefactors, royalties on the N. side (l.), clerics on the S. (r.). In the clerestory are apostles, prophets, and martyrs, some of them with the faces of prominent Victorian divines. The chimes of the *tower clock* (1793), installed by the Rev. J. Jowett of Trinity Hall, and possibly composed by a musician named William Crotch (then an undergraduate), were subsequently widely copied, and are familiar everywhere as the chimes of Big Ben beside the Houses of Parliament.

About 30 yds down Trinity St. (r.) is the small Dec. church of *St Michael*, built in the early 14C by Hervey de Stanton (d 1327), who is buried in the chancel. It was long used as a chapel for Michaelhouse, also founded by de Stanton (see Trinity College, p 120). Now no longer needed for worship, the main body of the church has been converted into a meeting room, though the Founder's Chapel is intact (key at Great St Mary's) and occasionally used for services.

Almost opposite Great St Mary's, across King's Parade, is the *Senate House (Pl. B7; no adm unless open for use), designed by James Gibbs (who was also then working on St Martin-in-the-Fields, London, and on the Radcliffe Camera, Oxford), as part of a plan which envisaged an exactly matching building opposite, and a linking N.–S. range between, intended to house George I's recent gift of some 30,000 books.

This was the occasion for the famous verses:

> The King, observing with judicious eyes
> The state of both his Universities
> To one he sent a regiment. For why?
> That learned body wanted loyalty.
> To t'other he sent books, as well discerning
> How much that loyal body wanted learning.

Only the Senate House ever materialised; built between 1722 and 1730 in the Palladian style, it consists of one long room with ante-room and galleries. The plasterwork ceiling is by Artari and Bagutti, and the handsome woodwork by the James Essexes, father and son. There are statues of the Duke of Somerset (Rysbrack) and Pitt (Nollekens). All university ceremonies and large gatherings take place here, Congregations are held three times a term, at which degrees may be conferred, while the most splendid occasion is the summer General Admissions, when honorary degrees are bestowed, and a procession of richly robed university dignitaries, led by Esquire Bedells carrying maces, wends its way right round and into the building.

Immediately behind the Senate House are the *Old Schools* (entrance in Trinity Lane, but no adm for visitors), dating from between 1350 and 1476. They were the first university (as opposed to college) buildings, and provided a Divinity School, meeting rooms, a chapel, and accommodation for the growing library. In the intervening centuries they have undergone such radical alterations that little of the medieval structure is now visible, except on the S.W. side; this, with its handsome gateway, was originally the Old Court of King's College (1457–76), sold to the university in 1829 when King's New Court was built. The Palladian range on the E. side, facing King's Parade, was built in the 1750s (by Stephen Wright); again it was the only part to be completed of a much more grandiose scheme. The Old Schools now house university offices and the Law Faculty.

Directly across Senate House Passage is **Gonville and Caius College** (Pl. B7; always known as Caius, pron 'Keys'). It was founded as Gonville Hall in 1348 by Edmund Gonville, a Norfolk parson, on the site where Corpus Christi is now. Gonville died in 1351, entrusting his college to William Bateman, Bp of Norwich, who moved it in 1353 to its present position next to Trinity Hall, which he himself had just founded. He renamed it the 'Hall of the Annunciation of the Blessed Virgin Mary', and the Annunciation is still shown on the college seal. In 1557 the college, which was not prospering, was refounded by another Norwich man, John Caius (the latinised form of Keys) who became Master in the following year. He had been a student at Gonville Hall in 1529, and afterwards a Fellow, before going to Italy to study medicine. He was for a time Professor of Greek Philosophy in Padua; on returning to England he achieved great renown as a doctor and was court physician in turn to Edward VI, Mary Tudor, and Elizabeth I. Although imbued with the New Learning, Caius had a great respect for tradition, and retained not only Gonville's old buildings, but also his name in the title of the new foundation. In 1565, at 4 a.m. on 5 May (sunrise by the old calendar, and judged to be an auspicious hour) the first stones were laid of his new Caius Court. He ordained that for health reasons it should be of three sides only, to admit sunlight and fresh air (a pattern followed by a number of later colleges); he also laid down strict rules on cleanliness and behaviour. A true Elizabethan, he delighted in 'conceits' and embellished his buildings with many symbolic 'devices' (including a column carrying sixty-six sundials) most of which have now disappeared. His grandest device, however, in part remains. This is the 'academic path' he designed for his students, leading from the Gate of Humility (originally at the Trinity St. entrance, now in the Master's garden), along a narrow passage to the Gate of Virtue, the other side of which was the Gate of Wisdom, on the E. side of Caius Court. Finally the Gate of Honour (S. side of Caius Court) took the successful scholar to the Schools. These gates are among the earliest and most interesting Italian Renaissance style buildings in the country. The Gate of Honour with its six sundials was restored in 1958 to celebrate the four hundredth anniversary of the refounding of the college.

Caius died in 1573, after some years of increasingly unhappy relations with his own Fellows and with other college Masters, which culminated in 1572 with a raid on his rooms and the destruction of the Catholic vestments and vessels he had carefully preserved.

The medical tradition of the college, established even before the time of Caius himself, still survives. Until the 19C there were also strong traditional links with the county of the founders; it was 1852 before a Master was elected who did not come from the diocese of Norwich. Caius men wear blue gowns faced with black. This distinctive pattern was adopted in 1837.

Alfred Waterhouse in flamboyant mood: Caius College, the south front of Tree Court

The main entrance leads into TREE COURT, originally dating from the early 17C, when benefactions from the Master, Thomas Legge, and a distinguished medical Fellow Dr Perse (who also founded the Perse Grammar School), financed an expansion of the college. It was entirely rebuilt 1868–70 by Alfred Waterhouse in flamboyant French chateau style, all towers, pinnacles, turrets and ornamental flourishes. Niches on the outer side carry busts of benefactors and famous members. Opposite the gatehouse the Gate of Virtue leads into CAIUS COURT (1565–67), unpretentious and domestic-looking, except for the resplendent *Gate of Honour* (l.).

On the N. side (r.) is the *Chapel*; built before 1375, it was greatly altered in 1637, when the E. end was extended, the wood-panelled ceiling with its cherubs and rays of light installed, and Dr Caius's monument moved from over his grave to the N. wall (l.), where there is also a monument to Dr Perse (1615).

On the S. side is a similar monument to Dr Legge (1607) and near it, behind a hinged panel above the stalls, the old piscina of the 14C chapel. In 1716 the exterior was faced in stone and the E. end again rebuilt. Finally, in 1870 Waterhouse added the apse, decorated with mosaics (by Salviati) portraying 'scenes of instruction'. The beautiful altar frontal, the cross and candlesticks (1958, by Gerald Benney) commemorate the quatercentenary of the refounding.

A passage W. (l.) of the chapel leads into GONVILLE COURT. Although the oldest, it was 'classicised' in 1753 by the then Master, Sir James Burrough (cf Peterhouse). On the W. (l.) side is the *Hall*, rebuilt in 1853 by Anthony Salvin. It has a handsome hammerbeam roof, and a gallery with the Royal Arms above. Behind the dais, in a curtained glass case, is the flag flown at the South Pole in 1912 by Scott's last expedition, of which Edward Wilson (an exhibitioner of Caius) was medical officer, and a member of the small party which perished with Scott on their return journey to base. Portraits of distinguished Caians include those of Dr Caius, Bp Cosin, Sir Thomas Gresham and Professor Seeley.

In 1903 the college expanded across Trinity St. with ST MICHAEL'S COURT (by Sir Aston Webb, designer of Admiralty Arch in London), enlarged by Murray Easton in 1934. Across the river off Queen's Road is *Harvey Court*, built in 1961 (see p 156).

FAMOUS MEMBERS: Thomas Gresham, founder of the Royal Exchange in London, 1519–79; William Harvey, physician and discoverer of the circulation of the blood, 1578–1657; Jeremy Taylor, theologian and divine, 1613–67; William Wilkins, architect, 1778–1839; John Venn, logician, inventor of Venn diagram, 1834–1923; Edward Wilson, Antarctic explorer, member of Scott's last expedition, 1872–1912; J.E. Flecker, poet, 1884–1915, and Nobel prizewinners Sir Charles Sherrington, physiologist, 1857–1952, Max Born, physicist, 1882–1970, and many others still living.

At the bottom of Senate House Passage, to the l. is **Clare College** (Pl. A8), founded as University Hall in 1326 by Richard de Badew, then Chancellor of the University, and refounded in 1338 by Elizabeth de Clare, grand-daughter of Edward I. The name was then changed to Clare Hall, and became Clare College only in 1856. Its elegant simplicity and the beauty of its setting make Clare one of the most immediately attractive and romantic looking of colleges at either Oxford or Cambridge.

Its largely uniform appearance is due to its complete rebuilding in the 17C. This was predominantly the work of John Westley and of the famous Grumbold family, between them responsible for many fine Cambridge buildings. It is a most interesting example of English

Renaissance architecture, Gothic heavily overlaid with Italianate Classical, although many of the more Gothic elements, such as battlements and pointed windows, were further 'classicised' in the 18C. Begun in 1638, the great court was not complete until 1693, partly because of the long interruption caused by the Civil War (the Parliamentarians seized the accumulated building materials to refortify the castle; however Cromwell did, honourably if belatedly, pay for them).

The handsome Baroque gateway, whose fan-vaulting is some of the last to be done in England, is approached down a long path between lawns; on the N. side is the *Chapel*, entered through a passage at the upper r. side of the court. It replaces a Tudor Chapel (members of the college previously worshipped in St Edward's church, see p 113), and is a purely classical building designed by Sir James Burrough in 1762, and completed after his death by James Essex. A feature of the ante-chapel is the high timber lantern, the only one of its kind in Oxford or Cambridge. The spacious interior has a barrel-vaulted plasterwork ceiling and contemporary panelling, furnishings, and altar-piece (an Annunciation, by Cipriani). On the N. side (l.) are modern stained-glass windows, commemorating two Fellows – Hugh Latimer, one of the 'Oxford Martyrs' (see History, p 11), and Nicholas Ferrar, founder in 1625 of the Little Gidding religious community, whose small church appears in the picture. His earlier support of pioneering ventures in Virginia led in the 18C to a considerable American connection with the college. In the S. side window the founder, de Badew, offers his college to the Virgin and Child.

The *Hall* (up the steps in the centre of the N. side) dates from 1688, though the ceiling and the woodwork above the dais are late 19C. Its portraits include a number of 18C statesmen, and one of Lord Cornwallis, whose surrender at Yorktown in 1781 marked the end of the American War of Independence. Over the doorway of the Small Hall, across the passage, is a 15C stone panel carved with the college arms, sole survivor of the medieval buildings.

The gateway on the W. side leads to the river and to *Clare Bridge, built in 1638 by Thomas Grumbold, and the oldest surviving in Cambridge. It is beautifully carved and surmounted by fourteen stone balls, one of which has a segment missing. There are various explanations for this, ranging from an undergraduate wager to a 'fault' in the stone. Through the wrought-iron gates (1714) a lime avenue leads past the Fellows' Garden (r., open Mon–Fri 2–4.45, but a good view at any time from the path) to another gateway (also 1714) and Queen's Road. Across this is the college's *Memorial* and *Thirkell Courts* (see p 158). Clare also has a graduate hostel below Castle Hill (see p 159).

FAMOUS MEMBERS: Hugh Latimer, 1485?–1555; Nicholas Ferrar, 1592–1637; Lord Cornwallis, English Commander-in-Chief in the American War of Independence, afterwards Governor-General of India, 1738–1805.

Immediately N. of Clare is **Trinity Hall** (Pl. A8), the only old college to retain that designation, although its original title was in fact 'The College of the Scholars of the Holy Trinity of Norwich'. It was founded in 1350 by the Bp of Norwich, William Bateman, who the following year also refounded Gonville Hall (see above, p 115). The two colleges, by his express intention, had 'a league of amity and support' which long continued. As well as being an eminent churchman Bateman was a leading authority on canon and civil law, and his college was founded to provide men trained in law, who could replenish the ranks of the profession decimated by the Black Death of 1345–47. It remained a college of lawyers, specialising after the Reformation (when canon law was abolished) in civil law, until well into the 19C; most of its Fellows had large legal practices, many in London, where Trinity Hall established and controlled *Doctors Commons*, a centre for those engaged in civil law, which existed until 1856. The consequent coming and going between Cambridge and

London probably influenced the Fellows of Trinity Hall, who in the 17C made financial provision for the improvement of roads leading into Cambridge. With monies from their bequests milestones were also set up. These bore the college insignia, and one can be seen in Trumpington Rd (W. side) almost opposite Brooklands Av. Although studies are now diversified the strong traditional connection with the law remains. The college also has a formidable reputation on the river, dating from the 1880s and 1890s.

The entrance, in Trinity Lane, leads into the principal court. Although the buildings are among the oldest in Cambridge, its appearance is of 18C, the original medieval fabric having been refaced in stone and 'classicised', during the Mastership of Sir Nathaniel Lloyd, by Sir James Burrough and James Essex, and the upper (E.) side rebuilt after a fire in 1852, by Salvin. On the lower S. side (l.) is the *Chapel*, 15C but completely remodelled c. 1730. The piscina is the only visible relic of the old building, as at Caius tidied away behind a hinged panel (S. side). The roof, splendidly renovated, is decorated with heraldic emblems, a guide to which hangs on the l. inside the ante-chapel screen.

In the archway opposite the main gate is the entrance to the *Hall*, again of the 18C, though over the panelling behind the dais a Norm window from one of the houses on the site in Bateman's time is a reminder of the college's antiquity. There is the usual impressive array of portraits.

Through the archway are the charming gardens giving on to the river, and r. the *Old Library* (usually open in term 10–2), an attractive Elizabethan brick building with crow-step gables. Inside it remains practically unaltered, and retains the old arrangement of sloped reading desks, benches, and chained books (cf Merton College and the Bodleian Library, Oxford).

In the 19C and 20C the college expanded on both S. and N. sides. Built into the gatehouse facing Garret Hostel Lane (N.) is the 14C gateway, which originally formed part of the Porter's Lodge on the S. side where New Court is now. In the 1960s and 1970s further accommodation was built in Huntingdon Rd, between Fitzwilliam and the playing fields.

FAMOUS MEMBERS: Sir John Paston, of the 'Paston Letters', 1442–79 (also Peterhouse); Stephen Gardiner, Bp of Winchester, famed for persecution of Protestants under Mary Tudor, 1483–1555; Lord Howard of Effingham, admiral, and commander of the English fleet against the Spanish Armada, 1536–1624; Robert Herrick, poet, 1591–1674 (a block of the new flats in Huntingdon Rd bears his name); Lord Chesterfield, statesman, wit, letter-writer, 1694–1773; Richard Fitzwilliam, founder of the Fitzwilliam Museum, 1745–1816; Bulwer Lytton, novelist and statesman, 1803–73; F.D. Maurice, theologian and social reformer, 1805–72 (see also St Edward's church, p 113); Leslie Stephen, man of letters, agnostic, mountaineer, father of Virginia Woolf and Vanessa Bell, 1832–1904.

Beyond the corner of Garret Hostel Lane, Trinity Lane turns sharply r. and rejoins Trinity St., where there are some pleasant bow-fronted shops and 18C houses. Shortly on the l. is ***Trinity College** (Pl. B5), largest and grandest of the Cambridge colleges, and in many ways comparable with Oxford's largest and grandest—Christ Church (p 52).

Henry VIII founded Trinity College in 1546, as one of his last acts, to this end taking over two existing colleges, King's Hall and

Michaelhouse, and enriching them with valuable endowments of money and property, much of it derived from the newly-suppressed monasteries. King's Hall already had a long royal connection, having been established by Edward II in 1317, as a training-ground for public servants, and continuing, with some fluctuations of fortune, to enjoy the royal patronage of his successors. Initially it drew its scholars principally from the choristers of the Chapel Royal, hence their designation as 'King's Childer', a name also given to the lane that formerly ran past the college. Michaelhouse was a more modest establishment. Its founder, in 1324, was Hervey de Stanton, Chancellor of the Exchequer to Edward II, who also built St Michael's church (see p 114), and it never enjoyed the same wealth and prestige as its neighbours.

The present magnificent appearance of Trinity is largely due to Thomas Nevile, appointed Master by Elizabeth I in 1593 (see below). Subsequent Masters and eminent members down the centuries have added to the splendour both of its buildings and of its reputation as a centre of academic distinction, and the home of scientific enquiry and liberal-minded ideas.

The Trinity gown is dark blue. The boat club is known as 'First and Third Trinity'.

The Great Gate lies back from Trinity St. across a cobbled forecourt with l. the entrance to Angel Court (1959), and r. a small lawn on which grows an apple tree directly descended from Isaac Newton's tree at Woolsthorpe Manor, which first set him thinking about 'the notion of gravitation'. Newton was one of Trinity's most famous members; the rooms where he lived and wrote his 'Principia Mathematica' are r. of the Great Gate (staircase E.; no adm).

The impressive turreted brick *Gatehouse*, dating from the early 1500s, belonged to King's Hall; it bears the name of Edward III and royal coats of arms. It also carries outside a statue of Henry VIII and inside statues of James I, his wife Anne and son Charles (Charles I). All these were put up by Nevile, c. 1615. Henry VIII grasps not a sceptre but a chair-leg—an undergraduate joke which has now become a hallowed tradition.

*GREAT COURT is the largest in Cambridge or Oxford (approx 340 x 288 ft). It was created by Thomas Nevile between 1597 and 1615, replacing the jumble of miscellaneous buildings and open spaces belonging to Michaelhouse (of which virtually nothing is left) and King's Hall. Its predominantly Tudor-Gothic style has survived numerous restorations. Nevile retained from earlier buildings only the Great Gate, and on the N. side (r.) the Chapel (1555–67) and *King Edward's Tower* (1428). This had been a gatehouse of King's Hall; Nevile moved it stone by stone to its present position, and installed the statue of Edward III (wearing Elizabethan armour, and impaling three crowns on his sword), and a clock (replaced in 1726 by the present one, which strikes the hour twice). Behind the tower is *King's Hostel*, another relic of King's Hall.

The *Chapel* (usually open; services Sun 9 and 6.30, Wed 6.30), largely the gift of Mary Tudor, was mainly constructed of materials acquired through the demolition of Ramsey Abbey and the Franciscan Friary which stood where Sidney Sussex College is now.

Outside a simple Perp.-style building, inside its appearance is mainly of the 18C, when the highly controversial Master of the time, Richard Bentley, put in the screen, panelling, and magnificent canopied

reredos. His tomb-slab is on the S. (r.) side of the altar rails, but does not record his Mastership, of which he was deprived but which he never relinquished.

In the ante-chapel are statues of great Trinity men, including Francis Bacon, Lord Macaulay, Tennyson (with his pipe, partly concealed in laurel leaves), all 19C, and one of *Newton (by Roubiliac, 1755) which inspired Wordsworth's famous lines: 'The marble index of a mind for ever/Voyaging through strange seas of thought, alone'. There are also numerous wall-monuments. Sorrowfully impressive in their seeming endlessness are the names of the 1000 sons of the college killed in the two World Wars, those of the first at each side of the altar, those of the second in the ante-chapel.

Near the centre of the court is the beautiful canopied fountain (1610). Its water was supplied from a pipeline laid by the Franciscans in the early 14C from springs over a mile away across the river (Conduit Head Rd, beyond Churchill College). On the S. side is *Queen's Gate* (1597) with a statue of Nevile's royal patron Elizabeth I. The W. side of the court is dominated by the *Hall* (possibly open mid-morning and early afternoon, entrance r. in the passage up steps). Paid for by Nevile, and built by the famous Cambridge master-mason Ralph Symonds, it is closely modelled on the Middle Temple in London. 103 ft long and 40 ft wide, it is the largest in the university. The style is again Perp., vast windows with heraldic glass, and hammerbeam roof topped by an attractive hexagonal lantern. The gallery is a riot of Elizabethan decoration. Henry VIII presides from his portrait above the dais; on his r. (looking down the Hall) is his daughter Mary Tudor and beyond her are Masters. On his l. is the Duke of Gloucester, aged six, by Reynolds (the boy was destined for Trinity, but died young), beyond him distinguished members of the college.

The Screens Passage leads W. into NEVILE'S COURT (1612), down steps adjoining the classical rostrum built (almost certainly to Wren's design) across this side of the hall, to bring it into harmony with the rest of the court, whose Italianate cloisters and Renaissance elegance are an interesting contrast to Great Court. The classical effect of the whole was accentuated by 18C renovations and alterations. At the far end is Trinity's crowning glory, the great *Library, designed by Wren and built in 1676–90 by Robert Grumbold (open Mon–Fri 2.15–3.45 or 4.45 in summer; Sat in full term 10.30–12). In the Baroque style, it is of cream-coloured Ketton stone, and carried on a cloister; along the roof balustrade are statues symbolising Divinity, Law, Physics, and Mathematics (by Cibber). The entrance is in the r. corner. The lofty interior (190 ft long), with its perfect proportions, great windows, and beautiful furnishings 'touches the very soul of any one who first sees it' (Roger North, 1695). The decorative lime-wood carving is by Grinling Gibbons, and a number of the wonderfully lively busts by Roubiliac. The window at the far end (by Cipriani, 1774–75) depicts Fame presenting Newton to George III, who sits enthroned among lightly-draped nymphs, cherubs, and clouds, while Bacon looks on, somewhat askance, notebook in hand. Over all broods Byron; his life-size statue (by Thorvaldsen, 1829) was rejected by Westminster Abbey in disapproval of the poet's morals. Newton's personal library is in the adjacent shelves.

Displayed in covered glass cases down the centre aisle are some of the library's many treasures. Older MSS and books (l., facing up the room) include 8C Pauline epistles, the *Trinity Apocalypse, a Gutenberg Bible of 1456 (first printed book), a first folio Shakespeare, and Milton's 'Comus'. Among later MSS and books (r. side) are works by Bertrand Russell, Housman's

Classical Baroque splendour: the interior of the Wren Library, Trinity College

'Shropshire Lad', Wittgenstein's notebook, and A.A. Milne's 'Winnie-the-Pooh'. Also on show are letters of Robert Louis Stevenson, George Eliot, Trollope, Livingstone, Faraday, and many others. This is just a random selection from an exhibition which repays hours of study.

Beyond the library are the college 'Backs' and a bridge (1765) over the river. To the S. (l.) are NEW COURT (neo-Gothic by Wilkins, 1923–25) and BISHOPS HOSTEL (1669–71). Arthur Hallam, to whom Tennyson was so devoted, had rooms in New Court; he had wished to go to Oxford, and in an early letter referred to Cambridge disparagingly as 'this college-studded marsh'.

In the 19C Trinity, like Caius later, expanded across Trinity St., into WHEWELLS COURT (Salvin, 1859–68). The gloomy Gothic Revival buildings were financed by the energetic and generous Master of the time, Dr Whewell, and are liberally adorned with his insignia. Alongside is the Wolfson Building (1971), and the college also has a hostel near the University Library, off Burrell's Walk.

FAMOUS MEMBERS: John Fisher, bishop and martyr (Master of Michaelhouse) 1469–1535; Francis Bacon, philosopher and statesman, 1561–1626; George Herbert, poet and divine, 1593–1633; Andrew Marvell, poet, 1621–78; John Dryden, poet and dramatist, 1631–1700; Lord Melbourne, statesman, 1779–1848; Lord Byron, poet, 1788–1824; Lord Macaulay, historian and poet, 1800–59; Alfred, Lord Tennyson, poet, 1809–92; W.M. Thackeray, novelist, 1811–63; J.M. Neale, hymnologist, 1818–66; Charles Stanford, composer, 1852–1924; A.E. Housman, poet, 1859–1936; Bertrand Russell, philosopher and mathematician, 1872–1970; R. Vaughan Williams, composer, 1872–1958; G.M. Trevelyan, historian, 1876–1962; A.A. Milne, writer (creator of Winnie-the-Pooh), 1882–1956; L.J.J. Wittgenstein, philosopher, 1889–1951; Shri Jawaharlal Nehru, first Prime Minister of India, 1889–1964.

Scientists and Nobel Prizewinners (a selection only): Isaac Newton, 1642–1727; George Airy, astronomer, 1801–92; Arthur Cayley, mathematician, 1821–95; Francis Galton (Eugenics), 1822–1911; James Clerk-Maxwell, physicist, organiser of the Cavendish Laboratory, 1831–79; George Darwin, astronomer (son of Charles Darwin), 1845–1913; J.W.S. Rayleigh, physicist, Nobel Prize, 1842–1919; J.J. Thompson (Master), mathematician and nuclear physicist, Nobel prizewinner (as were seven of his assistants), 1856–1940; F.G. Hopkins, biochemist (vitamins), Nobel Prize, 1861–1947; William and Lawrence Bragg, father and son, physicists, Nobel Prize, 1862–1942 and 1890–1971; Lord Rutherford, atomic physicist, 1871–1937; Sir James Jeans, astronomer, 1877–1947; Arthur Eddington, astronomer, 1882–1944; A.V. Hill, physiologist, Nobel Prize, 1886–1977; Sir George Thompson, physicist, Nobel Prize, 1892–1975.

Members of the Royal Family: Edward VII, George VI, H.R.H. The Prince of Wales.

Also numerous statesmen, bishops, scholars, men of letters and scientists, too many to detail.

North (l.) of Trinity College, Trinity St. becomes St John's St. On the r. is the *Selwyn Divinity School* (Basil Champneys, 1878–79; no adm). On the l. is *St John's College (Pl. B5; men only. Closed mid April–end May), until overtaken by Trinity the largest college in Cambridge, and still second only to its immediate neighbour. It was founded in 1511 with benefactions from Lady Margaret Beaufort; she had died in 1509, shortly after plans for the college were first proposed by John Fisher, who was left to carry out her intentions (for details about both see Christ's College, p 135). It replaced the 13C Hospital of St John. Rebuilding began at once, only the chapel of the old hospital remaining. Fisher's concern for the new college continued until his death on the scaffold in 1535; in his hands both its finances and its scholarship prospered. As an enthusiast for the New Learning and friend of Erasmus he early introduced the study of Greek.

Strongly Royalist in the Civil War, St John's suffered severely during the Parliamentary occupation of Cambridge; the Master and many of the Fellows were expelled, and the First Court was used as a prison.

During the 19C the college acquired a great reputation for athletic prowess. Its boat club (Lady Margaret Boat Club or LMBC), founded in 1825, is the oldest in Cambridge, and the challenge by one of its members to Oxford in 1829 was the forerunner of the famous Boat Race. The word 'blazer' is said to derive from the scarlet jackets worn by LMBC men.

The magnificent *Gate-tower*, of brick and stone, is best seen from across the street. It carries the emblems of Lady Margaret Beaufort, mythical creatures known as yales supporting the Lancastrian arms, the Beaufort portcullis, and Tudor rose, the background sprinkled with daisies and forget-me-nots growing from a well-populated rabbit warren. (For further details and explanations see Christ's College.) Above is a statue of St John (1662); the heavy linenfold-panelled doors are original (1515).

FIRST COURT, though built 1511–20, was much altered in the 18C, when the S. side (l.) was refaced and sash windows inserted. Over G staircase (no entry) an inscription 'Stag Nov 15 1777' records a stag

St John's College

Queen's Road

Northampton Street

Merton Hall

School of Pythagoras

Early 13C

Bin Brook

Magdalene College

Magdalene Street

Cripps Building
Mid 20C

New Court

The Backs

Early 19C

Bridge of Sighs

RIVER CAM

Bridge Street

Third Court
17C

Library

Late 19C

Trinity College

Second Court
Late 16C

Chapel Court

North Court
20C

Hall

Mid 19C

First Court
16C
Refaced
18C

Chapel

Early 16C

St John's Street

N

finally brought to bay by the local hunt half way up the stairs. On the N. side (r.) is the *Chapel* (usually open Mon–Sat 9–12, and Tues–Fri 2–4. Choral services, during Full Term only, Sun 10.30 a.m. and 6.30 p.m.; Tues–Sat 6.30 p.m.). It was entirely rebuilt by Sir George Gilbert Scott in 1866–69; attendance at Chapel was then compulsory, and the college had outgrown the old one. In High Vict-Gothic style, with a polygonal apse, it cannot be said to harmonise with its surroundings. The huge tower, modelled on Pershore Abbey, which is so prominent in the Cambridge skyline, was not part of Scott's design and the expense of its building was for long a heavy financial burden on the college. During this century it has become the custom on Ascension Day (Thur ten days before Whit Sunday) for a special hymn to be sung from the top (cf Magdalen College, Oxford); the choir has a long tradition of excellence.

In the ante-chapel are relics of the previous building. On the S. wall (l.) are the three arches of Bp Fisher's chantry (1525), with, set between two of them and protected by glass, a fragment representing the hand of Christ. Opposite is the tomb of Hugh Ashton (1522), one of Lady Margaret's officials. Typical of the time are the corpse below, and the rebus (a kind of visual pun) of ash-tree and barrel, or tun, on the tomb and railings. Other relics of the past, in the chapel itself, are the 13C piscina S. (r.) of the altar, and the 16C end stalls.

Opposite the main gate a handsomely carved archway surmounted by a statue of Lady Shrewsbury (see below) leads into the Screens Passage; r. is the *Hall* (no adm), mostly original though enlarged by Scott in the 1860s, when heating was installed to replace the charcoal brazier then still in use. The hammerbeam roof and much of the linenfold panelling dates from the 1530s; the heraldic glass is mostly Vict. SECOND COURT, built in 1598 partly with benefactions from Mary Cavendish, Countess of Shrewsbury (daughter of the great Derbyshire builder Bess of Hardwick) is the work of Ralph Symonds (see also Trinity, Emmanuel, and Sidney Sussex) and Gilbert Wigge, whose plans, the oldest surviving in Cambridge or Oxford, are in the library. As required in the contract, the style is the same Tudor-Gothic as the First Court before its 18C face-lift. Elizabethan decorations, such as strapwork, alone indicate its later date. A passage on the N. side (r.) leads to CHAPEL COURT (1885) and NORTH COURT (Sir Edward Maufe, 1939). Over the archway E. (r.) is a carving of Fisher's coat of arms (Eric Gill).

The gate-tower on the W. side of Second Court is embellished with Cavendish and Shrewsbury coats of arms (stag's head and dog respectively) and another statue of Lady Shrewsbury. Until 1859 its top storey was an observatory. The gateway leads into THIRD COURT. On the N. side (r.) is the Library (no adm) built in 1624; the interior is unchanged, and it houses a valuable collection of MSS and books. The rest of the court was built after the Civil War, 1669–72. On the W. side the famous so-called '*Bridge of Sighs*' (closed to visitors) leads to NEW COURT, to which there is also an entrance from the Backs. Leave Third Court by a passage S. (l.), turn r. through the elegant wrought-iron gates (1711) on to Kitchen Bridge (Robert Grumbold, 1709) and go in under the 'Wedding Cake' gateway, which is such a dominant feature of the Cambridge scene. This route gives delightful *views of the Backs, the 'Bridge of Sighs' and New Court (Rickman and Hutchinson, 1824). With its vaulted cloisters, battlements, and pinnacles, in the then newly fashionable neo-Gothick style, it is in complete contrast to the rest of St John's, a romantic fairy-tale flight of fancy. Its construction on a boggy riverside site was a herculean task; all the waterlogged soil had to be removed and replaced by timber foundations and huge cellars.

Opposite the 'Wedding Cake' a passage leads to the *CRIPPS BUILDING (Powell and Moya, 1964–67), given in one enormous benefaction by the Cripps Foundation. It is an exceptionally attractive composition, almost as much photographed as the 'Bridge of Sighs'. It extends W. across the Bin Brook into open ground which until 1959 belonged to Merton College, Oxford. Here stands one of

Modern Cambridge at its best: Cripps Building, St Johns College

the oldest buildings in Cambridge, the *School of Pythagoras* (c. 1200); the reason for its curious name is unknown. It has recently been converted for modern use, as has *Merton Hall* (16C) behind it (no adm to either).

FAMOUS MEMBERS: Thomas Wyatt, poet, 1503–42; Roger Ascham, scholar and tutor to Elizabeth I, 1515–68; William Cecil, Lord Burghley, chief minister to Elizabeth I, 1520–98; Robert Herrick, poet, 1591–1674 (also Trinity Hall); Erasmus Darwin, a scientific man of letters and grandfather of Charles Darwin and Francis Galton, 1731–1802; William Wilberforce, who brought about the abolition of the slave trade, 1759–1833; William Wordsworth, poet, 1770–1850; Lord Palmerston, statesman, 1784–1865; John Herschel, astronomer, 1792–1871; Louis Leakey, anthropologist, 1903–72; Nobel prizewinners Sir Edward Appleton, physicist, 1892–1965, and Sir John Cockcroft, nuclear physicist, 1897–1967. Also many archbishops and bishops.

Magdalene College (Pl. A4; pron 'Maudlin', men only) can be reached through the Porter's Lodge of St John's Cripps Building or via Bridge St. (a continuation of St John's St.) and Magdalene Bridge (cast iron, 1823) after which the name changes to Magdalene St. The only one of the older colleges across the river, it was charmingly described by Thomas Fuller in 1655 as the 'Trans Cantine Anchoret' (quoted by Edmund Vale, 'Little Guide to Cambridge', p 160). It was founded in 1542 by Thomas Audley, who had recently acquired great wealth through the dissolution of the monasteries. Its history, however, long predates this, since from the mid 15C the Benedictine abbeys of East Anglia (Crowland, Ely, Ramsey, and Walden) had a community here, where their monks could live while studying at the university, each probably maintaining its own 'house' (cf Worcester, formerly Gloucester, College, Oxford, p 86). At some stage this establishment received financial help from the Duke of Buckingham (executed for treason in 1484), and acquired the name 'Buckingham College'.

The founder of 1542 gave it little beyond its name, its motto 'Garde ta Foy' ('Keep Faith', or less reverently, 'Watch out for your liver'), and the proviso that its Master should in perpetuity be appointed by the owner of his great property at Audley End, near Saffron Walden. In the early 20C, through a long series of inheritances, this right devolved upon the title-holder of the Braybrooke family, who is also college Visitor.

Magdalene has an interesting link with the United States. In the mid 17C, when it was something of a Puritan enclave, a number of its members settled in New England, where one of them, Henry Dunster, became the first President of Harvard University (see also Emmanuel College, p 153). The post of Master at Harvard had been intended for the Moravian educationist Comenius, though he never took up the appointment. Dunster, however, always regarded himself as Comenius's deputy, and therefore used the title 'President' (a Cambridge term for Vice-Master); hence, possibly, the designation of the President of the United States.

An extremely influential Master (1915–25) was the author A.C. Benson. His books were enormously successful, and he lavished his consequent wealth on the college, being responsible for many of the 20C additions and alterations. He was also reponsible for a strong connection with his old school, Eton.

The spelling of Magdalene with a final 'e' which distinguishes it from Magdalen College, Oxford, dates from the early 19C. Before that it was spelt either way indifferently.

An attractive Renaissance gateway (1585) leads into FIRST COURT, which until the 18C comprised the whole college. The N. (l.) and S. (r.) sides were the old 15C Buckingham College; over the staircase doorways are modern versions of the coats of arms which indicated to which abbey the 'house' belonged.

The *Chapel* (N. side, usually open), though built c. 1480, has suffered many changes; 'classicised' in the 18C, it was 're-Gothicised' (largely by Pugin) in the mid 19C. In the ante-chapel, r. of the entrance, is a small modern bronze of Henry VII, aged seven.

Opposite the entrance gate is the Screens Passage, and (l.) the *Hall* (usually open), built in 1519 but inside completely remodelled in the early 18C, when a ceiling was put in, the Royal Arms (Queen Anne's) installed over the dais, and the uncommon double staircase built, leading to the gallery and combination room. It incorporates decorative woodwork from the old hall. There is a fine display of armorial bearings. Behind the dais are those of Audley, Sir Christopher Wray (who built the W. side of the court and the gateway) and of the Dukes of Buckingham and Suffolk (also benefactors). Audley's arms appear again in the middle window, E. side (16C). Otherwise the heraldic glass is all 20C, and commemorates distinguished members of the college; it was selected and paid for by Benson. Portraits include those of the founder and benefactors (on the dais) and of Samuel Pepys, Charles Kingsley, and Lord Tedder (on the stairs). The hall is still lit only by candles.

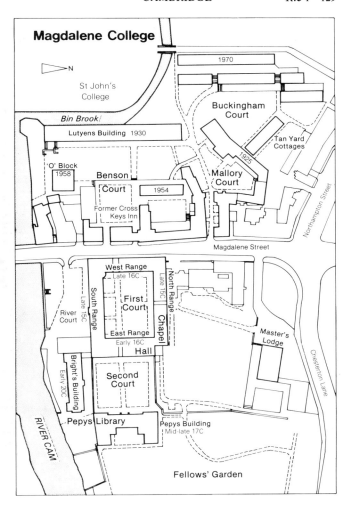

Magdalene College

N

St John's
College

Bin Brook

Lutyens Building 1930

1970

Buckingham
Court

Tan Yard
Cottages

'O' Block
1958

Benson
Court

1954

1925

Mallory
Court

Former Cross
Keys Inn

Northampton Street

Magdalene Street

West Range
Late 16C

First
Court

South Range
Late 15C

North Range
Late 16C

River
Court

East Range
Early 16C

Chapel

Master's
Lodge

Chesterton Lane

Hall

Bright's Building
Early 20C

Second
Court

Pepys Library

Pepys Building
Mid-late 17C

RIVER CAM

Fellows' Garden

In the SECOND COURT is the *Pepys Library (open Mon–Sat
2.30–3.30, also beginning of Easter Term–end Aug 11.30–12.30, or as
announced on a notice in the gatehouse). The building is a curious
mixture of styles, probably accounted for by the changes of fashion
occurring during the sixty years it took to build (c. 1640–1700).
Pepys's Library was installed here, after various moves, in 1742 (as
recorded on the facade).

Stringent conditions accompanied Pepys's bequest. The books were to be
kept in their specially-made glass-fronted cases, none were to be added, and

a periodical inspection was to be made by Trinity College (the other possible legatee). As well as superbly-bound books, the library contains *Pepys's famous diary, written in his own shorthand (with an account of Charles II's escape after the battle of Worcester as told by the King himself). Also on show are reminders of Pepys's days as Secretary of the Navy Board—Drake's pocket book, Elizabethan charts, and plans of Henry VIII's Navy. In the case between the windows is a manuscript translation of Ovid's 'Metamorphoses' made for Caxton. Pepys acquired the first part. The second, long thought lost, appeared in an auction sale in 1966 and was secured for Magdalene through the generosity of Mr Eugene Power of Ann Arbor, Michigan, USA.

S. of the library, facing the river, is Bright's Building (1909, by Sir Aston Webb, who also built Admiralty Arch). N. is the *Fellows' Garden* (open 2–4), and W. across more gardens is a further block, built and designed by Benson.

Further expansion took place from the 1920s onwards across Magdalene St., both by the adaptation of old houses and by some new building; *Lutyens Building*, 1930, is said to have been paid for from the royalties of 'Land of Hope and Glory', whose words Benson wrote; *Buckingham Court* (David Roberts, 1970) abuts on to St John's Cripps Building, and is clearly distinguished by its fiery red colour. The conversions (mostly by David Roberts) form an exceptionally attractive miniature townscape; the two 'courts' are named after *Benson* (l.) and *Mallory* (r.), the climber who perished near the summit of Everest in 1924.

FAMOUS MEMBERS: Henry Dunster, first President of Harvard, d 1659; Samuel Pepys, diarist, 1633–1703; Charles Kingsley, novelist, 1819–75; Charles Parnell, Irish Nationalist, 1846–91 (long practically disowned); G.L. Mallory, mountaineer, 1886–1924; Air Chief Marshal Lord Tedder, Deputy Supreme Commander Allied Forces, Second World War, 1890–1967; P.M.S. Blackett, physicist, Nobel prizewinner, 1897–1974.

The neighbourhood N. of Magdalene is described on p 159. Back in Bridge St., *St Clement's Church* (usually locked) is on the l. between Thompson's Lane and Portugal Passage. Basically EE, it has been much altered by the addition of an incongruous tower in 1821, and by Vict restorers. Its services are Anglo-Catholic in character. Shortly beyond it, just before Bridge St. becomes Sidney St., is the church of the Holy Sepulchre, usually known as the *Round Church* (Pl. B5). Dating from the early 12C, it is one of the few round churches in England. Its Norm appearance, however, is almost entirely due to 19C rebuilding by Salvin, under the direction of the Cambridge Camden Society or 'Ecclesiologists' (see p 13). The conical roof is likewise 19C. It is now the centre of Cambridge's vigorous Evangelical churchmanship. The door is nearly always wide open, and on a dark day the brightly-lit interior beckons warmly.

Behind it, in Round Church St., is the *Cambridge Union Society*. Founded as a debating club in 1815, it was suppressed two years later for debating politics, but restarted in 1821 on condition that no discussions took place on the politics of the last twenty years. It moved from the Red Lion Inn in Petty Cury to its present building (Alfred Waterhouse at his most strident) in 1866. Debates (nowadays of course on modern issues) are held Mon and Fri at 8.15 p.m. Visitors may attend as guests of members, though several days' notice is required.

To the S.E. of the Round Church is Jesus Lane, on the l. of which is the Pitt Club and (in Park St.) the *Amateur Dramatic Club* theatre. Further down is *Wesley House*, a Methodist training college, and beyond it *Jesus College* (Pl. B6), founded in 1496 by John Alcock, Bp of Ely and Comptroller of Works to Henry VII. Its position, somewhat away from the town centre, and its spacious grounds, are a reminder that this was once the site of the Nunnery of St Radegund

Jesus College Gate-tower and the 'Chimney' approach

(established 1135). By the late 15C, when Bp Alcock suppressed it in order to found his new college in its place, the community had dwindled to two—one of them allegedly imbecile. Alcock retained the conventual buildings, though vigorously adapting and adding to them, and architecturally Jesus is one of the most interesting colleges in Cambridge.

The massive three-storey *Gate-tower*, approached by a long passage known as 'The Chimney' (cf Trinity College, Oxford) was built by Alcock c. 1500. Above the central niche is a cock perched on a globe; this is Alcock's rebus and occurs ubiquitously on buildings and in stained glass.

The range W. (l.) of the gate until 1570 housed the grammar school attached to the college. In FIRST COURT the range opposite the gate is 17C, but deliberately designed to harmonise with the conventual buildings on the E. (r.) side, where a carved ogee-headed doorway, again surmounted by the cock, leads into *CLOISTER COURT. This was the heart of the old nunnery, to which Alcock added the third storey, the beautiful timber ceiling of the cloisters, and of course his rebus. On the N. side is the *Hall* (the first in Cambridge to be placed upstairs), Alcock's rebuilding of the nuns' refectory, with a magnificent chestnut-wood hammerbeam roof, and large oriel window. The heraldic glass on the r. was previously in the chapel, that on the l. is by William Morris (1875). There are interesting portraits: above the dais the founder (an imaginary likeness), Mary Queen of Scots, and Cranmer. Others of distinguished Jesus men include Flamsteed, Malthus (by Linnell), S.T. Coleridge as an old man, and Steve Fairbairn (d 1938), the great rowing·coach who brought Jesus to its pre-eminent position on the river. Outside the hall, steps lead up to the *Old Library* (no adm), which remains much as Alcock left it, complete with his books, and his cock in the window-glass.

Beyond the hall entrance, on the E. side of the cloisters, are the beautifully carved EE arches which once led into the Chapter House. Concealed for 350 years by Alcock's alterations, they were rediscovered during restorations in the summer vacation of 1840. Only one undergraduate, Osmond Fisher, and one don were in residence. In spite of Fisher's enthusiasm for the medieval gem orders were given for the arches to be plastered in, and it was not until 1873, when Fisher was himself a Fellow, that they were again revealed.

The huge and magnificent *CHAPEL on the S. side of the court is one of the most exciting in Cambridge. It has a complicated architectural history. Originally the conventual church, also serving St Radegund's parish, it was a cruciform building of EE design though with Norm work on the N. side. Alcock reduced its size by removing the side aisles and converting the W. end of the nave into rooms and part of the Master's Lodge. He also installed new windows (in the Perp. style) and furnishings.

In the late 18C this interior was 'classicised' but of this phase virtually nothing remains, for in 1845 under the influence of the Gothic Revivalists of the Cambridge Camden Society a complete restoration began whose object was to return the chapel to its 13C pre-Alcock state. What we see now, therefore, is partly genuine Norm and EE, and partly a brilliant realisation of their vision of the ideal medieval church.

Anthony Salvin restored the original choir roof, and built the organ chamber on the site of the old N. choir aisle. Later Pugin replaced Alcock's E. window with one in EE style, and filled it with glass inspired by the windows of Chartres Cathedral, to which he made a special visit. While there he purchased a sackful of fragments from a window under repair, and incorporated these with his own work, so that parts are in fact 15C Chartres glass. He also designed the floor tiles, organ panels, and some of the stalls, in which he used pieces of Alcock's carved woodwork. This had been sold to Landbeach church (about 5 m. N.E. of Cambridge) during the 18C alterations, and the college now made strenuous though only partly successful efforts to recover it. The lectern was given by Lord Brome, and is copied from one in the Brome family chapel.

The second phase of restoration, begun in 1864, provides a feast for admirers of the Pre-Raphaelites, for the delicate and colourful *ceilings were painted by William Morris, and the side-windows designed by Burne-Jones and Ford Madox Brown, except for one in the S. transept which is by Morris (bought 1900). The tower, which G.F. Bodley (who took charge after Pugin's death) considered unsafe, was narrowly saved from demolition by the intervention of Sir George Gilbert Scott, whose son was Bodley's assistant.

The striking green and gold altar frontal is by Barbara Dawson (1971); Pugin's frontal is in a glass case in the S. transept. Below it, slightly r., is the tomb-slab of a 13C benefactor of St Radegund's. Final reminders of the chapel's 13C origin are the columns (part of the N. aisle) outside in the cloister wall. They were exposed when the War Memorial was installed.

To the N. and W. of Cloister Court are PUMP COURT and SECOND COURT, both 19C. To E. is the very spacious CHAPEL COURT, also partly 19C, completed on the S. side by Morley Horder in 1931 (coat of arms by Eric Gill). The striking building N.W. of Second Court is by David Roberts, 1963–66.

The grounds of Jesus are open and roomy. Sadly the pleached limes which were such an attractive feature of Chapel Court were cut down in 1979, but the college still possesses a mulberry tree planted for James I, and the great plane trees, from the Vale of Tempe in Greece, planted in 1801 in the Master's and in the Fellows' gardens. Round the latter are massed crocuses, and in spring the gate into Jesus Lane is left ajar so that passers-by can look in.

FAMOUS MEMBERS: Thomas Cranmer, Abp to Henry VIII and Edward VI, compiler of the English prayer book, 'Oxford Martyr', 1489–1556; Laurence Sterne, novelist, 1713–68; Thomas Malthus, economist, 1766–1834; S.T. Coleridge, poet, 1772–1834; Humphrey Davy, chemist, inventor of the miner's safety lamp, 1778–1829; A. Quiller-Couch, man of letters, 1863–1944 (see also Trinity College, Oxford).

Opposite Jesus College, in Jesus Lane, is *All Saints* church (1864), designed by G.F. Bodley and decorated by William Morris, Burne-Jones, and Ford Madox Brown. It is permanently closed, and its fate awaits decision (1981). Next door is *Westcott House*, a Church of England training college. The wall beyond it is the boundary of **Sidney Sussex College** (Pl. B5) whose main entrance is in Sidney St. (l. at the top of Jesus Lane). This small college was founded in 1596 under the will of Lady Frances Sidney, wife of the Earl of Sussex. The head of the Sidney family (of Penshurst, Kent) is still the Hereditary Visitor, and the family crest, a porcupine, appears in various places on the buildings. These are on the site of the Greyfriars' convent, dissolved in 1538, whose chapel had formerly served the university for large gatherings and ceremonies (cf Great St Mary's, p 113). Nothing remains of the conventual buildings, however, for they had already been demolished to provide material for Trinity College.

The purpose of the new foundation was to train men for ministry in the Reformed Church, and its statutes were closely modelled on those of Emmanuel College. During the religious controversies of the 17C its tendency was strongly Puritan, in spite of which in the Civil War it remained loyal to the King, and suffered the consequent ejection. of its Masters and Fellows. Oliver Cromwell did not intervene to spare his old college.

The present appearance of Sidney Sussex is largely due to the restoration and alterations carried out in neo-Gothick manner by Sir Jeffry Wyatville in 1821–32. He built the central Porter's Lodge, covered the old buildings with Roman cement, and added the battlements, crow-step gables, and ornamental chimney-tops which are all such distinctive features. HALL COURT (l., by Ralph Symonds, 1598) stands where the conventual buildings stood. On the N.E. side is the *Hall* (open when the staff are there, or by arrangement); it was completely remodelled inside in the mid 18C, when a ceiling was put in below the old hammerbeam roof, and the walls panelled. The soft grey of its present decoration is most pleasing. Portraits include one of the three of Oliver Cromwell owned by the college, and may be the one that he instructed should be a true likeness 'warts and all'.

On the N. side of the court a passage leads to CLOISTER COURT (J.L. Pearson, 1891). To the r. of the Porter's Lodge is CHAPEL COURT. Ahead (S.) is Sir Francis Clerke's Building (1628). To the E. (l.) is the *Chapel*, which replaces two former ones. On the site of the friars' refectory, it runs N. and S. instead of the usual E. and W.—perhaps a deliberate Protestant disregard of tradition (cf Emmanuel College). The original simple chapel of 1600 was replaced in the late 18C (by James Essex), and this again was rebuilt and greatly enlarged 1912–23 by T.H. Lyon, in a freely Renaissance style. It has a barrel-vaulted ceiling decorated with the theme of the 'Benedicite'—all God's living creatures. The woodwork is rich in symbolic carvings, and the windows carry the armorial bearings of benefactors. Above the bronze and marble altar hangs a painting of the Holy Family (Giovanni Battista Pittoni, 1687–1767) which was also the altarpiece in Essex's chapel. A statue of St Francis is a reminder of the medieval friars.

In the ante-chapel windows are mosaics composed of 13–14C glass; large quantities of fragments were excavated in the garden in 1959, and there are similar mosaics in the old library (no adm). Also in the ante-chapel a tablet records the burial near by of Oliver Cromwell's head, which after many vicissitudes found a resting place in his old college in 1960.

SOUTH COURT (1938) and GARDEN COURT (1923) lie S. and E. of the chapel. Beyond looms the menacing BLUNDELL COURT (Howell, Killick, Partridge, and Amis, 1969), gloomy in purple brick and dark grey aggregate. The gardens, once bounded to the E. by the King's Ditch, are exceptionally large and beautiful.

FAMOUS MEMBERS: Oliver Cromwell, 1599–1658; C.T.R. Wilson, physicist, Nobel prizewinner, 1869–1959.

On the corner of Sidney St. and Market St. (S. of Sidney Sussex) is *Holy Trinity* church, mostly 14C and 15C. Historically it is linked with the Evangelical movement, a leading protagonist of which, Charles Simeon, (d 1836) was vicar for fifty-four years. Left of the busy road junction, where Sidney St. becomes St Andrew's St., is **Christ's College** (Pl. B8), originally founded as God's House c. 1436 by William Byngham, rector of St John Zachary church in London (burnt down in 1666). The intention was to provide a supply of trained teachers for schools, and studies were secular rather than theological. Established near Clare College, which gave it some assistance, it moved to the present site in the 1440s, when the whole area S. of Clare was cleared to make way for King's College.

In 1505 it was refounded, as Christ's College, by Lady Margaret Beaufort, mother of Henry VII, and 'a scholar, a gentlewoman, and a saint', who had already founded professorships of Divinity at both Cambridge and Oxford and was shortly to found St John's College (see p 124; Lady Margaret Hall, Oxford, is also named after her). Her close friend, confessor, and adviser was Bp John Fisher, formerly Master of Michaelhouse (see p 120), then President of Queens', Vice-Chancellor, and later Chancellor of the University (he was executed in 1538 for refusing to recognise Henry VIII as supreme head of the Church). Both were deeply interested in the New Learning, and classical studies formed part of the new regime.

In Elizabethan times Christ's tended religiously towards Puritanism, but then and later always showed a marked moderation and tolerance of outlook.

The superb *Gate-tower* closely resembles that of St John's, but the display of Lady Margaret's insignia is even richer and more complicated. The Beaufort arms are supported by yales—fabulous creatures similar to antelopes, but with the great asset of being able to move their horns independently (as made clear by the curious angles at which they are set). Around them are the Beaufort portcullis and coronet, the Tudor rose and royal crown, and at the sides the Welsh dragon and greyhound, supporters of the royal arms. Daisies (marguerites), perhaps recalling Lady Margaret's name, forget-me-nots recalling her motto (souvent me souvient), and plentiful rabbits fill in the background. The linenfold-panelled doors are the originals, but have several inches cut off at the bottom to adjust them to the changed street-level (notice also the staircase steps just inside the gate).

The appearance of FIRST COURT was much altered in the 18C (probably by James Essex) when the brick and clunch used by the 16C builders was cased in Ketton stone, the battlements replaced by balustrades, and the windows sashed. Opposite the entrance is the Master's Lodge, whose oriel window (l.) carries the same Beaufort emblems as the gatehouse. This upper floor was Lady Margaret's lodging; the room still has its Tudor fireplace. Next to it was a tiny oratory with an oriel window (rebuilt 1899) opening into the ante-chapel (it can be seen in the ante-chapel S. wall; cf New College, Oxford).

The *Chapel* is entered through the black and white door l. of the large oriel. Like the rest of this range it dates from the old God's House, although it was completely classicised in the 18C. However some ancient features remain: behind hinged panels on the N. and S. sides are doorways formerly leading respectively to a side chapel and the Master's Lodge, and in the windows on the N. side is some of the oldest glass in Cambridge. The larger figures (c. 1475) are possibly St Gregory and Henry VI, the smaller (c. 1505) Henry VII, Lady Margaret, and Edward the Confessor. The magnificent brass lectern is also 15C. Lady Margaret's greyhounds were added later. On the N. wall is a handsome monument to two close friends, Sir John Finch and Sir Thomas Baines (Joseph Catterns, 1684). The E. window (1912) shows First Court as it appears in Loggan's print of 1688, with above it the Risen Christ, and below Lady Margaret, Bp Fisher, and Edward VI.

The *Hall*, E. (r.) of the Master's Lodge, was rebuilt in Gothic style by George Gilbert Scott the Younger in the 1870s. Some of the woodwork in the screen was in the Tudor hall. The coats of arms over the gallery arches are those of Bp Fisher, with (l.) William Byngham and (r.) the first Master, John Sycling (Sir Ninian Comper, 1939). There are portraits of Lady Margaret, John Milton (also a bust, copied from an original in the Senior Combination Room), Charles Darwin, Lord Mountbatten of Burma, and several Nobel prizewinners.

A passage r. of the hall leads into SECOND COURT. Opposite is the sumptuous classical *Fellows' Building* (1624), on whose N. side a restored 16C doorway opens into the *Fellows' Garden* (open 10–12.30, 2–4). At the far end is a mulberry tree (one of several in the grounds) vaguely associated with Milton. These trees are descendants of some of the 300 planted in 1608 at the request of James I, who wished to encourage silk manufacture. Unfortunately the wrong species was chosen, and all the silk worms died. Near by is an outdoor bathing pool, whose water is still supplied by Hobson's New River (see p 150 and Emmanuel College).

Additions were made to Second Court in the early–mid 19C, and Third Court was built at various times between 1889 and 1953. N. of it, backing on to King St., is NEW COURT (Denis Lasdun, 1970) which inevitably recalls the Mappin Terraces in Regent's Park.

FAMOUS MEMBERS: John Leland, antiquary, 1506–52; John Milton, poet, 1608–74, and his friend Edward King, lamented in 'Lycidas'; Charles Darwin, 'Origin of Species', 1809–82; Jan Smuts, S. African statesman, 1870–1950; Lord Mountbatten of Burma, royal sailor and statesman, 1900–1979; C.P. Snow, novelist, 1905–80.

Opposite Christ's College Petty Cury leads back to Market Hill.

2 WEST AND SOUTH OF MARKET HILL

From the top side of Market Hill St Mary's Passage leads to KING'S PARADE, the heart of visitor's Cambridge, dominated by the soaring splendour of King's College Chapel, world-famous alike for the superlative quality of its architecture and of its choral music. **King's College** (Pl. D1; no adm to any building exc the chapel) was founded as 'The King's College of our Lady and St Nicholas in Cambridge' in 1441, by Henry VI (the 'Royal Saint' of Wordsworth's sonnet), and began quite modestly with provision for a Rector and twelve scholars, to be housed in a building N. of the chapel, opposite the entrance to Clare. This was the *Old Court*, now part of the University Offices (see p 115). But in 1445 the King devised a much more ambitious scheme, which envisaged a foundation of a Provost and seventy scholars, to be drawn from his newly established school at Eton, with a series of magnificent buildings ranged round a huge court. The whole plan was evidently based on William of Wykeham's New College at Oxford. To clear the chosen site, S. of Old Court and Clare, the recently-opened God's House had to be removed (see Christ's College, p 135), the church of St John Zachary pulled down (see St Edward's church, p 113), houses and wharves along the river demolished, and roads diverted. Of all the grand plans only the chapel was ever realised, for in 1455 the Wars of the Roses broke out, and in 1461 Henry VI was deposed.

Apart from the completion of the chapel (see below) no more building was done until the 18C, the only living accommodation being the Old Court. In 1724 James Gibbs, then busy with the Senate House, made plans for a new great court, but, history repeating itself, again only one part of the plan materialised, the *Fellows*, or *Gibbs, Building* opposite the entrance gates. Nearly 100 years elapsed before the court was completed, in romantic neo-Gothick style, by William Wilkins, who built the screen and gatehouse facing on to King's Parade, and the S. (l.) range which includes a splendidly medieval-looking *Hall* (no adm), now rather uneasily accommodating modern bar and self-service arrangements. Outside the gatehouse is a domed Vict post-box, a much-loved feature of the local scene.

Until the 1870s only Etonians were admitted to King's, and its members were exempt from university examinations. After these somewhat inhibiting privileges were removed the college expanded rapidly and quickly established a tradition of intellectual pre-eminence, particularly on the arts side, which is still maintained. It was one of the first men's colleges to admit women (1972).

Further buildings were added in the late 19C—*Chetwynd Court*, behind Wilkins' S. range (1873 by Scott), *River Court* (1895 by G.F. Bodley), and *Webb's Court*, W. of Chetwynd (1907 by Sir Aston Webb). Across the river is Garden Hostel (1950), and on Market Hill is Market Hostel (1960). In the late 1960s King's and St Catherine's next door joined forces to build the complex (by Fello Atkinson) of small courts, dining and concert halls, in and over the narrow space of King's Lane. It is familiarly known as 'Cats and Kings'.

FAMOUS MEMBERS: Christopher Tye, musician, c. 1500–73; Francis Walsingham, statesman, c. 1530–90; John Harrington, inventor of the water-closet, 1561–1612; Edmund Waller, poet, 1606–87; George Monk (Duke of Albemarle), soldier and statesman, 1608–70; Charles 'Turnip' Townshend, statesman and agriculturalist, 1674–1738; Robert Walpole, statesman, 1676–1745, and his son

Horace, wit and man of letters, 1717–97; M.R. James, scholar and writer of ghost stories, 1862–1936; Roger Fry, art critic, 1866–1934; E.M. Forster, novelist, 1879–1970; Maynard Keynes, economist, 1883–1946; A.V. Hill, physiologist, Nobel prizewinner, 1886–1977; Rupert Brooke, poet, 1887–1915; P.M.S. Blackett, physicist, Nobel prizewinner, 1897–1974.

Across a wide expanse of grass is **King's College Chapel**, open as follows: Term: Mon–Sat 9–3.45, Sun 2–3 and 4.30–5.45. Vacation: Christmas (from 1st Jan) 9–4; Easter 9–5; Summer, mid June–end Aug 9–5.45, 1st Sept–early Oct 9–5 (Sun 10.30–5). Choral services in term Tues–Sat 3.30, Sun 10.30 and 3.30 (none in vacation).

It is perhaps one of the greatest, as also the latest, medieval buildings of England, and indeed of Europe, Wordsworth's 'immense/And glorious work of fine intelligence'. The richness and variety of its decoration and furnishing reflect the changes in taste, largely due to the Renaissance, which took place during the 100-odd years it took to complete. Perhaps they also reflect the difference in outlook between the founder and his more worldly successors.

Work began in 1446, under Henry VI's master mason Robert Ely, but stopped abruptly in 1461 when the king was defeated at the battle of Towton. One great stone, half cut at the time, remained untouched for over two centuries and was eventually used as the foundation-stone of the Gibbs Building. Some progress was made between 1476 and 1483, but it was not until Henry VII visited Cambridge with his mother Lady Margaret Beaufort (see Christ's and St John's Colleges, pp 135, 124) in 1506 that vigorous building began again, this time directed by John Wastell. The stonework was finished by 1515, but much remained to be done inside, and it is to Henry VIII that the chapel owes the superb woodwork and windows.

The plan is simple—a great rectangle 289 ft long, 40 ft wide, and 80 ft high, spanned by fan vaults of exquisite delicacy, and lit by windows so enormous that the building seems walled in glass. Over the S. porch are the royal arms of Henry VII, supported by Tudor dragon and Beaufort greyhound. These emblems and other insignia of the royal family, Beaufort portcullis, French fleur-de-lis, Tudor antelope, rose, and crown, are the principal motifs of the carving throughout the chapel.

The *screen* which divides the ante-chapel from the choir is an outstanding example of Renaissance woodwork, every inch richly carved. It bears the initial of Henry VIII (the donor) intertwined with that of his queen, Anne Boleyn, whose family crest of a falcon also appears alongside the Tudor rose. Surmounting the screen is the organ; the case dates from 1686–88, but incorporates part of an earlier one. The trumpet-blowing angels were copied from old designs in 1859.

On the E. side of the screen in the aisle is an early 16C bronze lectern, engraved on one side with roses and on the other with the four evangelists and their beasts and topped by a small statue of Henry VI. The *stalls* are contemporary with the screen, and by the same craftsmen; above are heraldic panels (1633) showing on the N. side (l.) royal arms and those of Eton and Oxford, and on the S. the arms of King's College and Cambridge. The *altarpiece* is Rubens's 'Adoration of the Magi' (1634) given to King's in 1961. Its installation

King's College Chapel: 'that branching roof/Self-poised, and scoop'd into ten thousand cells'

necessitated the removal of panelling and the steps on which the altar then stood, and at the time aroused much controversy. The modern gold, bronze, and blue altar frontal was designed by Joyce Evans, and embroidered by Elizabeth Geddes. S. of the altar is the *War Memorial Chapel*, which contains facsimiles of Rupert Brooke's sonnets 'The Soldier' and 'The Dead'.

All the *windows* (except the W. window, a 19C Last Judgement) are by the famous glaziers Bernard Flower and Galyon Hone working with Flemish craftsmen c. 1517–47. Each contains four scenes, divided vertically by a light showing prophets and martyrs, horizontally by a stone transom. Beginning on the N. side, W. end, they tell the story of the Virgin, and the life of Christ up to the Passion, which is depicted in the E. window. The theme is continued on the S. side with the Resurrection, Pentecost, Acts of the Apostles and finally the Assumption of the Virgin.

Between the chapel and the river is a sweeping lawn, and across the bridge (1871) King's 'Backs', in spring carpeted with crocuses and, later, daffodils. The *view back towards the college and chapel is well worth the short walk.

Immediately S. of King's is **St Catharine's College** (Pl. D1), founded in 1473 by Robert Woodlark, Provost of King's, to serve as a chantry and for the study of philosophy and theology. He provided only for a Master and three Fellows and there were no students until after the Reformation (mid 16C). It was known as Katharine Hall until the 1850s (cf Clare College).

Nothing remains of the original buildings. The three-sided front court, closed on the Trumpington St. side only by fine iron railings (1779) was built in various stages between 1675 and 1757; of mellow brick, in restrained Baroque style, it makes a particularly attractive and individual contribution to the local scene. Seats round the sides (many of them memorial) are pleasantly welcoming. The rather unadorned early 18C *Chapel* (r.) has a handsome reredos and organ gallery.

Fronting on to Trumpington St. on each side of the front court are buildings closely in harmony with it, but in fact dating only from the 20C: *Woodlark* (S., 1951) named after the founder, and *Hobson* (N., 1930) named after Hobson the carrier (see p 150) whose George inn once stood here. Beside it was the Bell inn, bequeathed to St Catharine's in 1626 by the Master of Caius, Dr Gostlin, much to the chagrin of his own college. Of this only the 1820s facade remains; behind is the new complex built jointly with King's (see p 137). The large *Hall* (W. side) has four very striking steel chandeliers. There are more buildings (1870s–1930s) and the Master's and Fellows' gardens (no adm), behind the S. range of the main court, towards Silver St. On the W. side a gate leads out into Queens' Lane.

FAMOUS MEMBERS: James Shirley, dramatist, 1596–1666; John Addenbrooke, founder of Addenbrooke's Hospital, d 1719.

Almost opposite St Catharine's W. gate is the entrance to ***Queens' College** (Pl. C2; open throughout the year 2–4.30, exc during examinations, early May–mid June, when it is entirely closed; fee charged March–end Oct; visitors enter and leave by the Queens' Lane gate, and should follow the route described). This college, whose head is President, not Master as elsewhere, has three founders. In 1446 Andrew Dokett, rector of St Botolph's church, first established it as St Bernard's College; two years later it came under the patronage of Margaret of Anjou, the young queen of Henry VI (who had just founded King's College next door), and was renamed The Queen's College of St Margaret and St Bernard 'to laud and honneur the sexe feminine'. Soon after, the Wars of the Roses broke out; in 1461 Henry VI was deposed and the Yorkist Edward IV became King. His queen, Elizabeth Woodville (a former lady-in-waiting to Margaret) became the college's new patron and gave it its first statutes. She did not dishonour the memory of her old mistress, but merely gave the college the new style of Queens' rather than Queen's. The changes in royal patrons, who also included Richard (III) of Gloucester, account for the many elaborations of the college arms.

Queens' College: the Gate-tower and Old Court

In the early 16C, shortly after the Presidency of the saintly John Fisher (see also Christ's and St John's Colleges, pp 135, 124), Queens' had the distinction of playing host to his friend Erasmus, the great Renaissance scholar who introduced the study of Greek into Cambridge and Oxford. He was a most difficult guest, full of complaints, particularly about the college beer, 'raw, small, and windy ... I am being killed with thirst'. However he found English girls 'divinely pretty, soft, pleasant; gentle and charming as the Muses'.

The magnificent *Gate-tower* has richly carved and coloured vaulting, and on the outer side a statue, possibly of Andrew Dokett. OLD COURT was built in two stages 1448–49; the vertical join in the brickwork can be clearly seen on the S. (l.) side. On the N. (r.) is a large sundial (1733) which also tells moon-time, and the old chapel and library (no adm to either).

Over the doorway W., opposite the gate-tower, is the college coat of arms (1575)—those of Margaret of Anjou, showing quarterings of the many countries to which her father laid claim. The door (original) leads into the Screens Passage and (r.) the *Hall, recently restored (1980) and a glorious riot of colour and decoration. Although the basic structure is 15C, the interior has been radically altered twice, first (by James Essex) in the 1730s, to which date belong the panelling, screen, and 'reredos' behind the high table, and secondly (by G.F. Bodley) in the 1850s. He removed the 18C plaster ceiling, restored the timber roof, exposed the old fireplace, and built the louvre (which the hall, having a fireplace, would never in fact have needed). Roof and walls were decorated by William Morris, who also, with Ford Madox Brown, designed the exceptionally attractive tiles over the fireplace; they represent the months of the year, the saints of the college, and the two queens. Through the Screens Passage is *CLOISTER COURT (1460–95), with its warm red brick and intimate atmosphere one of the most pleasing in Cambridge. On the N. side (r.) is the half-timbered *President's Gallery*, added c. 1540, when long galleries were a fashionable feature of gentlemen's houses.

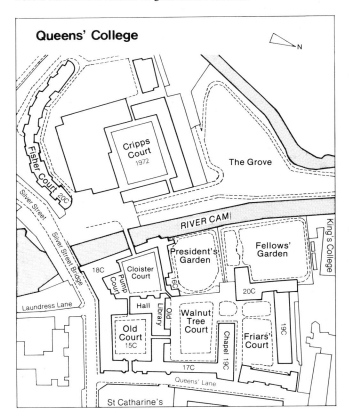

On the S. side (l.) is *Pump Court* (James Essex, 1756); its rather gaunt appearance is in marked contrast to the cosiness of the cloisters. Behind it (E. corner) can be seen the tower where Erasmus had his rooms (no adm). The passage on the W. side leads on to the wooden bridge (often, though wrongly, called the *Mathematical Bridge*); it is copied from the original Chinese-style design of 1749. Straight ahead is the striking new CRIPPS COURT (Powell and Moya 1972; cf St John's College, Cambridge, and Wolfson College, Oxford), while l. is *Fisher Court* (1936), of which there is a better view from Silver St. There is a short riverside walk (r.) to the Grove.

Back over the bridge in Cloister Court a passage N.E. (l.) under the President's Gallery leads into WALNUT TREE COURT, of which the E. side (r.) was built in 1616 (enlarged 1778). Beyond it is FRIARS COURT (of various dates from 1862, the W. side by Sir Basil Spence, 1959). Between is the *Chapel, built by G.F. Bodley in 1889–91. Like the Hall it presents a brilliant spectacle of colour.

Queens' Lane is reached by returning to Old Court through the passage immediately opposite the chapel door.

FAMOUS MEMBERS: Erasmus, scholar (resident c. 1511–14), 1466–1536; John Fisher, Bp and martyr, 1469–1535; Thomas Smith, statesman and scholar, d 1577; Thomas Fuller, antiquarian, author of 'Worthies of England', 1608–61; Isaac Milner, mathematician and divine, 1750–1820; Osborne Reynolds, mathematician and engineer, 1842–1912; Charles Villiers Stanford, composer and organist, 1852–1924; T.H. White, author ('The Once and Future King'), 1906–64.

At the S.E. (r. out of Queens') end of Queens' Lane is Silver St.; on the r. are various university offices and lecture rooms, once part of the Cambridge University Press, whose Pitt Building (1821) is at the top of the street. Its architecture is so ecclesiastical that it has been called the 'Freshmen's Church', from the old joke of directing newcomers to it on Sunday. It was built with money left over from subscriptions collected for a memorial to William Pitt.

A short way N. (l.) along Trumpington St., across the road, is **Corpus Christi College** (Pl. D1; familiarly 'Corpus'), which was founded in 1352 by the united religious guilds of Corpus Christi and the Blessed Virgin. It was strongly religious in character; all members were in holy orders, and chantry duties were incumbent on them. These were carried out in the neighbouring church of St Benedict or Bene't (see below) which served as the college chapel until 1579, and the foundation was long known as Bene't's College.

In the riots of 1381 the college was a particular object of attack; this was perhaps due to resentment of its prosperity and the wealth of the guilds which supported it, and also to the extreme unpopularity of its patron the Duke of Lancaster. The buildings were sacked and college records burnt on Market Hill.

The entrance gate leads into New Court, in the N.E. (far l.) corner of which is a passage into *OLD COURT, completed in 1377 and until the 19C the college's sole building. Though buttressed for strength in the 15C and 17C, it remains outwardly much as it was in the 14C, and is the best example in Cambridge of a medieval college court. A passage on its N. side leads to some 20C additions. NEW COURT was built by William Wilkins (1823–27), in the neo-Gothick style he had also adopted at King's. His plans involved the complete destruction of the old chapel given to Corpus in 1597 by Nicholas Bacon, and subscribed to (it is said) by Sir Francis Drake. The new *Chapel*, extended 1870, has stall-backs and some canopied seats from the old one (no adm, but it can be seen through a locked glass door installed after serious thefts). In the *Hall* (N., or l.) which has a richly decorated timber roof, is a fine collection of portraits among which perhaps the most interesting is a painting on wood, dated 1585, of a young man thought to be Christopher Marlowe. It was found among builders' rubbish during repair work in 1955.

On the S. side (r.) is the *Old Library* (open Tues, Wed, Thur, 2.15–4 Oct–end Apr, 2.15–4.45 May–end Sept, but enquire at Porter's Lodge). It houses the priceless collection of MSS and books bequeathed by Matthew Parker (Master 1554, and later Abp of Canterbury), and containing much material rescued from monastic libraries dispersed after the Dissolution. Among its treasures are a MS of the Anglo-Saxon Chronicle, Geoffrey of Monmouth's 'Historia Britanniae', the 12C rhymed chronicle 'Brut', and a 12C 'Life of Charlemagne'. Parker left strict instructions for its care, which included an annual surveillance by Caius and Trinity Hall. In the 1960s Corpus established a postgraduate hostel, Leckhampton House, off Grange Rd (see p 157).

FAMOUS MEMBERS: Matthew Parker, Abp of Canterbury, 1504–75; Nicholas Bacon, statesman, father of Sir Francis Bacon (Trinity), 1509–79; Christopher Marlowe, dramatist, 1564–93; John Fletcher, dramatist, 1579–1625; Sir George Thomson, physicist, Nobel prizewinner, 1892–1975.

On the N. side of Corpus Christi is *St Bene't's* church; the tower is early 11C and the tower arch at the W. end a particularly good example of Saxon work. The rest of the church is mainly 13C and 14C, much restored. The elegant little font is 18C. In c. 1500 Dr Cosyn, Master of Corpus, added two chapels, one above the other, on the S. side, and connected them with the college by a gallery. They now serve as a vestry and a college room. Fabian Steadman, who perfected the art of change-ringing, and after whom various 'changes' are named, was parish clerk in the 17C (tablet). Until the 1940s the incumbent was nearly always a Fellow of Corpus.

S. of Corpus Christi is the church of *St Botolph* (14–15C, heavily restored late 19C). He was a patron saint of travellers and churches of this dedication were usually near city gates, in this case Trumpington Gate. The four bells are exactly as they came from the foundry in 1460, and there is a particularly handsome font-case and cover (1637).

Beyond St Botolph's, Pembroke St., becoming *Downing St.*, runs E. (l.), a rather cheerless thoroughfare on each side of which is a large complex of Science Faculty buildings of many dates from the 1860s to the 1970s. THE NEW MUSEUMS (N. side, l.) came first, built on the site of the old Botanical Garden. Embedded in this gloomy and confusing medley is the *Zoology Museum* (open Mon–Fri 2.15–4.45) and the small white semi-circular *Mond Laboratory*, decorated with a crocodile in tribute to Lord Rutherford (nicknamed 'The Crocodile'). Near it a passage leads into Free School Lane, where the *Whipple Museum of the History of Science* (open Mon–Fri 2–4) is housed in the original hall of the Perse School (17C). On the Downing side (S. side, r.), through the Vict-Gothic portal, are (l.) the *Sedgwick Museum of Geology* (open Mon–Fri 9–1, 2–5; Sat 9–1 in term only) and (r.) the *Museum of Archaeology and Ethnology* (open Mon–Fri 2–4, Sat 10–12.30).

On the corner of Pembroke St. is **Pembroke College** (Pl. D3; men only), founded in 1347 by Marie de Valence, widowed Countess of Pembroke, and close friend of Lady Elizabeth de Clare, founder of Clare College. It was known as Pembroke Hall until the 1850s.

Although it is one of the oldest colleges in the university, only its 14C gateway on to Trumpington St. still presents its medieval appearance. The N. and N.W. sides of OLD COURT are basically the original, but the crumbling clunch walls were refaced partly in brick (1633) and more extensively in stone c.1712, the first to receive this treatment, afterwards employed so widely elsewhere in Cambridge. Pembroke was also the first to have its own chapel, licensed in 1398. In 1663–65 a new *Chapel* was built (S. side, r., in Old Court). The donor was Matthew Wren, Bp of Ely (d 1667), who had studied at Pembroke and later became Master of Peterhouse (qv). His High Church sympathies earned him eighteen years in the Tower; soon after his release at the Restoration in 1660 he commissioned his nephew, Christopher Wren, to design a chapel for his old college. It was Wren's first building to be completed (he was also then working on the Sheldonian Theatre in Oxford), his first church, and the first classical building in Cambridge. The sanctuary, entered between massive Corinthian columns of Italian marble, was added by G.G. Scott the Younger in 1880. On its S. side (r.) is the 14C piscina from the old chapel, and the chair of Nicholas Ridley, Bp of London and one of the 'Oxford Martyrs' (see p 11), a former Master. Matthew Wren's cushions of turkey-work (a particular kind of stitchery) are still in use in the stalls.

The old chapel (N.W. corner, l. in Old Court) was converted into a *Library* (now used for various gatherings; open by written appointment). It was given a *plasterwork ceiling of exceptional gaiety and charm: scrolls and swags, open books and putti and birds flying across a pale blue sky (by Henry Doogood, 1690).

Opposite the entrance gate is the *Hall* (usually open in the morning). This, and the buildings S. of the chapel (c. 1890) are by Alfred Waterhouse, who had recently done Tree Court at Caius. As there, he made no attempt to harmonise his designs with their surroundings. The hall was lengthened and a ceiling installed in 1925, and the whole much simplified in the late 1940s. The admirable Master's Chair (David Pye, 1965) is the first piece of official Cambridge furniture in the mid-20C style. As well as many interesting portraits there are busts of William Pitt and the famous 19C mathematician Sir George Gabriel Stokes, who founded a number of Pembroke scholarships.

Behind the hall is IVY COURT; the N. (l.) side is of 1614. The S. side (1659) is named after Sir Robert Hitcham of Framlingham, with whose bequest it was built, and carries his coat of arms. On the upper floor are the *rooms occupied by the poet Thomas Gray* from 1755 till his death in 1771 (open by written appointment; see Peterhouse for the story of his migration to Pembroke). During restoration work wall-paintings were discoverd behind the panelling; there are two life-sized drawings of decorations on Wren's chapel (perhaps the working drawings of the architect or his master mason?), and a picture of a red-haired, bearded man, whose presence is an intriguing mystery.

To the E. of Ivy Court are more buildings by G.G. Scott the Younger (1878) and Caröe (1907), and a few 20C additions. The gardens are extensive and beautiful; on a mound near the pond in the Fellows' Garden (private) is a mulberry tree descended from that associated with the poet Edmund Spenser.

FAMOUS MEMBERS: Nicholas Ridley, Bp and martyr, 1500–55; Edmund Spenser, poet, c. 1552–99; Richard Crashaw, poet, 1613–49; Thomas Gray, poet, 1716–71; William Pitt the Younger, statesman, 1759–1806; George Gabriel Stokes, mathematician and physicist, 1819–1903; and many archbishops and bishops.

Shortly beyond Pembroke, across Trumpington St., is the 14C church of *St Mary the Less* (Pl. D3), or Little St Mary's, a beautiful example of Dec. style architecture; until 1632 it served as the college chapel for Peterhouse, which takes its name from the former church on this site—St Peter without Trumpington Gate. On the N. and S. side are the remains of chantry chapels (presumably for Masters of Peterhouse); the present vestry, below which is a tiny rib-vaulted crypt, was also at one time used as a chantry, and an oratory built over it connected with the college by a covered gallery (cf St Bene't's and Corpus Christi). At the W. end on the N. wall is a memorial to Godfrey Washington, vicar 1705–29, who from his coat of arms was evidently of the same family as the President of the United States.

At the bottom of Little St Mary's Lane is the *Museum of Classical Archaeology* (open Mon–Fri 9–1, 2.15–5; Sat 9–1 in term only).

Peterhouse (Pl. D3; men only; never Peterhouse 'College') is the oldest college in Cambridge, founded by Hugh de Balsham, Bp of Ely, in 1284, on much the same lines as Merton College, Oxford, founded twenty years earlier. From the first its studies were to be secular rather than theological, perhaps reflecting the Benedictine founder's wish to counteract the influence of the Friars, so dominant in Cambridge at the time. Initially de Balsham lodged his students in the Hospital of St John which preceded St John's College, but this was not a success, and after three years they moved to houses on the present site.

During the religious and political upheavals of the mid 16C the fortunes of Peterhouse were guided by Dr Andrew Perne (Master 1553–89), who so skilfully adjusted his opinions to the many changes of wind that the weather-vane he put up was regarded as something of an emblem, and his initials 'A.P.' which formed part of its design were said to signify 'A Protestant', 'A Papist', or 'A Puritan' (it is now on the church of St Peter in Castle St.). He was an early advocate of improved sanitation for the town (see p 107, and Hobson's Conduit, p 150). In the Civil War Peterhouse paid dearly for its High Church and Royalist sympathies, and its chapel was a particular target for the iconoclasts.

The buildings are mostly much older than they appear, the 15C and 16C walls having been faced with stone on the inner side in the 18C. The original medieval walls can still be seen outside, from Little St Mary's Lane. In FIRST COURT, immediately l. of the 18C entrance gate, is the Old Library (adm by written arrangement only), in which until recently was housed the splendid collection of MSS and books, 'the worthiest in all England', bequeathed by Dr Perne. Some of the old fittings survive. Opposite (r. side) is the *Burrough's Building* (1738–42) designed by the talented amateur architect Sir James Burrough, Master of Caius. On its top floor the poet Gray had rooms in 1742–56; he had a morbid dread of fire, and the iron bar for his fire-escape can still be seen from the street, near Little St Mary's church. Heartier members of the college made him the butt of practical jokes, and it was their raising of a false fire-alarm that eventually precipitated his departure to Pembroke. The story that he descended into a tub of water is, alas, fictional.

The court is dominated by the *Chapel*, built 1628–34 while Matthew Wren, who later gave Pembroke its chapel, was Master. It is a most interesting mixture of Gothic and Renaissance styles. Originally of brick, it was, like the rest of the buildings, later refaced in stone. The attractive flanking colonnades were rebuilt by Robert Grumbold c. 1709. Many of its decorations and most of its windows were destroyed in 1643 by William Dowsing, who 'pulled down two mightie great Angells, with wings and divers other Angells, and the four Evangelists, and Peter with his Keies over the Chappell Dore, and about 100 cherubims'. The E. window (1639), based on Rubens's 'Le Coup de Lance' and possibly by Bernard van Linge, happily survives. The remaining windows have 19C Munich glass, which greatly darkens the interior. Over the altar is a Gothic 'Pietà', installed in 1941 in memory of the social historian Eileen Power (Postan).

On the S. side (l.) of Old Court is the *Hall* (entered from the Screens Passage). It dates from 1290, but was virtually rebuilt by George Gilbert Scott the Younger in 1870, and decorated by William Morris, who also designed the daisy-pattern tiles of the fireplace (itself early 16C, with a 17C fireback carrying the arms of James I). The windows are by Morris, Burne-Jones, and Ford Madox Brown, and commemorate benefactors and distinguished members of the college. Eighteen small portraits on wood (16C) also record benefactors,

An interesting mixture of Gothic and Renaissance styles:
Peterhouse Chapel

Fellows, and Masters. On the r. side of the high table a doorway, probably 16C, once led to a spiral stairway connecting with the Master's apartments.

To the W. of Old Court are Gisborne (neo-Gothick, 1825) and Fen Court (1939); S., through the Screens Passage a path leads into the *Deer Park* or *Grove*, once the grounds of the ancient Friary of the Penance of Jesus. There have been no deer since the 1930s. At the far end, in the Scholars' Garden, is an eight-storey brick tower-block (Sir Leslie Martin, 1953), given by and named after an old scholar of Peterhouse, William Stone, who died in 1958 aged 101. A path leads out into Trumpington St.

FAMOUS MEMBERS: Sir John Paston of the 'Paston Letters', 1442–79 (also Trinity Hall); Thomas Campion, poet and musician, 1567–1620; Richard Crashaw, poet, 1613–49; Thomas Gray, poet, 1716–71; Henry Cavendish, scientist, after whom the Cavendish Laboratory (where his library is housed) is named, 1733–1810; Charles Babbage, scientist, 1792–1871; William Kelvin, mathematician and physicist, 1824–1907.

The handsome building backing on to Peterhouse gardens is the *Fitzwilliam Museum (Pl. D3; open Tues–Sat downstairs only 10–2, upstairs only 2–5; Sun all rooms 2.15–4.55), one of the oldest public museums in Britain, and certainly among the finest. It was founded by the bequest of Viscount Fitzwilliam in 1816; the massive neo-classical building was designed by George Basevi, and started in 1837. Later work was done by C.R. Cockerell (cf the Ashmolean Museum, Oxford) and the interior completed by E.M. Barry in 1875. There have been many additions since, as the museum's collections have grown.

As only half the museum is open at a time, except on Sunday afternoon, a visit needs to be planned with some care, and the pleasant coffee and snack bar over the museum shop (S. end, l.) can be useful here. The floor plans show how the exhibits are grouped; the following guide to 'highlights' is necessarily both selective and somewhat subjective.

Lower Floor. At the bottom of the stairs is the WEST ASIATIC ROOM, with Syrian and Phoenician ivories and reliefs (9C–5C B.C.) including the huge Ashurnasirpal II, King of Assyria. In the EGYPTIAN ROOMS (r.) are exhibits from the pre-Dynastic to the pre-Coptic periods; specially striking are the *Shrine of Nekbet* and the *sarcophagus lid of Ramasses III*, King of Egypt 1198–1166 B.C. The GREEK ROOM contains pottery, statuary, grave-reliefs (a charming one of two boys with hoops), and seals. In the window is the **Dexamenos gem*. Among the exhibits in the ROMAN ROOM are: the Pashley sarcophagus, and a child's sarcophagus (early 2C A.D.); the mosaic fountain niche from Baiae (c. A.D. 50), and an Etruscan funerary couch carved in bone. The LOWER MARLAY GALLERY has European porcelain and silver, and in cases down the centre a superb **collection of books and MSS which includes a first edition of Milton's 'Paradise Lost', a second folio of Shakespeare, Keats's 'Ode to a Nightingale', letters of Shelley, Tennyson, A.E. Housman, Walter de la Mare, and Rupert Brooke. Music MSS include works of Vivaldi, Bach, Handel, Mozart, and Purcell. At the far end of the gallery is the great marble **figure of 'Glory'* by Baratta. The GLAISHER ROOM is devoted to European pottery; almost opposite the entrance is a Wedgwood copy of the 'Portland Vase' which belonged to Darwin.

The ORIENTAL ROOMS (r.) display Chinese lacquer, carvings, and ceramics, and beyond is Korean ware, Japanese weaponry, lacquer, and Chinese snuff boxes. Through the TEXTILE GALLERY is the ANTHONY DE ROTHSCHILD ROOM, with more marvellous MSS both European and Islamic, ivories, crystals and jewellery, and the most ancient works in the museum, Paleolithic drawings from the Dordogne (far end, l.). The ARMOURY (off which is the SMALL HENDERSON ROOM, displaying English and Irish table glass, stained glass and pewter) leads into the NEAR EASTERN ROOM where the most interesting exhibits are a Persian painted 'Hawk', and the glass lamp of Emir Shaikhu from his mosque in Cairo. From here are steps to the entrance hall.

Upper Floor. This floor is devoted to pictures. At the top of the stairs (r.) are three galleries of the British school, late 16C–mid 20C, displayed with contemporary furniture, ceramics, drawings, and busts. The collection includes works by *Hogarth, Reynolds, Constable, Sickert*, and *Augustus John*. In desk cases are notable drawings by *William Blake*. In the central bay of ROOM III (at the top of the stairs), are Italian portraits of Englishmen abroad. ROOMS IV AND V (l.) contain French paintings of mid 17–20C; in ROOM IV are works by *Oudry, Vouet, Poussin* (Deposition), *Corot, Delacroix* (**Odalisque), *Rousseau*, and *Decamps*, and in ROOM V by *Boudin, Fantin-Latour, Degas* (**Au Café), *Renoir* (**Coup de Vent), *Monet, Cézanne, Gauguin, Pissarro, Sisley, Matisse* and *Picasso* (**Man's Head). The UPPER MARLAY GALLERY displays early Italian paintings, notably *Simone Martini's* polyptych showing Sts Ambrose, Michael and Augustine, (l. side), *Domenico Veneziano's* Annunciation and *Lorenzo di Credi's* Martyrdom of St Sebastian. This room leads back into the COURTAULD GALLERY, where there are later Italian pictures with work by *Tintoretto, Bassano, Palma Vecchio*, (Venus and Cupid), *Titian* (Venus; Tarquin and Lucretia), *Veronese* (Hermes), and drawings by *Leonardo da Vinci, Michelangelo, Titian, Tintoretto*, and *Tiepolo*.

Lobby
Museum
Shop

Music
Ms

Butler Reading
Room

(Students only)

Mellon
Rare Books

A. de Rothschild
Manuscripts

Textiles

Small Henderson
Glass

European Armour

Near Eastern

Korean
Ware

Oriental

Glaisher
European Pottery

Chinese

Coins & Medals

Study
Room

Lower Marlay
European Porcelain & Manuscripts
Silver

Fitzwilliam Museum

Lower Floor

Founder's
Library
(not normally
open)

Roman

Down

West Asiatic

W.C.

Greek

Entrance

Egyptian

In the FOUNDER'S ROOM, l. past the *Broughton flower paintings* at the top of the stairs, are beautiful Dutch landscapes by *Cuyp, Ruisdael, Hobbema*, and *Van Goyen*, and portraits by *Rembrandt* and *Frans Hals*. At the other end of the Courtauld Gallery (r.) are pictures of the *Flemish and Spanish schools*, including a *Murillo*, oil sketches by *Rubens*, and three *Van Dycks* (notably a Madonna and Child). The OCTAGON ROOM has changing displays of watercolours and drawings, and the final room is devoted to 20C works; especially striking are *Graham Sutherland's* *Deposition and *Ben Nicholson's* *White Relief. There are bronzes and drawings by *Henry Moore*. Special exhibitions are mounted in the ADEANE ROOM beyond (normally entered from the other end, up stairs from S. lobby).

Opposite the Fitzwilliam Museum is *Addenbrooke's Hospital*, founded with a bequest from John Addenbrooke (d 1719), a Fellow of St Catharine's, and opened in 1766 (New Addenbrooke's Hospital is in Hills Rd, on the outskirts of Cambridge). Further on (r.) are the Engineering Laboratories and the *Leys School*, founded (for Methodist boys) in 1875. In Lensfield Rd (l.) is the *Scott Polar Research Institute and Museum* (open Mon–Sat 2.30–4; may be closed on Bank Holidays).

At the junction of Trumpington St. and Lensfield Rd stands *Hobson's Conduit* (Pl. D6), moved here in 1856 from its original site on Market Hill, where it had been dispensing fresh water since 1614. Beyond it, beside Trumpington Rd, flows the pleasant little watercourse which is all that can now be seen of the Cambridge New River, or Hobson's Brook, constructed in 1610, shortly after the making of London's New River. It carries water from springs about 3 m. S. to this point; from here, in the past, an open stream flowed down Trumpington St. (its memory survives in the very wide roadside channels) to wash out the King's Ditch, and pipes took supplies of drinking water to the conduit on Market Hill. Another leet was made in 1630 which flowed E. to St Andrew's St., from which water was piped to Emmanuel College and thence to Christ's (whose pools still make use of it). A moving spirit in the scheme was Thomas Hobson (d 1631), a prominent Cambridge citizen, landlord of the George inn, the 'University carrier' on whose death Milton wrote two semi-humorous poems, and the originator of the expression 'Hobson's choice', from his insistence that clients hiring his horses should take the one that had been longest in the stable, and not select their own mount.

About ¼ m. further on is the *University Botanic Gardens* (open Mon–Sat 8–7.30 or dusk if earlier; Sun in summer 2.30–6.30 exc from Trumpington Rd gate; other gates in Hills Rd and Bateman St.). The gardens began in the 17C on the site now occupied by the New Museums and were moved in 1846.

Also opposite the Museum, Fitzwilliam St. runs E. to Tennis Court Rd. Just to the r. is an entrance to **Downing College** (Pl. D4) but the main gate is in Regent St. (turn l. to Downing St., then r. into Regent St.). It was founded in 1800 under the will of Sir George Downing (1683–1749) grandson of Emmanuel Downing, who was one of the founders of Massachusetts, and son of George Downing, one of the first graduates of Harvard. He himself was not an admirable character. The provisions of his will were so complicated, and gave rise to so much litigation, that fifty years elapsed between his death

Hamilton Kerr

Adeane
Special
Exhibitions

20th
Century
Painting &
Sculpture

Prints

Founder's
Room

Dutch

Students' Room
& Offices

Broughton
Flower
Paintings

Octagon

W.C.

Courtauld Room
Later Italian Paintings
and Majolica

Flemish
&
Spanish

Graham
Robertson
Room

Upper Marlay
Early Italian Paintings & Majolica

Fitzwilliam Museum

Upper Floor

V

French Painting
Mid 17C to 20C

IV

Sculpture

III
Italian
Paintings of
Englishmen
Abroad

Gallery

I
Drawings
Busts
Furniture

British
School

II
Paintings

Neo Classicism: Downing College

and the establishment of his college. By that time the money available had greatly dwindled.

The buildings, set round a huge and rather draughty grass court, were designed on a grand scale by William Wilkins in neo-Grecian style. Of his plans, only the E. and W. ranges were ever built (finished 1875 by E.M. Barry). In the centre of the N. side (Sir Herbert Baker, 1931) is the *Chapel*, designed by A.T. Scott and completed in 1953. Its cool simplicity and pale woodwork are restful and pleasing. In the apse windows is a semi-abstract depiction of the 'Four Horsemen of the Apocalypse' (L.C. Evetts, 1963) and let into the floor on the S. side of the altar is a small square of Greek marble from a Byzantine church in Sparta, the site of which was excavated by W.L. Cattle, Senior Tutor of the college. The beautiful altar frontal is by Barbara Dawson. In the ante-chapel is an attractive sculpture—'Mother and Child'.

The *Hall* (l. at the far end of the great court), recently enlarged, has a portrait of the first Sir George Downing, on loan from Harvard, of the second Sir George (the founder), and various other members of the family; also of F.R. Leavis (1895–1978), the influential and controversial literary critic, and a former Fellow.

Famous Members: J.M. Neale, hymnologist, 1818–66 (Chaplain); C.M. Doughty, explorer and poet, author of 'Arabia Deserta' 1843–1925; E.R. Lankester, zoologist, 1847–1929; also a number of distinguished lawyers, including Edward Christian, 1758–1823, C.S. Kenny, 1847–1930, and F.M. Maitland 1850–1906.

Opposite Downing College is one of the many open commons in Cambridge, *Parker's Piece* (Pl. D2/4). It belonged originally to Trinity College, and takes its name from an early tenant, Edward Parker, the college cook; in 1613 it was exchanged with the town for some land which is now Trinity 'Backs'. During the 19C it was much used as a games field. Just S. is *Fenner's*, the university Cricket Ground, overlooking which, in Mill Rd, is *Hughes Hall*, founded in 1885 as a women's teacher-training college, but now admitting both men and women graduates to study a variety of other subjects as well. It has been an Approved Society of the university since 1969. About 1¼ m. up Hills Rd is *Homerton College*, also an Approved Society (since 1977), whose students all read for the Education Tripos (B.Ed.). Its origins go back to an 18C academy for training Congregationalist teachers, but it has long been non-denominational.

A few minutes' walk N. (l. coming out of Downing) is **Emmanuel College** (Pl. D2; familiarly 'Emma'), founded in 1584 by Sir William Mildmay, a former member of Christ's College, and a staunch Puritan, to train men for Protestant ministry in the church. Questioned by Elizabeth I, to whom he was Chancellor of the Exchequer, about his 'Puritan foundation', Mildmay replied 'No Madam, far be it from me to countenance anything contrary to your laws; but I have set an acorn, which, when it becomes an oak, God alone knows what will be the fruit thereof'. Somewhat ironically his acorn was planted on the site of a Dominican friary (dissolved in 1538) of which the chapel, correctly oriented, became the college dining hall, and the refectory, which ran N. and S., became the college chapel. This may have been a deliberate demonstration of Puritan disregard for ritual and religious tradition (cf Sidney Sussex College).

During the 1630s when, under Abp Laud's regime, Puritans were in great disfavour, many Emmanuel men sought religious liberty in America; of the first hundred graduates who settled in New England a third were from this college. Newton, Massachusetts, was renamed Cambridge in honour of one of them—the preacher Thomas Shepherd—while another, John Harvard (BA, 1632), was the major benefactor of the first university in America, which bears his name. The link between Harvard and Emmanuel is preserved in the Lionel de Jersey Harvard Studentship, awarded each year to a graduate of Harvard.

Emmanuel's Puritanism found favour during the Civil War and the Commonwealth, when it supplied no less than eleven heads of colleges to replace those Masters ejected for their High Church and Royalist sympathies. But with the Restoration, and the Mastership of William Sancroft (later Dean of St Paul's, and then Abp of Canterbury), it gradually lost the religious allegiance it had been founded to nurture.

The job of converting and adding to the monastic buildings was given to Ralph Symonds, and was his first major undertaking in Cambridge (cf St John's, Trinity, and Sidney Sussex), though little is now visible of his work. On the N. side (l.) of FRONT COURT is the *Hall* (originally the monastic chapel, see above). Reconstructed by Symonds in 1584, in the mid 18C it was refaced in stone by James Essex, and given its handsome plasterwork ceiling (the old hammer-beam roof survives above). The 'reredos', screen, and furnishings date mostly from 1694, the high table having 'barley-sugar-twist' legs typical of the period. Over it is a portrait of the founder. In the lobby to the Upper Hall and kitchens (no adm) are remains of a window and door-arch of the priory church. Essex also built the W. (entrance) side of the court.

Opposite the gateway is the *Chapel*, with its most attractive flanking cloister, built for William Sancroft and completed in 1677. It was designed by Sir Christopher Wren (cf Pembroke College), who was also then working on St Paul's Cathedral in London. Most of the woodwork is original (carved by Cornelius Austin); the altar rails were formerly three-sided, and when the two sets of side-rails were removed in the 1880s to accommodate a third step they were reset into panelled wooden chests. The altar-piece is 'The Return of the

Prodigal Son' (Amigoni), presented in 1734. On the altar is a war-memorial cross (1951) and a strikingly beautiful modern *frontal (by Beryl Dean) with the CHI RHO monogram surrounded by flames and palms in silver raised-work.

On the S. side (r.) of the court is the *Westmorland Building*, which in the early 18C replaced Symonds's original range. It was named after the Earl of Westmorland, who largely paid for it, and whose coat of arms is over the doorway. Running S. at right-angles to it is the pleasant *Old Court* (formerly the Brick Building) of 1633. Beyond this is the modern SOUTH COURT (1966) and the Library (1910 and 1930).

A passage l. of the chapel leads to NEW COURT (actually the oldest part of the college) on the r. of which is the *Old Library* (no adm). This was the original priory refectory, which Mildmay converted into a chapel; it became the library when the Wren chapel was built. It is now used for concerts and social gatherings. Behind a hinged panel can still be seen the ancient clunch and rubble of the medieval wall, and between ante-room and main room the chapel screen of 1584. The other buildings of the court are 19C and 20C; on the N. side a subway leads under Emmanuel St. into NORTH COURT. The charming Elizabethan herb garden was laid out in 1961.

To the E. are spacious gardens; the pools here and in Chapman's Garden (N. of Old Court) are fed with water from the New River (see p 150).

FAMOUS MEMBERS: John Harvard, principal benefactor of Harvard University, 1607–38; William Sancroft, Dean of St. Paul's during much of its building, Abp of Canterbury, one of the 'Seven Bishops' who defied James II, 1617–93; William Temple, diplomat and essayist, to whom the 'Letters of Dorothy Osborne' were written, 1628–99; William Law, divine, author of 'The Serious Call to a Devout and Holy Life', 1686–1761; Thomas Young, physicist, egyptologist, polymath, 1773–1829. Nobel prizewinners: Gowland Hopkins, biochemist, discoverer of vitamins, 1861–1947; R.G.W. Norrish, chemist, 1897–1978. Swift's Gulliver, of 'Gulliver's Travels' (published 1726) went to 'Emanuel College in Cambridge at Fourteen Years old, where I resided three years, and applied myself close to my Studies'.

Shortly N. beyond Emmanuel College, Petty Cury leads back to Market Hill. On the l. is the church of *St Andrew the Great* (19C), grim, gloomy, and usually locked. It contains monuments to Captain Cook, 'circumnavigator of the globe' (d 1779) and his family, transferred from the earlier church on this site.

3   ACROSS THE RIVER

Cambridge began to spread west of the river only in the late 19C, and of the buildings described in this route the majority are 20C, and in the main belong to the great period of university expansion after the Second World War. Visitors only interested in historic Cambridge, and with limited time, need not in fact cross the river at all (except to see Magdalene College, for which see pp 127–130). Nevertheless, not to look at what has happened in the last hundred years, and especially in the last thirty, would be to go away from Cambridge with a very unbalanced picture, and to miss some stimulating visual experiences.

From Silver St. to Castle Hill (about 1 m.)

It is worth pausing on the bridge in Silver St. to look up-river at the old mill-pool, the weir, the 'island', and—usually—boats. On the E. side (l.) is *Laundress Green*, where much of the university's washing used to be hung out to dry, and the *University Graduate Centre* (no adm; designed by Howell, Killick, Partridge, and Amis, 1964).

Across the water is **Darwin College** (Pl. C4; no adm), of which the best view is from the bridge, or the terrace of the Anchor Inn. It is a graduate college, established in 1965 by Caius, St John's, and Trinity; its buildings incorporate Newnham Grange, the former home of Sir George Darwin and his family, and the Hermitage, both so vividly described in 'Period Piece' by Gwen Raverat (Darwin). The

Hermitage was also the first home of New Hall (see p 159). Straight ahead is Sidgwick Avenue, on the l. of which is *Ridley Hall*, an evangelical Church of England training college, and immediately beyond it **Newnham College** (Pl. C3), founded for women (and still only for women) in 1875, largely under the aegis of Henry Sidgwick, a leading figure in the women's education movement in Cambridge (for details of which see History, pp 13–14). His ideas were more liberal and flexible than those of Girton's founder, Emily Davies, and their differences of opinion led to the almost simultaneous establishment of two separate women's colleges. Newnham's life began in 1871 with five students in a house in Regent St. (Sidgwick's 'little garden of flowers') presided over by Miss A.J. Clough, who became the first principal. She was succeeded by Mrs Sidgwick, and the college became the Sidgwicks' home. His liberal outlook and genial personality seem to have left their mark on Newnham, whose buildings are on a deliberately domestic scale, and, uniquely, are arranged in a series of self-contained houses (linked by passages), so that students belong to the smaller community of a house as well as the larger community of the college.

The *original entrance* was in Newnham Walk (turn r. at the end of Ridley Hall Rd), which ran right through the college site until Sidgwick Avenue was made (at Henry Sidgwick's expense). It still provides the best approach. The early buildings (1875–1910) were all by Basil Champneys, Dutch red brick with white dressings and shaped gables (cf his work at Lady Margaret Hall, Oxford). The *Hall* of the house known as Clough (seen by arrangement) has a ceiling by Sir George Frampton, designer of the Peter Pan statue in Kensington Gardens, and the Edith Cavell statue in St Martin's Place, London. In the gardens, on whose grass you may walk, is the *old laboratory* used by science students before they were admitted to university facilities. It is now used by the visiting Arts Scholar. Additional buildings belong to 1938 (W. side) and the 1960s (E. side).

Harvard University's first woman professor (of Astronomy, 1956) was an old Newnhamite—Mrs C.H. Gaposchkin (Payne).

Opposite Newnham is the **University Arts Faculties** site (the 'Sidgwick site'), a complex of individually-styled buildings (Sir Hugh Casson and Neville Conder, 1952 onwards) providing libraries, lecture rooms, two halls and a buttery, loosely grouped round a podium which, with its benches and tables and newly-planted trees, has something of the village-green community atmosphere. The roof-lines offer some visual excitement. On the N. side is the controversial *History Faculty Building* (James Stirling, 1965; cf the Florey Building of Queen's College, Oxford, p 64), two six-storey blocks of fiery red brick set at right angles, with a receding pyramid of glass between. The effect is not improved by venetian blinds hanging at crazy angles behind most of the 'windows'. In the N.E. corner of the site is Caius College *Harvey Court* (Sir Leslie Martin, 1960), an inward-facing three-sided court with rooms in stepped-back terraced tiers, an arrangement affording the occupants little privacy.

On the corner of Sidgwick Avenue and Grange Rd, beyond the Sidgwick site, is **Selwyn College** (Pl . C3), founded in 1882 to provide a university education for young men of the Church of England unable to afford the fees of the older colleges (cf Keble College, Oxford). It is named in honour of George Augustus Selwyn, first Bp of New Zealand, an influential and greatly admired man (d 1878). Its denominational character, and somewhat unusual charter, which made no provision for Fellows, long delayed Selwyn's full acceptance as a college. It was recognised as an Approved Foundation in 1923, and as a college in 1958. Although never confined to theological studies, a very high proportion of Selwyn men did, until recent times, go on to take Holy Orders.

The red brick Tudor-style buildings, set round a spacious court, were mostly designed by Sir Arthur Blomfield. Opposite the entrance is the *Chapel*; the side windows (Kempe) depict saints and church leaders, the E. window Christ in Majesty. Behind the altar, against a white wall, is a sculpture of Christ ascending (Karin Jonzen, 1958). Set into the altar is the pectoral cross of Bp Patteson of Melanesia, friend and colleague of Bp Selwyn. His combined bible and prayer book are in the vestry, and his staff in the chapel above. The trowel used at the laying of the foundation stone is on the N. wall below the sanctuary steps. On some of the stalls are carved the heads of contemporary statesmen (1895). On the S. side of the court is the *Hall* (1905), approached up a double flight of steps over which appears the rebus, three apples and a tun, of the then Master, Richard Appleton. In 1967 Selwyn expanded across Grange Rd into Cripps Court.

Opposite Selwyn a private road leads to *Leckhampton House* (no adm) a graduate hostel for Corpus Christi College. In the grounds is a sculpture, 'Seated Figure' by Henry Neave.

Turning S. (l. out of Selwyn) along Grange Rd, and then r. at Barton Rd, one comes to (r.) **Wolfson College** (off Pl. C5) founded in 1965 as University College and renamed in 1973 in recognition of a large benefaction from the Wolfson Trust. It is principally a graduate college, fostering connections with Continental and other overseas universities, and with business and administrative circles. The buildings (Ferrey and Mennim) incorporate Bredon House, formerly occupied by a professor of botany and consequently having beautiful gardens. The grounds are open to visitors (keep to the paths).

To the N. (r.) of Selwyn along Grange Rd, then soon l., in Herschel Rd is *Clare Hall* (Pl. A7), a graduate establishment founded in 1966 by Clare College, but now independent. The buildings (by a Scandinavian architect, Ralph Erskine) provide both single and family accommodation.

Immediately beyond Herschel Rd is **Robinson College** (off Pl. A7), the first in Cambridge to be founded for both men and women. It has been entirely financed by a Cambridgeshire businessman, Mr David Robinson. The first graduates were admitted in 1977, and undergraduates in 1979. It was formally opened by the Queen in 1981.

The red-brick L-shaped buildings, with very large grounds beyond, were designed by Gillespie, Kydd and Coia (and at a later stage by Yorke, Rosenberg, and Mardall). The massive gatehouse, approached by a ramp, is reminiscent of a castle; the *Chapel*, with John Piper glass, is to the r., the Hall straight ahead. Communal rooms face outward to the roads, private ones inwards to the quiet of the court.

On both sides of Grange Rd beyond Robinson are college sports grounds, and on the l. *St John's College Hostel* and Girton's *Wolfson Court* (in Clarkson Rd; by David Roberts, 1969).

Opposite Robinson, Burrell's Walk leads back to Queen's Rd past (l.) *Trinity College Hostel* (no adm). On the r. is the **University Library** (Pl. A7; open Mon–Fri 9–7.05, Sat 9–1. Accompanied visitors admitted; unaccompanied visitors shown round Mon–Fri 3 p.m., the tour lasting about ½ hr). Built in 1931–34 by Sir Giles Gilbert Scott, it is one of the country's most important libraries, with over four million books, MSS which include the 6C Codex Bezae, one of the five great uncial MSS of the Gospels, and a magnificent collection of Caxtons including his 'Historyes of Troye' (1475–76), the first book printed in English, and the only perfect copy of his 'Golden Legend' (1483). There is often a special exhibition in the long first floor corridor.

Immediately next to the library, facing on to Queen's Rd, is *Clare Memorial Court*, also by Sir Giles Gilbert Scott, built in the 1920s as a memorial to men killed in the First World War. It is pleasantly spacious and restful, of pale grey brick in neo-Georgian style. In the 1950s *Thirkell Court* was added on the W. side, as a memorial to men killed in the Second World War. The sculptures in the grounds are Henry Moore's 'Falling Warrior' and Barbara Hepworth's 'Two Forms (Divided Circle)'. Clare Bridge, and shortly N., Garrett Hostel Lane, lead back to the city centre.

About ⅓ m. N. of Clare Memorial Court, Queen's Rd joins Northampton St. (r.) and Madingley Rd (l.). Opposite the junction is *Westminster College*, a Presbyterian training college (1899), and in Lady Margaret Rd (r. off Madingley Rd) *Lucy Cavendish College*. This began informally in the early 1950s, to provide a social focus for senior women graduates working in the university but not attached to a college, and grew by 1965 to the status of an Approved Society. A few (mostly mature) undergraduates are now also admitted.

About ⅓ m. along Madingley Rd is **Churchill College** (off Pl. A3; entrance in Storey's Way), founded in 1960 to promote scientific and technological studies, though not exclusively devoted to them. As a memorial to the achievements of Sir Winston Churchill it attracted benefactions and gifts from all over the world; Sir Winston himself took a close interest in its progress, and presented to it the monies subscribed for his eightieth birthday present, and his priceless collection of papers. Now one of Cambridge's largest colleges, Churchill was also one of the first three men's foundations to admit women (1972).

The low brick, wood, and concrete buildings (Richard Sheppard and Robson) follow the traditional plan of connecting courts, and form an intricate complex. Through the massive entrance, with bronze doors (Geoffrey Clarke), a corridor of 225 ft runs the whole length of the college. The *Hall* is r., up a wide flight of stairs, on which is an impressive bust of Sir Winston (Oscar Nemon); the hall is entirely glass-panelled on the inner side and so can always be seen. The roof consists of three concrete tunnel-vaults, resting on exposed beams; the walls are wood-slatted, and the tables lit by low-slung copper strips. In the *Library* (no adm), given by the Transport and General Workers' Union in memory of Ernest Bevin (d 1951), the great trades unionist and wartime statesman, is a magnificent Lurçat tapestry presented by Gen. de Gaulle. Sculptures on the lawns are by Henry Moore and Barbara Hepworth.

Away at the furthest end of the grounds is the *Chapel*, not in fact a college chapel, but privately subscribed for and maintained. No chapel was included in the original plan, as it was considered inappropriate to a community of many religions or none, devoted to secular studies. The chapel is a Byzantine-style building with central altar; the windows, designed by John Piper and made by Patrick Reyntiens, are a memorial to the first Master, Sir John Cockcroft, and the bell was given by the Board of Admiralty, of which Sir Winston was several times First Lord.

Beyond Churchill are sports grounds and university scientific laboratories (no adm to any).

Northampton St. runs E. (r.) from the junction with Queen's Rd. On the r. is the back entrance to St John's Merton Hall and Cripps Building (see p 126), on the l. is *Kettle's Yard Art Gallery*, with a collection of modern pictures, and frequent exhibitions of modern arts and crafts (open daily 2–4; special exhibitions Mon–Sat 12–6, Sun 2–6). On the corner of Castle St. is the *Cambridge and County Folk Museum*, housed in the 16C former White Horse Inn (open Tues–Fri 10.30–5; Sat 10.30–1, 2–5; Sun 2.30–4.30; closed most Bank Holidays).

From Castle Hill to Girton (about 2 m.)

On the r. of Castle St. is the great artificial grassy mound of Castle Hill; nothing remains of the Norm castle. Below it is St Giles Church, 19C, but incorporating fragments of its 12–13C predecessor, beyond which (in Chesterton Lane) is Clare College *Castle Hill Hostel*, consisting of two older houses and a new building by David Roberts (1957–58). On the l. is the tiny church of *St Peter* (usually locked), early 13C but rebuilt with the old materials c. 1780. The Norm font is decorated with mermen.

Further on (about 6–7 mins walk), down Mount Pleasant, is *St Edmund's House*, which began in 1895 as a residential centre for Roman Catholic priests studying in Cambridge. It is now an Approved Foundation (1975) of the university and as well as some priests admits lay men and women graduates and a few mature undergraduates, who need not be Roman Catholics. It remains an essentially Christian community.

About 5 mins walk beyond is *New Hall (Pl. A1; call at the Porter's Lodge), founded in 1954 as Cambridge's third college for women, and still admitting only women. It began life at The Hermitage in Silver St. (see Darwin College, p 155) and moved to its present site in 1962. The eye-catching buildings (by Chamberlain, Powell, and Bonn) are faintly reminescent of the Taj Mahal, of pure white brick and concrete, and arranged round sunken courts with pools and fountains. In the centre rises the segmented dome of the hall roof, surrounded by four half-domed towers which contain the four staircases that approach the *Hall*, a cruciform room hung with modern pictures and lit with grey-glass-shaded lamps. The Library (no adm) is on two levels, arcaded bookshelves above, reading cubicles below. The undergraduates' rooms, arranged in pairs, are also on two levels, the upper one reached by ladder-like steps; a novel, if hardly practical, idea (of course no adm).

Next door is **Fitzwilliam College** (Pl. A1) whose history begins in 1869 with the Non-Collegiate Students' Board, set up to administer the affairs of men who wanted to study at the university but who could not, or did not wish to, belong to a college (cf St Catherine's College, Oxford). The first premises were in Trumpington St., opposite the Fitzwilliam Museum, from which it takes its name, and as Fitzwilliam Hall, later House, it became a centre for non-collegiate students, who always included a high proportion of graduates studying for higher degrees. It moved to its present site in 1963, and became a full college in 1966.

The buildings are by Denis Lasdun, long low uniform ranges of dark-grey brick, in marked contrast to the white curves of their neighbours. Over the *Hall*, which has a flat roof, is a distinctive fluted canopy on slender concrete columns.

Fitzwilliam has three Nobel prizewinners among its past members, including Sir Charles Sherrington, physiologist, 1857–1952 (also Caius).

On the outskirts of the town (about $1^1/_2$ m.) is **Girton College**, the first residential college in Britain to offer a university education for women. It was founded in 1869 by the educational pioneer Emily Davies, with the support and encouragement of such leaders of the Women's Movement as Barbara Leigh Smith (afterwards Mme Bodichon) and a number of liberal-minded Cambridge men (see p 13 for details on the history of women in the universities). Miss Davies's insistence on women fulfilling exactly the same examination requirements as men, and the rigid discipline she imposed, led in time to some conflict with both her colleagues and her students; she resigned in 1904.

The College began at Hitchin, a place discreetly removed from Cambridge, yet accessible to visiting lecturers from the university. It was greatly disapproved of by the more conservative, and even referred to by an indignant clergyman as 'that infidel place'. In 1873 it moved to its present spacious site on the outskirts of Cambridge near the small village of Girton, from which it took its name. Men are now admitted.

The original red brick Vict-Tudor buildings were designed by Alfred Waterhouse (see also Caius and Pembroke Colleges), and the same style was followed in subsequent additions (some by his son Paul, and grandson Michael, with Sir Giles Gilbert Scott). An innovation was the arrangement of rooms on corridors, instead of staircases as in the older colleges. In the large Hall are portraits of, among others, Emily Davies, looking deceptively mild, Mme Bodichon, and Lady Stanley of Alderley, an early benefactor. The chapel has embroidered kneelers and an altar-frontal designed by Jennifer Gray (1965) and another frontal by Leila Kerr (1978). The college also owns a fine set of embroidered wall-panels (1902) by Lady Carew (seen by prior arrangement). The beautiful grounds were originally laid out c. 1900 by the then Mistress, Miss Elizabeth Welsh.

In 1969 Girton's centenary was marked by the opening of the new residential block, **Wolfson Court**, in Clarkson Rd (see p 156).

ENVIRONS OF CAMBRIDGE

On foot

The various commons on the edge of the city centre offer some pleasant short walks. On the E. side are *Jesus Green*, and *Midsummer Common* where a path beside the river, opposite the college boathouses, runs from Victoria Bridge to Elizabeth Way (about ³/₄ m.). On the S.W. side there are numerous paths across *Lammas Land*, *Sheep's Green*, and *Coe Fen*, beginning in Mill Lane (l., just before Silver St. Bridge).

With transport

The *American Military Cemetery* is about 4 m. N.W. of the city, along Madingley Rd past Churchill College. It commemorates American servicemen based in Britain who were killed on operations. It has beautifully landscaped gardens and a chapel in which is a mural map of the war in Europe.

Stourbridge Chapel is about 1¹/₂ m. S.E. along Newmarket Rd, on the l. immediately over the railway bridge, at the edge of Stourbridge Common, which was once the scene of the great annual fair (see p 107). It is now a dreary industrial wasteland, though the tiny 12C church stands in an oasis of green. It was the chapel of the leper hospital maintained by the monks of Barnwell Priory. It was evidently re-roofed in the 14C, but not very skilfully, as many of the vertical timbers have no supporting corbals below. For long it was used simply as a store, and at fair-time as a beer-house. Through the enthusiasm of Westcott House students, one of whom 'discovered' it while walking on the common, the chapel was in the mid 19C restored to religious use, and completely renovated by Sir George Gilbert Scott, who inserted the Norm style W. window. It is now cared for by the Cambridge Preservation Society, and well worth a visit in spite of its bleak surroundings (key at house near by).

The *Gog Magog Hills*, about 4 m. S.E. (leave Cambridge by Hills Rd), rising to 222 ft, are the highest ground for miles. They are crossed by the old Roman 'Via Devana', and on top is Wandlebury Camp, an Iron Age fort. The area is maintained by the Cambridge Preservation Society; there are nature-trails and picnic places.

Trumpington is about 2¹/₂ m. S.W., the old village lying r. of the busy main Trumpington Rd. In the church is the second oldest brass in England—Sir Roger de Trumpington, 1289. Past the church, on the Grantchester road, a footpath l. (about ¹/₄ m.) leads to *Byron's Pool*, where 'his ghostly lordship' swam in his undergraduate days. The close proximity of the M11 motorway is not conducive to poetic imaginings.

Grantchester, immortalised by Rupert Brooke, can be reached from Trumpington (1 m.), from Grantchester Rd, l. off Barton Rd past Wolfson College, or—most pleasantly—by a footpath near the

river, which starts at the end of Grantchester St. (beyond the junction of Newnham Rd and Fen Causeway). In the church are memorials to the poet, whose name is also recalled by an inn and various tea-gardens etc. in the village. The Old Vicarage (private), at which he lodged for a time, is below the church near the river, where

> 'The chestnuts shade, in reverend dream,
> The still unacademic stream.'

Picture Credits

Thanks are due to the following for permission to reproduce pictures:

The Librarian, Newnham College, Cambridge, page 14
J. Allan Cash Limited, page 21 (top)
Cambridge Evening News, page 21 (bottom)
Oxfordshire County Libraries, pages 54, 96 and 98
National Monuments Record, pages 68, 89, 131, 147 and 152
Howell Killick Partridge and Amis and Brecht-Einzig Limited, page 93
Victoria and Albert Museum, page 116
Donald W. Insall, photograph by Colin Westwood, page 123
John Laing Limited, page 127
The Provost and Fellows of King's College, Cambridge, photograph by John Leigh, page 139
John Leigh, page 141.

INDEX

Figures in *italic* refer to illustrations, those in **bold** type to main entries. Asterisks indicate pages on which a person's name appears among the 'famous members' of a college (see p 6).

Typeset by Coats Dataprint Limited, Inverness
Printed in Great Britain by Fletcher & Son Limited, Norwich